Dr. John Doran

Memories of our Great Towns

Dr. John Doran

Memories of our Great Towns

ISBN/EAN: 9783337371166

Printed in Europe, USA, Canada, Australia, Japan

Cover: Foto ©ninafisch / pixelio.de

More available books at **www.hansebooks.com**

MEMORIES

OF

OUR GREAT TOWNS

WITH

Anecdotic Gleanings

CONCERNING

THEIR WORTHIES AND THEIR ODDITIES

[1860—1877]

BY DR. JOHN DORAN, F.S.A.

London
CHATTO AND WINDUS, PICCADILLY
1878

TO THE READER.

DR. DORAN'S last book demands a word of introduction. For fourteen years the genial Author carried on in the pages of the *Athenæum* that charming series of papers which dealt annually with the locality selected for the approaching meeting of the British Association for the Advancement of Science. Last year, with the kind concurrence of the Proprietors of the *Athenæum*, it was determined that these papers—so brimful of pleasant chatty interest and antiquarian lore—should be collected and republished. Accordingly the Author set about their revision. After finishing *London in the Jacobite Times* he took a short holiday, and on returning to town completed his task. On the second day of January—then in his usual happy spirits, and apparently in his usual health—he called on the printer, and with his own hand delivered the packet containing all the corrections in the contents of this volume.

CONTENTS.

	PAGE
DONCASTER	3
ON THE ROAD	31
CAMBRIDGE	47
BATH	75
BIRMINGHAM	95
NOTTINGHAM	117
DUNDEE	139
NORWICH	161
EXETER	187
LEICESTER	231
LIVERPOOL	247
EDINBURGH	269
BRIGHTON	293
BRADFORD	317
BELFAST	343
A TRIP TO LONDONDERRY	361
BRISTOL	373
GLASGOW	393
PLYMOUTH	427

I.
DONCASTER.
1860.

DONCASTER.

1860.

HORACE WALPOLE was building his new tower at Strawberry; Boswell courting the notice of Mrs. Rudd; Cook starting on his last voyage; the Duchess of Kingston in jeopardy for bigamy; the Court in dismay at the news from America—the provincials there were melting for bullets the leaden statue of their '*late* king,' George III.; Charles Fox, no longer Tory, was in ecstasies that the Americans were quietly setting about governing themselves in face of the enemy; and Jack the painter was trying to fire the ships and stores in Portsmouth harbour,—when all the clubs and coteries, whose attention was divided between 'sport' in particular and things in general, forgot the outside world, and began to canvass the enlivening matter of the new stake proposed for Doncaster.

The corporation there, when the last quarter of the last century opened on it, had reached the end of its tether with respect to liberality. It had subscribed its few pounds for 'plates,' and it had appealed to the gentlemen of the county for aid. It had never been so active since the period when municipal— But we will not fall back into the annals of a corporate town. 'Turpe est homini nobili ejus civitatis in quâ versetur, jus ignorari,' no doubt; but *we* do not translate this passage as meaning, 'Every gentleman who frequents Doncaster Races ought to know the character and history of its corporation.'

Of the difficulties of writing history in connection with any subject we have had innumerable instances. That of the St. Leger affords one more to the accumulated number. Authorities differ as to the identity of the winner of the first '*Sillinger.*' The Peerage claims it for the man who had been, and was again to be, Prime Minister; namely, the Marquis of Rockingham, with his Sampson filly in 1776. The Baronetage claims it for Sir Thomas Gascoyne, with his famed Hollandaise in 1778. The two statements are easily accounted for. In the year 1776 there appears for the first time, on a Doncaster card of the races, the entry for 'A sweepstakes of 25 guineas each, for three-year-olds. Colts 8 stone, fillies 7 stone 12 lb., in one 2-mile heat.' The cards for 1777 bear a similar record; but in the succeeding year, instead of 'A sweepstakes,' we find the words 'St. Leger's Stakes'—by which name cards and calendars have recorded the great contest ever since. In the first of the above-mentioned years Lord Rockingham was the winner; Mr. St. Leger's Scrub colt coming in ninth. In 1778, when the race first assumed the name of the most fashionable of gentlemen, Sir Thomas Gascoyne carried off the prize; Mr. St. Leger's Minor filly appearing ninth at the winning-post. At this result a shout was raised by the friends of the victor loud enough almost to have reached the family-house at Aberford, or to rouse the Judge Gascoyne so famous in history, who sleeps his long sleep in the fine old church at Harewood. That district of Yorkshire could talk of little else at the time. Compared with their great triumph, what was the opening of the vast new dock at Hull? The best to be said on both subjects was, that two memorable circumstances had occurred in the county in the same week. The dock, however, has been the more profitable triumph to its subscribers.

We have said that St. Leger was a fashionable gentleman. This is doing him but slender justice. He was a wit, who, for a quarter of a century or more, had kept his club alive, and the armchairs at White's filled with vivacious young fellows, long after the older rakes had gone to bed. He was lively, dashing, and, as will be the case with wits, often absurd. He was audacious too; for on one occasion, when exhibiting extraordinary alacrity to swear to some matter in a court of justice, the judge remarking, 'You are very ready, sir, I see, to take an oath,' he answered, 'Of course I am, my lord; my father was a judge!' This was a hit at some gentlemen of the time who held, or had recently held, the scales of justice.

Whether dating from Norman or Plantagenet, the blood of the St. Legers answers to the legend on their shield of arms: *Haut et bon.* Leaning on the shoulder of a knight of that name, William the Conqueror stepped ashore at Bulverhythe, near Hastings. The Kentish lands of Ulcombe rewarded that and other service. The name shines throughout the stirring period of the Crusades. Its glory might be said to have culminated when Sir Thomas St. Leger married Anne, the sister of Edward IV. and widow of the Duke of Exeter, were it not remembered how that termagant princess treated her second spouse even more infamously than she had treated her first. The Irish branch of the family, at the head of which is Viscount Doneraile, are descended, through the female line, from the famous old Lord-Lieutenant, Sir Anthony St. Leger. A branch more illustrious dignifies the English peerage in the ducal house of Rutland. The luckless fellow who married the royal virago Anne had a daughter by that tremendous lady, who espoused young George Manners, and their son was created Earl of Rutland, first peer of a house which from time immemorial has been distinguished by its love for, and patronage of, the national sport. *Their* motto, too, is not a bad one to run with to the winning-post: *Pour y parvenir* is the aim of every one there concerned.

It was not in compliment to either of these houses, however, that the new stake at Doncaster received the name by which it has become celebrated all over the world. The fact is that the collateral branches, known only by the old Norman appellation, were of considerable notoriety during the last half of the eighteenth century and also at the beginning of the present. Their names turn up everywhere: in pulpits and fat prebends; on the front and back stairs at Court; at the head of crack regiments and at the tail of scaling-ladders planted against American forts;

on the hot plains of India and on the dusty racecourses of Great Britain and Ireland. One of them, Anthony St. Leger, was located at Park Hill, near Doncaster. There were many of them; and 'so many men so many fortunes.' The luck of the Legers was as variable as that of racing. Its extremes may be noted by reference to two entries in newspapers of the last century. One of them indicates a social prize pleasantly won, in the announcement that 'John St. Leger, Esq., was married to Miss Butler, niece to Lord Lanesborough, 40,000*l.*' The other paragraph points to a man 'distanced' in his race of life. It informs us that on a certain day died, 'in a mean lodging at the Bowling Pins, Rolls-buildings, Fetter-lane, George St. Leger, Esq.' What a descent from the state once shared by a Plantagenet princess! What a contrast between life in the old manor-house of Ulcombe and death in a 'boozing-ken' off Fetter-lane!

Such were the St. Legers and their fortunes. We need hardly say that in racing, as in the ordinary affairs and contentions of life, the hero of yesterday is the vanquished of to-day, and the high-mettled racer, whose value is reckoned by thousands one year, can hardly realise a few ten-pound notes the next. Chester Billy swept the plain in the van of all competitors, and we have seen that once royally-owned steed painfully tailing it, in his old days, after the slow Boroughbridge harriers. Swiss, for which Lord Darlington gave 2600 sovereigns, was sold at Doncaster, six years afterwards, for 50*l.*! Petre's Theodore won, at the same place, an immortality of renown, as it was thought, by beating Orde Powlette's Swap, which subsequently beat Theodore with infinite facility. There, too, the great favourite of the hour, Birmingham, conquered the greater favourite, Priam; and then went with all his laurels to Holywell, where he was disgracefully vanquished by a third-rate cocktail! There was as much regret at this demonstration of the instability of fortune as there was ultra-measure of sorrow, a century ago, in Doncaster, at the sudden demise of the famous horse 'White Nose.' The sporting world looked on this event as a public calamity; and one enthusiastic amateur proposed that a monument should be raised in memory of the defunct—after the fashion of one which Lipsius declared he had seen in imperial Rome!

In those old days the spirit of sport was occasionally apt to run riot, and gentlemen addicted thereto would exhibit themselves, in the intervals of meetings, under exceptional circumstances; performing wonderful feats, and winning fame and guineas thereby. One of these uneasy individuals, athirst for glory, undertook to ride his own boar a match against time, and gained it. An officer of Marines betted deeply in his own favour that he would ride a blind horse a certain number of times round a course and up and down a portion of it without any reins in his hands. He accomplished his object by cutting the reins in two, and attaching the ends to each leg, by which his steed was safely guided. As late as 1786, just previous to the Doncaster meeting, the Steyne at Brighton was crowded with spectators to witness a match between an officer, with a jockey on his back (the rider weighing 7 stone 5 lb.), booted and spurred, against a stout bullock unmounted. In this contest the quadruped was defeated by the other animal.

The 'captains' of the last century were especially distinguished for their devotion to 'sport.' They were the crack riders in all matches. Doncaster was excited to a great pitch of enthusiasm, before the period when her enthusiasm was annually aroused on account of 't' Leger,' by a race of which the whole town formed but a portion of the course. On the 23d of August 1773, at six o'clock on a Monday morning, two gentlemen appeared at the corner of Portland-street, Oxford-street: one of them, Captain Mulcaster, on the mare of a friend, Captain Hay; the other, Mr. Walker, rode his own horse. They started thence on a race to York, two hundred miles, without changing steeds. It was such a race as Arabs ride, proving the strength and endurance as well as the speed of the horses. The first ninety miles were accomplished in six hours. The two gentlemen-jockeys passed the end of Doncaster racecourse nearly together early on Tuesday morning, amid such cheering as was never heard there again till the days of Hollandaise and Hambletonian. But Walker was at the time sorely distressed, and his steed altogether broke down when between Doncaster and Tadcaster. The captain went ahead, and reached Ousebridge, York, in forty hours thirty-five minutes after he and his companion had started from Portland-street— thereby winning four hundred guineas besides wagers. The winning mare drank twelve bottles of wine on her journey; and was well enough by Thursday morning to take a gallop on Knavesmire, the racecourse just outside the city of York.

Such was the feat of a gallant and active and brutal captain. During the time occupied by a portion of it, while the North was in an uproar on the passage of the mare and her rider, the King was on Kew-green, gossiping with Beattie and old Dr. Majendie, discussing the merits of books, canvassing questions of morality, weighing religious difficulties, comparing preachers, and, on the part of the King, expressing fears that manhood was losing its dignity, and that the English language was on the decline. Had he witnessed the ride from Doncaster to York he would, perhaps, have been confirmed in his opinion at the sight of the captain, but he would have been compelled to confess that the language had lost nothing in force, however it might have suffered in elegance of expression.

This was the period when Doncaster was 'looking up,' and becoming a formidable rival to York. The races in the former locality had, however, as much of a business aspect as one of pleasure. The old prints of the early races would lead us to infer that they were less cared for by the public than was the case in later years. There is, indeed, a substantial grandstand, but it is only thinly dotted over, here and there, by visionary-looking sportsmen, who might pass for ghosts permitted to revisit old haunts, in order that they might convince themselves of the unreality of their mundane pursuits. Then there is one solitary rumbling old coach, tottering its way to the subscribers' entrance, with marks about it of having been long in the family, and of having seen hard service on this and other occasions. Meanwhile, the race is in progress below, and the steeds engaged are jumping off the ground just as greyhounds do when they suspect a hare to be in their vicinity, and long to obtain a sight of him. As for the small public, it is divided into the indifferents and the unruly. The former are lounging upon, over, and against the rails, gazing in every possible direction, with respect to their bodies, and conveying an idea of a lunatic asylum out for a holiday. The unruly are running after the racers—satirical suggestion that these are not of the swiftest — stimulating them by shouting, waving of quaint old hats, flinging up of arms which look like legs, and indulging in various undescribable antics free from all supervision of the police. Such was the early picturesque idea of Doncaster! It had its poetical element also.

The poetry of the course—the songs having reference solely to the horses and their riders, with the feats accomplished by them—is not of a Pindaric and permanent character. It is rather hearty than elegant; in expression more rough than refined. You may hear a good deal of it in Doncaster in racing-time as you pass by tavern-doors, while foreign minstrels in the streets are winning a shower of fourpenny-pieces from the young ladies in an adjacent balcony, charmed by those vagrant reminiscences of favourite operatic ditties. Do not despise the humbler and heartier minstrelsy, nor, indeed, the feeling that can be gratified by the peripatetic company of melodists, but go on your way rejoicing, humming, if you will, the appropriate line of Horace:

'Denique non omnes eadem mirantur amantque :
Carmine tu gaudes, hic delectatur iambis.'

As matters of record, however, the racing ballads are worth collecting. They preserve the memory of many things besides the value of the horses, the merits of the riders, and the virtues of the gentlemen who own the one and hire the other. They who are curious in such literature may consult Ritson's *Poetic Garland*. Dr. Ingledew has inserted in *his* collection the metrical details of the never-to-be-forgotten race, or races, here between Flying Dutchman and Voltigeur; and, as a general and philosophical history of a racer in the abstract, no better is to be found than that given by Dibdin, whom, by the way, young yachtsmen are asking us to abuse as a naval poet, because his sea-terms are not strictly according to the grammar of gentlemen and lubbers afloat.

Doncaster has been especially fortunate in its racing poets. They have really struck a *sport*ive lyre, and they ride their Pegasus with loose rein, but with no lack of whip and spur to stimulate him to gamesomeness. The course has had, too, its wits as well as its bards; and half of what is attributed to the northern jockeys as mere ignorance is really to be laid to their appreciation of fun. When Alcides first appeared on the course, they knew well enough the quantity of the syllables, but they also knew the quality of the horse. They accordingly called him All Sides; and nothing could be more appropriate, for the nag was of the very thinnest, looked as if he were cut out of pasteboard, had no back, and, to completely authorise his nickname, never ran straight.

Nor were the north-country 'jocks' less witty on their masters than on the steeds. No name was better known at Doncaster, no man altogether so fortunate there for a time, as Mr. Petre. At that period, however, he exemplified the truth of the proverb implying that Love does not favour the favourite of Fortune. The lucky master of a racing-stud had been unsuccessful in more than one suit to very many ladies; and as he once walked on to the course Tommy Lye, that atomy in top-boots, remarked to his fellows, 'Eh, look oop, lads; yon's *Solicitor-General!*'

In the time of honest and ludicrous Tommy some changes had been established which rendered the races at Doncaster—but especially the St. Leger— more popular both with trainers and the people at large. The amount of subscription was raised to fifty guineas, and the weights were settled at 8 st. 6 lb. for colts, and 8 st. 3 lb. for fillies. The owner of the second horse, too, did not approach honour so nearly without reaping some of its substantial fruits, by receiving a hundred guineas out of the stakes. Thenceforth Doncaster became more 'fashionable' than any similar locality in the north.

A day there, when the place was really in its prime, was by no means an idle day for the gay people who were generally making nearly a week of it, and were often paying a guinea a night for their beds. The men began the morning, if last night's business had not incapacitated them, by hunting—cub-hunting, if they could get nothing better. They went out early, and were easily back for the races at two o'clock. These over they dined, and then went to the play, the capital York company supplying the actors, and the entire county and some districts beyond furnishing glowing samples of north of England beauty. This portion of the day's hard toil, or delicious pleasure, as some thought it, being concluded at a reasonable hour, the *élite* of the audience repaired to the ball, and so 'kept it up' till the gray dawn of a coming September morning. The dissipation was compounded for by small subscriptions to local charities and religious societies; a course the spirit of which was something akin to that of the famous Princess d'Harcourt, who both gambled and cheated till four o'clock in the morning, but who never went to bed till she had received the Sacrament at the hands of her chaplain.

Doubtless many of the nobility the most abandoned to the allurements of sport were influenced by principles superior to these. Among them we may mention the Marquis of Exeter, who once proposed that the race for the Riddlesworth Stakes should not take place on the Monday, as, in order to be present at them, he was obliged to do what he would rather avoid—namely, travel on the Sunday. General Grosvenor, if we remember rightly, treated the proposal with a laugh and a 'rider,' to the effect that the Riddlesworth Stakes, in such case, should be thenceforth called the '*Exeter Change!*'

In the early period of Doncaster races, previous to the '*Sillinger*,' the '*Coop*-day' was *the* day for lord and lout, for the Lady Clara Vere de Veres and the Cicely Jenkinses. For the whole country-side the Cup-day remains still the favourite of the week, and attracts its especial thousands in the north. When the Leger rose from its nine, ten, or a dozen subscribers to thirty or forty, at five-and-twenty guineas each, and to its seventy or eighty, at fifty guineas each, offering chances of fortunes to be won, requiring superior horses, and furnishing opportunities for realising great profits even by their sale if they distinguished themselves, it became an essentially fashionable stake, and the day of running for it an emphatically fashionable day. In its performance and its issues Yorkshire was indeed immensely interested; but the hopes, fears, delight, or despair of the 'country people' were all reserved for 't' race for t' coop.' It was the first prize the old corporations had ever subscribed for; and the example set by a sporting Queen in connection with the same subject had not lost its influence even on those unconscious of it.

We allude to Queen Anne. She not only gave cups to be run for in the north; but this remarkably placid woman was very eager as a runner of her own horses on the Turf. Pick's old *Historical Racing Calendar*, published yearly at York, from 1709 to 1785, affords evidence of this fact. The Queen entered her horses at York, to run for her own cups; but she does not appear to have been fortunate. In July 1712 her gray gelding Pepper came in fifth and third in two heats for her Majesty's hundred-guinea cup. In the following year her gray horse Mustard ran seventh and fifth for a similar prize; four-mile heats, it must be remembered, but the horses were six years old. At the summer meeting of 1714, Anne's bay horse Star won a plate of 40*l*. value, in four heats, thus lost and recovered—four, three, one, one. This was the sporting Queen's last triumph, one of which she was never conscious. After this royal race had been run, 'an express,' says old Pick, 'arrived with advice of the death of her Majesty Queen Anne, upon which the nobility and gentry immediately left the field and attended the Lord Mayor (Wm. Redman, Esq.) and Archbishop Dawes, who proclaimed his Majesty King George I., after which most of the nobility set off for London.'

The sun of York, as we have intimated, paled before Doncaster, which became a trysting-place for delegates from all the nobility, gentry, and commonalty with means of getting thither, from every part of the kingdom. Lady Pentweazle, in the old farce, regrets that less care is taken for the improvement of the race of men than for that of the breed of horses. Had her ladyship ever been at Doncaster the sight there would have cut the ground from under the basis of her regret. We pass over the distinguished people of now ancient days—Sir Charles Bunbury, whose system of running two-year-old horses has been ruinous in its consequences to the steed; the old Earl of Grosvenor, to support whom even the miser Elwes warmed into liberality, lent him 3000 guineas, and nearly broke his own neck in trying to cheat a turnpike for the sake of twopence, on his way home. We say nothing of the beautiful and audacious Mrs. Thornton, wife of a colonel who was chief of the Jockey Club and Prince of the Holy Roman Empire, a lady who rode races for thousands of guineas or hogsheads of claret, who dazzled the eyes as she flew by in her leopard-coloured tunic, coquettishly short enough to exhibit the smallest of feet, and the most richly laced of petticoats; a lady, in short, who was not only a Hippolyta but a Sappho; in her own case joyously recalling her old loves of the stables, and the feats she accomplished, as the jockey-poetess remarks,

'With my mare hard in hand and my whip in my mouth.'

Among the former glories who used to shine on Doncaster racecourse we will merely register the old Earl of Clermont, whom, once riding in a loose coat and a hood by the side of the Prince of Wales, people mistaking for the antiquated Princess Amelia, ascribed a virtue to 'Wales' which he did not possess, and thought him a model of a grand-nephew for taking such care of his aged kinswoman. Then there was Lord Foley, Fox's confederate, as he used to be called, whose horses, like Sackville Fox's, were generally anywhere but first at the winning-post. Greater than he was 'Old Q.,' the last Duke of Queensberry, whose death gave such regret to rascaldom and such wealth to the Yarmouths. Even

'The King—God bless him!—gave a *whew!*
Two dukes just dead—a third gone too!
What, what! could nothing save old Q.,
    The Star of Piccadilly?'

Equal in rank, more noble in spirit than old Q., was
c

the Duke of Grafton, who also often honoured the
St. Leger-day by his presence. He is said to have
been the person who conferred a rich living on a
hard-riding curate, for no other reason than that
the Duke having been 'spilt' in a ditch, the curate
called to him to 'lie still!' while he leaped over him.

The splendour of the show at Doncaster culminated in our fathers' days, or in the spring-time
of many of us, who remember, as if it were but
yesterday, when Petre's Rowton beat Voltaire and
Sir Hercules. In these practical days the train
simply discharges wagon-loads of noble, gentle,
and simple into the town. It was not so of yore.
There was then a *gathering* in its true and 'gradual'
sense. The divers roads brought a diverse company.
The great aristocracy of the county 'progressed' to
their lodgings or to the course like princes, in grand
state-coaches and six, with a score of grooms as
radiant as new liveries and old ale could make them.
There were their stately masters, Rockingham and
Fitzwilliam, Leeds and Cleveland, Harewood and
Wharncliffe, whose sons, cantering along the roads
in joyous groups, would have made a body of cavalry
as handsome as Pompey's, and less regardful of their
beauty. Sons of peers, many brothers together,
young squires—all lords of land, in hand or in hope
—it was a pleasant sight to see them! Protestant
or Catholic, there was a general fraternisation, and
the roads were merry with them—Fairfax, Lane
Fox, Markham of Beccles, Middleton Chaloner,
Vavasour, Bland of Kippax, Mitton, the Gascoynes
of Aberford, young Conyers Osborne, and three or

four of the brothers Lascelles, the eldest of them a 'curled son of Clinias,' and with a not more affable word for Lord George Bentinck or Osbaldiston than for Mr. Gully, who is riding down from Pontefract, and through whose hat Osbaldiston in a duel once sent a ball. 'Better there,' as Gully remarked, 'than through his head!'

Then what a gathering there used to be in the streets on the Monday before the races commenced! Debrett might have found there nearly all his 'peers,' Lodge his 'baronets,' and Burke all his 'commoners' of note. This sort of thing was at its height in 1829, the year when Rowton won. We never saw the territory of the old Saxon De Fossard,—of Tostig, son of Godwin,—of Robert Earl of Mortaigne,—of the Malolieus, or Mauleys,—and, finally, of the Corporation of Doncaster, so brilliant as in that year, when the famous Duchess of St. Albans held a little court on the sunny side of the street, where Norman and Saxon rendered homage to that queen for an hour, ere all, moving off to the races, were encountered by dozens of tract-distributors, solemnly pronouncing that the road to the course was the route to Hades, and something beyond.

Far be it from us to discuss how Lord Cleveland's Voltaire lost the Leger and won the 'Coop,' or how Mr. C. Horncastle played Figaro; and Mr. Leman Rede Charles XII., at the theatre. Let us rather show that the great meeting of 1829 was productive of good results, foreign to the races themselves, but a natural consequence of them. It was among the young beauties and handsome lords and squires, whose numbers rendered that especial assembling a thing to be remembered as a dazzling dream, that first sprang up the idea of that famous 'Charity Bazaar,' for the benefit of the County Hospital, which was subsequently held at York. At this bazaar the chief Yorkshire beauties presided, and their presence wrung poetry, good, bad, and indifferent, out of the hearts and inkstands of half the heirs apparent to Yorkshire estates, and others. Of all the rhymers, however, two only may be said to have knitted rhymes which well deserved to live. These were leisurely-made *impromptus*, the authors of which were Lord Mulgrave (the present Marquis of Normanby) and a youthful scion of a noble house, flaxen-haired, light-eyed, clear-skinned, and with a reputation from college which made the winners of cups, by horses or greyhounds, afraid of him, so much more glorious were the prizes he had carried off in university contests, where there was a cudgelling of brains. This last young poet, and then budding statesman, was Lord Morpeth, now Earl of Carlisle and Lord Lieutenant of Ireland.

Like true poets, these two young lords took the presiding beauties for the subjects of their lines; but while Mulgrave illustrated a group, Morpeth dashed into lyrical love with the whole bevy. The stanzas of either bard, however, present us with pictures of a past which may still interest us; and we give precedence to the sweep of the lyre effected by the rapt author of *Matilda*, as he beheld one of the fairest sights in Christendom—Lady Grantham and her two daughters, the Misses Robinson, officiating together at the same counter. Eurynome amid her three Graces was not a sight more fit to wake the lyre. That of Lord Mulgrave was touched to this tuning:

> 'See that fair troop at yonder stall,
> With one who shines above them all.
> They look a sister group; but *she*,
> The youngest beauty of the three,
> By dearer ties to them allied,
> Of British matrons is the pride.
> Look at her brow, so smooth and fair!
> Care has not found its impress there.
> Her raven locks are black, as when
> She first bewitched the eyes of men.
> Time has delayed for her alone,
> And Youth has marked her for its own.'

Lord Morpeth worshipped that fair mother too; but the young poet was subdued by the general loveliness. A 'card of the races' could not have been more precise to its purpose than his lyric list of the charms, the grace, the names, and merits of the ladies. Thus sang the bard,—and no wonder is it that he has remained a bachelor ever since:

> 'Lady, I covet not that radiant heap
> With more than all the rainbow's colours warm
> The rich mosaic of embroidery keep,
> The pencilled landscape and the painted form.
>
> If round my senses thou wouldst cast thy spell,
> If o'er my coffers thy dominion prove,
> Sell me the beauties that in Grantham dwell,
> Her mouth of softness and her smile of love.
>
> Sell me the loveliness, sedate and high,
> Twined in the bridal-wreath round Petre's head;
> The laughter-loving blue of Vernon's eye,
> Herbert's young bloom, and Milner's high-born tread.

> Sell me the smiles in Fox's dimpling face,
>   The form she borrowed from Titania's dance;
> Stourton's mild lustre, Duncombe's tapering grace,
>   Yorke's full bright orb, and Howard's kindred glance.
>
> Such are the peerless charms that price defy,
>   Above the weight of silver and of gold;
> For when thy winning voice would bid me *buy*,
>   I feel, alas! that I myself am sold.'

The Theban who sang the conquests in the course and other contests at the four great festivals of the Greeks may have produced more lasting lines than the above, born of Doncaster and York; but he produced none which present to us, as these do, the distinctive individuality of the beauties who shed lustre on the scene. The minstrels themselves may have forgotten the homage which they paid in rhyme, and which we commit to type from manuscript copies which were circulating at the time, and which were commented upon till another Leger occupied the souls of men. We will only remark that this autumn meeting fulfilled, in a certain degree, the desire expressed by Walpole, that races and county gatherings might produce that in which the games and assemblies of the ancients were fruitful,—bards to render attendant beauties immortal in deathless (or decent) verse.

We have alluded to the more exalted visitors who were to be habitually seen on Doncaster course; but the truth is, that the more eccentric characters were among the visitors of a lower grade. Some of these eccentric personages, however, contrived to get hanged. Such was the case, some half a century since, with Daniel Dawson, not better known at Doncaster than at Newmarket, and who employed himself, or was employed by others, in poisoning with arsenic the drinking-water of horses whose success in the future race was not desirable to Daniel or his patrons. Several steeds perished in this way at the hands of Daniel in the north, as well as at Newmarket. Ultimately a case from the latter locality was proved against him through the treachery of a confederate, and Daniel suffered death for it at Cambridge. Had he been a martyr in a good cause, he could not have died with more becomingness. Daniel complained of no one, did not even reproach himself; and expressed his satisfactory conviction that he 'should certainly ascend to heaven from the drop!' Brutal as his offence was, it seems ill-measured justice that takes a man's life for that of a beast.

Dawson is beyond our own recollection; but we can well remember a more singular and a much more honest fellow than himself, whose appearance on the Doncaster course was as confidently looked for and as ardently desired as that of any of the lords-lieutenant of the various ridings. We allude to the once famous Jemmy Hirst, the Rawcliffe tanner, whose last of about fifty visits to the '*Sillinger*' and '*Coop*' contests was made when he was hard upon ninety-one years of age. When Jemmy retired from the tanning business with means to set up as a gentleman, the first object he purchased was, not a carriage, but a coffin, depositing therein some of the means whereby he kept himself alive, namely, his provisions. The walls of the room in which this lugubrious sideboard was erected were hung round with all sorts of rusty agricultural implements. This lord of a strange household retained a valet and a female 'general servant.' His stud consisted of mules, dogs, and a bull; mounted on which he is said to have hunted with the Badsworth hounds. His most familiar friends were a tame fox and otter. He certainly rode the bull when he went out shooting, and was then accompanied by pigs as pointers. In fair-time, Hirst used to take this bull and a couple of its fellows to be baited, sitting proudly by himself while his valet went about collecting the 'coppers.' His waistcoat was a glossy garment made of the neck-feathers of the drake, from the pocket of which we have seen him issue his own bank-notes, bearing responsibilities of payment to the amount of '*Five* halfpence.' His carriage was a sort of palanquin, carried aloft by high wheels, and its chief peculiarity was that there was not a nail about it. This vehicle was really better known at Doncaster than the stately carriage of Lord Fitzwilliam himself. It was the boast of the proud and dirty gentleman who sat enthroned there, that he never had paid, and never *would* pay, any sort of tax to the King; and how he managed to shoot, as he did, without paying for a license, was best known to himself. He was the most popular man on the course, and, unlike very many who began rich and ended poor, Jemmy increased in wealth year by year. He was wont to contrast himself with 'the Prince's friend,' Colonel Mellish, who inherited an immense property, won two Legers in two consecutive years, 1804-5, and finally died almost a pauper. Jemmy had undoubtedly, in *his* view of things, done better than

Colonel Mellish; but the tanner through life never thought of the welfare but of one human being—that of James Hirst. He was as selfish as the butcher-churchwarden of Doncaster, who ruined the grand old tower of the church by placing a hideous clock-face in it, which was so constructed that no one could see the time by it except from the butcher's own door!

We should hardly render Hirst justice, however, if we omitted to state how such a great man departed from this earth. The folding-doors of his old coffin were closed upon him. Eight buxom widows carried his corpse for a *honorarium* of half-a-crown each. Jemmy had expressed a desire to have eight old maids to undertake this service, bequeathing half-a-guinea to each as hire. But the ladies in question were not forthcoming. So the widows were engaged in their place; but why the fee was lowered we cannot tell, unless it was to pay for the bagpipe and fiddle which headed the procession. All the country round flocked in to do Jemmy honour or to enjoy the holiday; and for many a year afterwards might the sorrowing comment be heard on Doncaster course, 'Nay, lad! t' Coop-day seems nought-loike wi'out Jemmy!' and the mourners took out his 'Fi-hawpence notes,' and compared their own touching respective memories of the departed glory of Doncaster.

At the close of Jemmy's career, that of wonderfully well-dressed members of the 'swell mob' was at its busiest, if not at its brightest. The latter, however, was only short-lived, let it be as temporarily prosperous as it might; and it bore a grand moral with it to those who witnessed its two extremes. We particularly remember a most illustrious party of this equivocal 'quality,' who really dazzled common folk by the splendour of their 'turn-out,' both as regarded themselves and their equipage. People took them for foreign princes, or native nobility returned from foreign climes, and not yet familiarly known to the public. This impression did not last long. The well-dressed, finely-curled, highly-scented, richly-jewelled strangers sauntering among the better-known aristocracy commenced a series of predatory operations which speedily brought them within the fastness of the town-gaol. No one who saw them there a day or two later, after seeing them on the course, will ever forget the sight and the strange contrast. Stripped of their finery, closely cropped, and clad in coarse flannel dresses, we remember them seated at a board with a hot lump of stony-looking rice before them for a dinner. They gloomily refused the wholesome fare; but four-and-twenty hours more, sharpening their appetites and demolishing its fastidiousness, subdued them to the level of their fortunes, and the prison provender was consumed with the calm dignity, but therewith the intense disgust, of philosophers and men of the world.

Altogether there was occasionally a very mixed society on and about the course; among the so to speak professional *habitués*, men who made a business of the pursuit there—who were actors rather than spectators, and all of whom have disappeared without leaving a successor in his peculiar line—we may mention the old Duke of Leeds, redolent of port; the white-faced Duke of Cleveland, 'the Jesuit of the ring;' Mr. Ridsdale, ex-footman, then millionaire, finally pauper; blacksmith Richardson, who, shaking his head at 'Leeds,' would remark of himself that sobriety alone had saved him from being hanged; Mr. Beardsworth, who had been originally a hackney-coachman, now sporting his crimson liveries; Mr. Crockford, who commenced life with a fish-basket; and the well-known son of the ostler at the Black Swan in York, wearing diamond rings and pins, betting his thousands, and looking as cool the while as if he not only largely used the waters of Pactolus, but owned half the gold-dust on its banks.

The two extremes of the official men as regarded rank were, perhaps, Lord George Bentinck and Mr. Gully, the ex-pugilist. The former introduced at Doncaster the signal-flag, to regulate the 'starts,' and he founded the Bentinck Fund (with the money subscribed for a testimonial to himself) for the relief of decayed jockeys and trainers. The two men were equal in one respect—the coolness with which they either won or lost. They who remember the year when Petre's Matilda beat Gully's Mameluke, and who witnessed the event and its results, speak yet with a sort of pride of Gully's conduct. He had lost immensely; but he was the first man who appeared in the betting-rooms to pay any one who had a bet registered against him, and he was the last man to leave, not retiring till he was satisfied that there did not remain a single claimant. He paid away a grand total on that occasion which, properly invested, would have set all the poor in Doncaster at ease for ever.

We have alluded to some of the most famous of running-horses; let us add, there was no instance of the same horse winning both the Derby and St. Leger stakes till the year 1800, when Kit Wilson's Champion carried off the two prizes. The old charm was broken; but the like feat has only been rarely accomplished since that time. Nearly half a century elapsed before it was repeated by Lord Clifden's (or rather Lord George Bentinck's) Surplice. Mr. Wilson won the two races, not only with the same horse, but the same jockey, Frank Buckle. Surplice was ridden in the Derby triumph by Templeman; at Doncaster by Nat.

Finally, this year much of the old excitement seems to have been aroused, and doubtless great will be the gathering where more than fourscore 'Legers' have been now decided. There are a few very old men toddling about the ancient town who, from the shoulders of their sires, saw the first race run when Lord North was the careless and good-natured Premier. To these the name of the present favourite, Thormanby, has a pleasant Yorkshire sound, and with them there *is* something in a name. With the issues of the coming race, however, we have nothing to do, except to remark on this occasion the possibility, though it be remote, of the success of what does not often deserve to succeed—namely, 'High Treason.'

II.
ON THE ROAD.
1864.

ON THE ROAD.

1864.

When the British Association first assembled at York, in the year 1831, it was encountered in some quarters by a storm of derision. The members were charged with being moved by vanity, and wiseacres foresaw that the result of their meeting would be valueless. There were not wanting other persons who were of opinion that the project would bear good fruit, and that the public would take great interest in the proceedings. How best to report the latter, and how swiftest to carry the reports to London, severely exercised the proprietors of journals. The time was the time before railways, and the flashing of reports along the electric wire was a phenomenon, if thought of by one or two, not even dreamed of by the public generally. The reports had to be translated from shorthand signs and symbols into readable text, and the manuscript was then despatched by post or by coach. In those days the Royal Mail carried such freight to or from London. They were well called *Royal*, or his Majesty's Mails; for when letter-carrying was first instituted it was for the King's use exclusively, and the 'people' were not considered. It was the King's convenience that was first thought of.

Long was the interval before poor wretches could send the tale of their wrongs, or ardent lovers transmit a record of the furnace in their hearts, from one end of the kingdom to another, at the small and uniform cost of one penny.

Some great thing was considered to have been achieved when, in Queen Elizabeth's days, the Archbishop of Canterbury could despatch a letter to a distance of sixty-three miles in forty hours. In France, however, there had been a better ordering of these things for a very long period. We had been slow to imitate Louis XI. by setting up post-horses; and it was not till the Stuart wore the crowns of England and Scotland that a great northern post was established, in order to bring London and Edinburgh into closer proximity. Even then the transport of individuals, rather than of letters, was the main business; but, again, in those rough-travelling times every traveller was any and every body's letter-carrier.

King James has the credit of having established something like an organised foreign post. But the machinery was often out of gear, and merchants and others frequently announced that they would carry letters abroad—of course, for a 'consideration' —in spite of the authorities, who had consigned the office, its emoluments and privileges, to the superintendence and advantage of duly-appointed officials. These foreign-post officials must have been more successful in their vocation than those who managed —or mismanaged—the inland post; for, in James's time, it was remarked that a man could more speedily receive a reply to a letter sent to Madrid than he could to one despatched to Ireland or Scotland. The fact is, that the home-post was in the hands of carriers and also of pedestrian wayfarers; and the former even could not convey a note to the North and bring an answer back under two months at the very earliest. Witherings, one of the chief postmasters of Charles I.'s days, reformed this abuse. He established a running-post, as it was called, between England and Scotland, the riders pushing forward night and day. And it was hoped, if the thing was not actually accomplished at the time, that the writer of a letter from London to Edinburgh would receive a reply within a week! When this running, or rather riding, post was established, very sanguine was Witherings, the Rowland Hill of his day. 'If the post,' he said, ' be punctually paid, the news will come *sooner than thought*.' He considered that news which passed from Edinburgh to London in three days and nights by relays of horses, whose swinging trot never ceased, was outstripping thought. He did not dream of the electric transmission of thought itself from one end of the world to another in fewer hours than his posts took days to outstrip thought, as he fondly imagined, between the chief cities of England and Scotland.

There was some danger at times that the packets intrusted to these mounted postmen—or much the same sort of postboys that Cowper has limned so artistically—should come to grief. To rob the post became part of the highway robber's vocation. The postboys, though never well armed, held their own in some very dramatic combats now and then between brigand and letter-bearer, on some wild moor or desolate road. Occasionally the highwayman blew out the postboy's brains, and galloped away with the bags. At others the plucky carrier of missives, if he lacked the means to shoot his assailant dead, contrived to maim and capture him, and a month or two later perhaps he trotted gaily at night past the dark gibbet on which the robber was swinging in chains. In the whole affair there was a dash of manhood, for the highwayman met his adversary face to face, and set his life on the venture. It was open war, such as legitimate kings practised, but which they punished with death in the persons of those who imitated them, and who provoked these little private wars for their individual profit.

One other peril threatened the letter-bags which were carried on horseback, before the mail-coach swept with them over well-made roads, under the care of the scarlet-coated guard and his armoury of horse-pistols and blunderbusses. If the postboy was a craven, he would dismount at some roadside inn, and take a draught of ale and courage at the bar, wherewith to dash more furiously across the neighbouring heath. In the old days these boys even looked shy at Turnham Green Common, which was then indeed of wide extent. These chicken-hearted Mercuries always pulled up in Hammersmith, and drank their pint before they faced the common. But in those days there were also petty-larceny rascals, who had no more spirit to pull out a pistol on a common than the craven postboy had to be exposed to its fire; and it was the work of these little larcenists to cut away the saddle-bags from the pony, which stood patiently at the door while the boy was drinking at the bar. Nevertheless, they who filched, and they who ignobly allowed themselves to be despoiled in this unseemly style, were held in contempt by braver fellows in their vocation. Between the latter many an encounter has taken place on a dreary waste or moonlit heath, which would not have disgraced those annals of chivalry which are apt to draw small distinction between *battle* and *murder*.

We must not overlook a third peril which beset letters in the good old times. There was a possibility of their being opened and read, ' with your leave, good seal!' by unauthorised people. Mr. Lewins* tells us that ' one of the ordinances published during the Protectorate sets forth that the Post Office ought to be upheld, not only because it is the best means of conveying public and private communications, but also because it may be made the agent in discovering and preventing many wicked designs which have been and are daily contrived against the peace and welfare of this Commonwealth, the intelligence whereof cannot well be communicated except by letters of escript.' We cannot but think, however, that Mr. Lewins has mistaken the signification of this passage, wherein he sees that ' a system of espionage was thus settled, which has always been abhorrent to the nature and feelings of Englishmen. But, perhaps,' he adds, ' we ought not to judge the question in the light of the present day.' It will bear such light, however; and so will the fact above

* *Her Majesty's Mails.*

recorded. The Commonwealth Government, as the words themselves show, did not authorise the spying into letters; it simply improved postal communication in order that its own means of intercourse with parties at a distance might be increased and facilitated.

On the other hand, there was something of meanness in the way the franking privileges were established by the Parliament of 1735. A committee reported to the Commons that 'the privilege of franking letters by the knights, &c., chosen to represent the Commons in Parliament, began with the creating of a Post Office in the kingdom by Act of Parliament.' It was proposed that the privilege should then be assumed and enjoyed by members, at least during each session of Parliament. Some few opposed the proposition as shabby. Sir Heneage Finch protested that it was a 'poor mendicant proviso, and below the honour of the House.' The Speaker, Sir Harbottle Grimston, when called upon to put the question, declared as he did so 'that he felt ashamed of it.' The Bill was carried by a large majority, and was sent up to the Lords, who at once rejected it. The dignity of the Peers seemed enhanced by the step; but the Commons ultimately comprehended the meaning of it. They inserted a clause providing that 'the Lords' own letters should pass free;' and *then* the Upper House recognised the presence in the Bill of a virtue which it had previously lacked, and passed it accordingly.

Poor people, meanwhile, had to pay exorbitant rates of postage, which continued down to a very recent period. Even persons belonging to the middle classes did not scruple to cheat the Post Office. On the covers of newspapers (which went free of postage) they wrote in milk; the writing when held to the fire became legible, and the newspaper went back again with an answer similarly inscribed. Another method was to dot such letters in the printed paper itself as served to convey the sender's meaning. Detection often ensued, for the postal authorities were wary; but nothing came of it. No signature was used by which the writer could be discovered, and the person to whom the paper was addressed simply refused to take it in, charged heavily as it was in such cases as a letter. Poorer people had other means of cheap communication. Children who went forth into the world, and who loved to let the old folk at home know that they were alive and well, and also to learn home news from them, not being able to pay a shilling, perhaps, for a letter, were wont, at periods agreed upon, to send blank sheets of note-paper properly addressed. It was in this address that the parties concerned read the domestic telegrams which they had been expecting; after looking at which they returned the letter as too expensive a luxury for them to purchase. Sackfuls of such letters were weekly carried backwards and forwards over the country for nothing. It took long years before the legislature found out that they would gain more by carrying letters for a penny, which was duly paid, than by asking a shilling, or whatever high charge the tariff allowed, and which they never received at all. The statistical logic of the day could not understand that pence could ever represent more than shillings; but when fifty penny letters took the place of a shilling one, the excellence of the arithmetic was indisputable.

Moralists used to shake their heads at the demoralised poor people who saved their money, heard from their friends, and made the Post Office serve them gratis notwithstanding. Yet it was what the richest in the land, and out of it too, were doing! Public officers could frank any weight 'On his Majesty's Service,' and under such pretence peers have received their top-boots and peeresses harpsichords or pianos. And as for English absentees in foreign lands, who were of 'quality,' as the phrase used to go, their ambassador's bag conveyed all of, and even more than, their correspondence, to their own advantage and the detriment of the postal revenue.

As in the Church, so in the Post Office there were reformers before the reformation. A metropolitan penny-post and parcels-delivery office was established in Charles II.'s reign. It was so novel and incomprehensible that the Protestants smelt a Popish plot in it. It was so profitable to Mr. Murray and his successor, Mr. Docwray, that the head of the Papists in England, the Duke of York, a large amount of whose revenue was charged on the Post Office, maintained that this private but authorised penny enterprise should be amalgamated with the General Post Office, and his income increased in due proportion to the increase of profits. Ultimately the amalgamation took place. The system died out, so far as letters were concerned, not in a penny, but in a 'twopenny-post' form. But Mr. Rowland Hill happily revolutionised the whole establishment.

When the Duke of York came to the throne, he had, as James II., the control of the Post Office revenue, and he abused the control and misapplied the revenue. One sample will indicate the quality of many. He granted a pension of 4700*l.* a year, to be paid out of the Post Office receipts, to Barbara Palmer, Duchess of Cleveland, the most shameless of his brother's mistresses. This pension is still paid to the Duke of Grafton as her living representative. The country has paid dearly for the honour of the first Duke of Grafton having been the illegitimate son of Charles II. and Barbara Palmer. The pension was granted one hundred and seventy-seven years ago, and if we multiply the years by the sum yearly received we shall find that the cost to the country of the very equivocal honour alluded to amounts to 831,900*l.* sterling in direct payments. If we count the interest, the sum will be many millions. Dealing with the dead and not with the living, we may say that if any of the five Dukes of Grafton who have passed away, and who belong to history, especially to the history of the Post Office, had been worth the money expended on them, one might hear of such iniquity with comparative patience. But we have not that consolation. Henry Fitzroy himself, the first duke, was a *roué* and an imbecile. His blustering and swearing and love-making son Charles was so loyal that when Pelham told him he should retire from the ministry as soon as the rebellion in Scotland was suppressed, Grafton exclaimed, 'Then, by G—! I hope you'll see it twinkle in the Highlands for a good while yet!' The annuity earned by Barbara Palmer out of the Post Office helped the third duke, Augustus—him whom Wilkes attacked and whom Junius has damned to everlasting fame—to maintain in splendour that handsome hussy Nancy Parsons, and perhaps helped Nancy to a dowry when she was espoused by the easily-pleased Lord Maynard. Without pursuing the subject further, we may say that these Post Office pensions were public robberies. Even that to Lawrence Hyde, Earl of Rochester, was not to be defended. It amounted to 4000*l.* per annum; but we cannot say whether it continues to be received by Lord Rochester's living representative, Lord Clarendon. We believe that it is not.

Of the old postboy time, when the boy did business on his own account as well as on his master's, this lively incident is told by the author already noticed:

'Some of these postboys were sad rogues, who, besides taking advantage of confusion in the two posts, were accustomed to carry letters themselves concealed upon them, and for charges of course quite unorthodox. In all records of the Post Office, principally the Surveyor's Book, referring to country post-offices from the year 1735, there are long complaints from the surveyor on this head. The following, " exhibiting more malice than good grammar," may be taken as a specimen, and will suffice to show the way things were managed at that date: " At this place (Salisbury) found the postboys to have carried on vile practices in taking the *bye-letters*, delivering them in this cittye and taking back answers, especially the *Andover* riders. On the 15th found on Richard Kent, one of the Andover riders, 5 bye-letters, all for this cittye. Upon examining the fellow, he confessed he had made it a practice, *and persisted to continue in it*, saying he had noe wages from his master. I took the fellow before the magistrate, proved the facts, and he was committed; but pleading to have no money or friends, desired a punishment to be whipped, which accordingly *he was to the purpose*. Wrote the case to Andover, and ordered the fellow to be dismissed, but no regard was had thereto; but the next day the same rider came post, ran about the cittye for letters, *and was insolent*. Again he came post with two gentlemen, made it his business to take up letters; the fellow, however, instead of returning to Andover, gets two idle fellows and rides off with three horses, which was a return for his master not obeying my instructions." '

Too much drink in the postboy is often set down as the cause of 'the stopping of the mails.' The letters that came or went by sailing-packets were frequently half-devoured by the rats. Transmission was everywhere slow. It was accelerated by Allen, and still further improved in 1782 by Palmer's mail-coach system, at which innovation many wise persons shook their heads in mistrust, seeing with the usual unswiftness of pace a break-neck running away towards the end of all things. It was much the same when railroads took the universal correspondence; and when Mr. Rowland Hill proposed the uniform penny stamp the secretary of the Post Office maintained that the revenue would not recover itself for half a century, and that the poor would not write. Lord Lichfield pointed to the absurdity of supposing that letters, the conveyance of which cost on an average twopence-halfpenny each, could ever be carried for a penny and have a profit on the transaction! The uniform rate was pronounced by Colonel Maberly to be 'impracticable;' and as to pre-payment he was sure the public would object to it, however low the rate might be.

The power of opening letters under a warrant—and the statute directed that there should be a fresh warrant for every letter, not a general one to open any—was framed by Lord Somers. It has been acted upon more or less, and more or less according to the statute, by all Governments. The inquiry, when Sir James Graham was implicated, has checked at least any violation of the statute. Mr. Lewins seems to think that the examination of foreign despatches sent by post was confined to England. It has been universal. Outrage of trust was most unpleasantly illustrated a few years back in Prussia, when some of the King's own letters were forwarded to the Emperor of Russia. The felony had been committed by Prussian noblemen, it was said, and great scandal ensued. When a British ambassador at a foreign court complained that despatches bore not the official seal from home, but that of the country to which he was accredited, he was coolly informed that the officer charged with reading despatches from foreign Governments had, by mistake, re-sealed them with the wrong stamp. 'But why have my despatches been opened?' asked the ambassador. 'Only that we might know what was in them,' is said to have been the aggravating reply.

A letter once posted can never be recalled. Mr. Lewins gives many examples of the results of this just regulation, from which we take one:

'A tradesman's daughter, who had been for some time engaged to a prosperous young draper in a neighbouring town, heard from one whom she and her parents considered a creditable authority that he was on the verge of bankruptcy. "Not a day was to be lost in breaking the bond by which she and her small fortune were linked to penury." A letter, strong and conclusive in its language, was at once written and posted; when the same informant called upon the young lady's friends to contradict and explain his previous statement, which had arisen out of some misunderstanding. "They rushed at once to the post-office; and no words can describe the scene: the reiterated appeals, the tears, the wringing of hands, the united entreaties of father, mother, and daughter for the restoration of the fatal letter." But the rule admitted of no exception, and the young lady had to repent at leisure of her inordinate haste.'

The following choice bit of statistics is notable for its singularity:

'It is a matter of notoriety, furnishing a fruitful subject for reflection and comment, that the great majority of complaints reaching the Post Office authorities take their rise with *clergymen*. As offering a curious commentary on the Divine injunction to be merciful, and to forgive "seventy times seven," we once saw a requisition from a clergyman for the dismissal of a post-office clerk—a man with a wife and several children, by the way—on the ground that he had twice caused his letters to be mis-sent, in each case losing the clerical correspondent a post.'

This reminds us of a defunct station-master (Mr. Mitchell) at Reading, who never heard, as he sat in his room, the noise of something wrong on the platform without quietly remarking, 'There's a disturbance on the platform. What *can* have put out the clergyman to-day?'

What is done with the millions of old letters that have passed through the post? When Sadi and his friend were in the garden of roses they both enjoyed the fragrance, but one took home a heap of flowers and enjoyed the delicious odour for months, even in the dried leaves. We may scarcely expect the same pleasure from old letters:

' So mournfully they bring again
    The past, with less of light than shade,
Before the mind; the pleasure, pain,
    The joy that gleamed out but to fade;

The sorrow we were wont to feel,
    The laughing tide of sunny youth,
And hopes and thoughts that used to steal
    About the heart, and seemed like truth.'

III.
CAMBRIDGE.
1862.

CAMBRIDGE.

1862.

The British Association first met at Cambridge, at the opening of its third session, in 1833. The members assembled in the same ancient town in 1845. For the third time Cambridge was the trysting-place of philosophers and others in 1862. On this last occasion, the *Athenæum* of September 27th said:

Cambridge will next week be crowded with inquirers, with philosophers and professors, with idlers and ladies; so that we need not solicit a hearing for some general gossip on what the students who bring something of their own to that place will find to interest and amuse them, either as sights or as memories, on the banks of the Cam.

With a difference, the town will be very like what it was in the olden time, when the place swarmed with students and monks—when between four and five thousand scholars taxed the resources of instructors, and a score of hostels held hundreds of philosophical and religious men, who did not indeed associate for the sake of science, but who were, nevertheless, busily employed in the composition of legends and cognate matter acceptable to the mental appetite of the period. The assembly next week will enrich the town and the neighbouring villages. In remoter times the reverse was the case, and twenty-three villages groaned under heavy impositions merely to support in comfort the one monastery of St. Giles.

The road to Cambridge, or rather the shire which surrounds it, is not now, as it was in William III.'s time, a vast and desolate fen, saturated with all the moisture of thirteen counties, and overhung during a great part of the year, as an historian has described it, 'by a low gray mist, high above which rose, visible many miles, the magnificent tower of Ely.' The roads are said to have been at that time the worst in the island; and in that dreary region, covered by vast flights of wild-fowl, a 'half-savage population, known by the name of the Breedlings, there led an amphibious life, sometimes wading, and sometimes rowing, from one islet of firm ground to another.' These were the 'Cambridgeshire Camels,' who went about on stilts, like the peasants of the Landes, but for different reasons. The philosophers who used to solemnly traverse the distance between London and Cambridge on horseback, or they who painfully coached it—a summer day's journey—went their way invested with the dignity of their vocation; but the dignity of a philosopher whirled along at the rate of a mile a minute is for the time annihilated. He can neither observe nor be observed; and yet in the county itself there is much that is worthy of observation.

We would recommend those who have leisure to

make such observation, to look well at the land as they wend or tarry; there is as much instruction in it as in any of the libraries. The mind's eye has often seen 'old John of Gaunt' in silken suit at lady's knee and on his own, or in panoply of war, or mantled and coroneted as a princely peer; but this Cambridgeshire land once saw 'time-honoured Lancaster' in another suit—the good warm attire of an honest country gentleman superintending the draining of his estate. John, indeed, was a great drainer, and helped to reclaim the lands which by injudicious management had been converted into fens. The pursuit was profitable for himself and others, and his name deserves to be remembered with that of Pallavicino, who rose up on Peter's pence, and spent the money in land and irrigation.

In Cambridgeshire, however, water has as often been let in upon the land as drawn from it. To raise the latter the muddy water of the Ouse has been thus let in upon it, with a result of elevating the soil two feet. The water, short of its deposit, was then thrown back by a mill. Irruption of this sort was always considered beneficial; a breach of bank, after the mischief was repaired, enriched the land more than 'soaking' did, because in the latter case the water came filtered. This draining and banking and enclosing will not, of course, account altogether for the great increase in the value of land hereabouts; but the system has much to do with it. In Henry VIII.'s time the value of the rectory of Doddington was 22*l*. Gooch's *Survey* sets it down in his time at 2000*l*., which, at the full tithe of what the land let

E

for, would have been, according to the same authority, 4800*l*. Much has been thought of the land growing turf here having been sold at fourscore pounds per acre. What the profit was to the purchaser we do not know; but we believe that it was not a tithe of that realised in the old brick-fields round London. Middleton mentions fields which, after producing 4000*l*. profit, became good grass-land by aid of town manure.

The deer which, in the olden time, as elsewhere at the present period, were addicted, at certain seasons, to dig up the land with their fore-feet, in holes to the depth of a foot, or even of half-a-yard, contributed a new word to our language. These were called 'scrapes.' For a wayfarer to tumble into one of these was sometimes done at the cost of a broken leg; and, ultimately, any Cambridge man who found himself in an unpleasant position, from which extrication was difficult, was said to have 'got into a scrape.'

The uplands consist chiefly of chalk hills, these being a portion of the great chalk formation which traverses the island from Dorsetshire to the Yorkshire coast. The *savants* will find profitable subject of discussion in the organic remains characteristic of the chalk and clunch beds of the county of Cambridge. The *savants* of some future century will, perhaps, occupy, if not perplex, themselves, should they ever come upon the remains of the *Prodigium Willinghamense*, with which England was busying itself above a hundred years ago. If Cambridgeshire were unable to boast of great men, it might be proud of its big boy—the big boy of Willingham. At the age of five years and ten months, in the year 1747, and the month of September, died young Tom Hall, more feet high than he was years old. Time could not sustain such a lusty youth, but handed him over to Death. Of all precocious lads, Willingham Tom was the most forward. When two years and some months of age, he fairly frightened the Royal Society itself—a body very much accustomed to deal with marvels. The baby was then nearly four feet high, and could throw, with ease, from his hand a blacksmith's hammer of seventeen pounds weight. Was not this a youth to startle his governess, to say nothing of his mother and sisters? Paterfamilias must have looked with as much alarm as affection on the son who, at five, wore a moustache on his lip, spoke in a bass voice that made his hearers shake again, and trod with the resounding step of a full-grown Polyphemus. Fancy such a juvenile hopeful seeking admission to a young ladies' school; how he would have fluttered the dovecot! To what uses might he not have been turned in taming the bullies in the Lower School at Eton! Had he lived and grown at his usual rate, a foot a year, what a desirable match he would have been at four-and-twenty! But the world could not bear with patience the baby Titan, whose foot at five years old was eight inches long, whose calf you could barely garter with a band of eleven inches, and who weighed fourscore and five pounds. And so, happily for himself and society, the boy died—*non flebilis occidit*, and the county philosophers of the day wrote treatises on him, speculated on his peculiarities, accounted, or thought they did, for his growth, and showered epitaphs upon him in poor English and more indifferent Latin. As a youth of the greatest weight in the county, the Willingham prodigy should not be altogether forgotten in the section of Physiology. They will find in him a true descendant of those stout men of these parts who alone stood their ground against the Danes when the rest of the East Angles fled, and kept the Norman out of Ely when all besides was his own. The philosophers will find that the Willingham prodigy was the last of that race of Cambridgeshire men who could carry eight bushels of barley on their backs, when half that quantity was a load for the men of other counties.

The spirit of the locality of the great assembly of next week is one to deepen and strengthen the modesty of the most modest and yet greatest of sages. Cambridge is a place of much learning, and not merely in the sense of that wag of Merton, who described his own college in the same words, because 'every fellow brought some learning to it, and took none away.' The ablest master will find here the name and the memory of a greater than he. The profoundest philosopher will meet with the effigy of him who laid the foundations of his philosophy, wanting which his own superstructure would not have been raised. Healer, if in conceit of thy power, unbonnet here to the great physicians who were before thee. Minstrel, however skilled in sweeping the lyre, the glorious shades of the most tuneful of all poets will encounter you here. Divine, not unworthily honoured, render homage here to the Titans of Divinity. Lawyers and legislators, the great fathers of whom you are the clever sons, have names inscribed here, in whose presence it behoves you to be humble-minded. The measure of the glory of Cambridge is full and overflowing. In the names of Bacon, Milton, and Newton we may resume the history of English intellect. Even the never-do-wells of the University—of some of whom it might be said, as Antonelli says to Lodovico,

'All the damnable degrees
Of drinking have you staggered through'—

had at least wit enough to write some of our raciest plays.

Divines, physicians, and poets cluster about Caius. What contrasts too among the first—Jeremy Taylor and Titus Oates!—the former born in, the very pride of, Cambridge, brought up in its free school, entering thence as a sizar at Caius, with his good father the churchwarden looking proudly on, having done his best to make his boy worthy of that to which he attained—a bishopric. Titus was a sizar like Jeremy; but that Rutlandshire (not Sussex) lad was a liar from the beginning—a fellow who stooped to rob his own tailor, and to deny his own rascality—who went to Salamanca for a degree, and ended with pillory and whip, a sore back, a crushed body, an unfailing appetite, and unquenchable impudence in prison. Shadwell, who smiles on us too, from Caius and Gonville, is of quite another quality, despite all Dryden's satire. Honest Tom was a respecter of truth; he honoured it in others and practised it himself. If he be not so well remembered now as many of his contemporaries, the reason may be partly found in the oracular judgment of Rochester, that if Shadwell had burnt all he wrote, and printed all he spoke, he would have shown more wit and humour than any other poet. But the most practically great of all the sons of Caius was William Harvey, the discoverer of the circulation of the blood. His native town never produced a second worthy; but how could a peer to him be expected from Folkestone?—a place so tortuous and confused that it is said to have been built one Saturday night in the dark, and around which the simple folk once raised their nets to keep out the smallpox! As we turn from Caius, we bow to the shades of Taylor, of Harvey, and other noble students, only wishing that they could elbow from the group that superlative scoundrel, Titus, whose very ghost seems all brazen and unabashed.

But if visitors or philosophers are in search of contrasts, let them look at the two shadows of old students, the one sedately walking, the other jauntily flirting about the vicinity of Trinity Hall. The former is solemn Tusser, who wrote the *Five Hundred Points of Good Husbandry*, and died a bankrupt gentleman-farmer, who was unable to apply them. The other is Mr. Stanhope, better known as *the* Lord Chesterfield, a finer gentleman than Titus Oates, but as little scrupulous as he in violations of truth. Do you not mind how he went up to Whitfield, and said, ' Sir, I will say to you what I will not say to other people—*how I admire you!*' Well, Whitfield, if he sneered at Stanhope, might himself smile greetingly at the clusters of good men and true, rustling in their gowns, as the sun shows them dimly about Corpus Christi. They are all clerics. There is worthy John Copcot, so lean by study and fasting, that a Dutch philosopher, one Drusius, once exhausted himself by making a joke of it, and addressed a letter, 'Manibus Johannis Copcot.' One as lean as Copcot is at his side, Dr. Stephen Hales, the vegetarian, who advocated total abstinence from strong drinks before Father Mathew was born, and who taught George III. his conjugations. Herring of Bangor is near them smiling satisfiedly as he looks over his sermon against the *Beggars' Opera*. But these, and Tennison himself, with others of like quality and vocation, fade into very weak shadows indeed, when Matthew Parker appears, 'mine own good master Parcare' of Latimer's letters. What beauty and dignity about that great primate, to know whose history is to know the ecclesiastical and literary history of his period! What a subject for a painter, that of Queen Anne Boleyn recommending to him, then her young chaplain, her little daughter Elizabeth! How well that daughter rewarded him for his faithful observance of her mother's recommendation! The greatest contrast here to Parker whom we can call to mind is that jolly, noisy, frolicsome prelate and earl, Hervey, Bishop of Derry and Earl of Bristol. He was as good-natured a graduate as Corpus ever sent forth into the world, which he enjoyed himself, and so liked others to enjoy, that his spirit probably did not object, when his body was brought home from the Mediterranean in a puncheon of rum, to the nightly practice of the sailors of 'tapping the bishop.' There is a story connected with the episcopal Earl of Bristol and his contemporary, Dr. Balguy, which concerns Cambridge teaching. It is well known that Bishop Hoadley, another distinguished Cambridge man, recognised the supremacy of the State in Church affairs. Dr. John Milner subsequently declared that by such a course, 'both living and dying, he undermined the Church of which he was a prelate.' Dr. Balguy was accustomed to defend the so-called Erastianism of Hoadley, and on one of these occasions, says Milner, 'having to discuss this subject with him, in the presence of Lord Hervey, Bishop of Derry, and others, I asked him whether, if he had accepted the bishopric (which he had refused) and the King had sent to him *a known, professing, and unbaptised Jew*, to be consecrated a bishop of the Church of England, he would consecrate him or not. His answer was, Yes, I would.' This story is told in Dr. Husenbeth's life of the Roman Catholic, Milner. But Cambridge need not be disturbed by it: Milner must have been deceived, or the Cambridge man, in sport, gave to the absurd query touching an impossible case a startling reply, the humour of which was lost on the querist. To take the reply as serious is a fair specimen of the *sancta simplicitas* of Milner, to whom the very name of Hoadley was an abomination.

But pass we on to King's, where the echoes ought to be musical still, for there, among other worthies, studied and sang Phineas Fletcher and Waller, who was not so desperately in love with Sacharissa as he pretended to be, nor pretended so ardently as the world, who do not read him, gives him credit for. But who are those two remarkable personages whom your mind's eye sees standing together, and your mind's ear detects holding colloquies upon politics? Walsingham and Walpole! Sir Francis and Sir Robert? Nay, if you lack contrasts, may you not find the strongest here? So it would seem; but think the matter over well, and you will find the seeming contrast shaping itself into the form of something like a parallel. The *men* were unlike; but the *ministers* had much in common. Both used spies and agents, were too wary to be abused by them, and had patience enough to let a plot be played just so far as to enable them to lay hold of the greatest number of plotters. At the end of their power and their lives, Walsingham did not leave wherewith to bury him, and Walpole bequeathed to his heir 40,000*l*. worth of debts. Turning hence to the shadows about Queen's, we recognise among them more divines and lawyers than politicians. *There* is quaint epigrammatic Fuller, of the 'Worthies,' and honest Sir John King, that marvellous lawyer, who actually returned to his clients the fees they had given him, when he was unable to render them equivalent service. Probably there will be few visitors at Cambridge who will remember the name of one of the ablest of the students of Queen's, Wasse, rector of Aynhoe; and yet it was of him that modest Bentley said, 'When I am dead, Wasse will be the most learned man in England.' Queen's, too, has its great subject of contrast in the persons of Sherlock and Hoadley. How capitally is the life-long character of each illustrated in that little incident of Hoadley coming away from an examination in Tully, with a sparkling compliment from his tutor! 'Ben,' said Sherlock, in his little jealous way, 'you made good use of L'Estrange's translation to-day.' 'No, Tom,' replied Ben, with that electric readiness which always rendered an attack upon him a matter of peril,—'no, Tom; I forgot to send the bedmaker to borrow yours, which is the only copy in college!'

Then is not this a singular company to be culled from the greater assembly of men who have made Jesus College famous? There is Flamsteed rapt in unveiling the splendid mysteries of the stars, and tickled at the simplicity of the laundress who takes him for a conjuror, and offers him half-a-crown. How marked the contrast between the great astronomer, whose mind was lifted to the empyrean, and Ockley, who was more sensual than any of the Saracens whose manners he described! Flamsteed snatched purity from the divine subjects of his study; Ockley, of the earth earthy, died of an easy-chair and two bottles of port a day. One other contrast we have here in Jortin and Sterne: the former of Huguenot blood, the good vicar who wrote such useful, but dry-as-dust, books; the latter, the parson whose charming and rascally stories equally delight us, the man of noble sentiments who was not above beating his wife. Christ's College cannot exhibit two men of its society more widely apart in their characteristics than these, even though one of them be Francis Quarles, who seems made up of heaven, honesty, and harmonious measures, and the other broad-spoken Paley, with his logical mind and his coarse accent; the latter expressing the conclusion arrived at by the former, that no government could sustain itself without a little 'corrooption.'

Paley had something of the roughness, but more than the reverence, of Boys, of Clare. When the latter was Dean of Canterbury, and about to preach at Paul's Cross, he parodied the Lord's Prayer in a spirit that would have made Sterne blush, and the 'Clare greyhounds' generally to drop their tails in shame. It commenced with 'Our Pope, which art in Rome, cursed be thy name;' asked him to 'remit our moneys which we have remitted for thy indulgences, as we send *them* back unto thee,' and concluded with, 'For thine is the infernal pitch and sulphur,' &c., *Amen!* Boys was a man who well illustrated the latter half of the old proverb, which says that 'A Boston horse and a Cambridge Master of Arts are a couple of creatures that will give way to no man.' Indeed, there was a good deal of stiffness about Cambridge 'Heads' generally. Among the clerics not one obeyed the behest of King Charles to leave off periwigs, tobacco, and reading their sermons.

There are other names upon which one comes with a sort of reverence, yet which are not too venerable not to be touched. When Dr. Warner poked his cane through the broken coffin, and turned upwards the red beard of good Dr. Caius, he instantly smoothed it straight again, and went away full of respectful reflections on the gentleman whose quiet he had invaded. So when passing Clare we see the shadow of the immortal Ridley, it is enough if we lovingly touch the hem of his garment, and bowing, leave to him his right of way. One would be divided between Edmund Spenser and Ridley, whose old church at Herne is still sanctified by his once presence there, were it not for another student of mark, but of quite an opposite quality. Both divines, both martyrs: the one, Ridley, grave, yet cheerful in his gravity, walking in the light of heaven and a good conscience, pure of life, forgetful only of self, sacrificing all for the sake of truth, and consecrated to Heaven by a baptism of fire. The other is a more modern personage, a saucy-looking gentleman, a divine by imposition of sadly-mistaken hands, a scamp by virtue of his own doings and sayings, a Christian gentleman who considered the 'heart of a man' as Macheath does when he sings that luxurious bit of morality to the rollicking tune in the Lancer quadrilles; a smooth clever knave, to whom honesty was burdensome; crafty, but caught at last in the web of his own cunning; a criminal, but not a martyr, one who was not burnt for the faith, but hanged for forgery. At what extreme ends of the scale of divines are Bishop Ridley and Dr. Dodd! Cambridge indeed may boast of every species of greatness in the character of her sons, Bacon, Spenser, Milton, Ridley, Latimer, and troops of as heart-thrilling names; and therewith Titus Oates and Dr. Dodd,—ay, and Scum Goodman, that luckier knave, the maintained lover of the Duchess of

Cleveland, a forger like the Doctor, a player and a plotter in King William's days, a dabbler too in murder, or in incentives to murder, who was expelled from Cambridge for cutting the picture of the Duke of Monmouth, the Chancellor, and who would assuredly, later, have gone ' westward ho !'—the London slang for the way to Tyburn tree,—had he not fled abroad to escape the consequences of being mixed up in the Sir John Fenwick business. The better men are here, however, in the majority; the worse appear only here and there, looking like the graduates in the goose-market at Sturbridge Fair, where Webster's Bellamont saw ' a number of freshmen stuck here and there with a graduate, like cloves with great heads in a gammon of bacon.'

Sturbridge Fair periodically, and Mrs. Aynsworth permanently, sensibly disturbed the propriety of the old University town. The former could not be put down, but the lady was banished the place on account of her evil life. She established herself at an inn at Bishop's Stortford, where she amassed such a fortune that she entertained the Vice-Chancellor and some of the heads of houses with a dinner off silver plate, bedding them afterwards on couches fit for kings, and refusing to make any charge for a hospitality which acquitted, as she said, a debt of gratitude. How slyly Mr. Pepys alludes to this painted piece of mischief when, in October 1667, his friends Lowther and Burford arrived with him and Mrs. Pepys at the Reindeer at Stortford: ' where Mrs. Aynsworth, who lived heretofore at Cambridge, and whom I knew better than they think for, do live. It is the woman

that, among other things, was great with my cousin
Barmston of Cottenham, and did use to sing to him,
and did teach me, "Full forty times over;" a woman
they are very well acquainted with, and is here what
she was at Cambridge, and all the good fellows of the
country come hither.' A glance at the internal arrangements of the hotel kept by the ex-alewife of the
University town is afforded us by the former student
of Magdalen and drinker of Mrs. Aynsworth's ale:
'To supper, and so to bed; my wife and I in one bed,
and the girl in another, in the same room, and lay
very well; but there was so much tearing company
in the house that we could not see the landlady; so
I had no opportunity of renewing my old acquaintance with her.'

In the following year we come upon evidence
tending to show that the resolutely dissolute University men were nothing the quieter for the banishment
of Mistress Aynsworth. At the end of May 1668
Pepys records: 'After dinner to Cambridge, about
nine at night, and there I met my father's horses,
with a man staying for me. But it is so late, and
the waters so deep, that I durst not go to-night:
but, after supper, to bed; and there lay very ill, by
reason of some drunken scholars making a noise all
night.' These roysterers were, doubtless, exceptional
personages. At all events, a University is to be
judged of by its best rather than its worst samples.
At the very time the drunken scholars were keeping
Pepys from sleeping, young Stillingfleet—that noble
object of emulation to all Cambridge students sincerely
preparing for 'divinity'—was electrifying the crowds

that packed St. Andrew's, Holborn, by the eloquent earnestness of his preaching. When rivals were contending for that London rectory, the Archbishop of Canterbury and the Bishop of London presented Stillingfleet to the Lord Treasurer, as the 'ablest young man to preach the Gospel of any since the time of the Apostles.' There will be no 'Section' so closely beset with listeners, next week, as St. Andrew's used to be, when countless thousands succeeded each other, all eager to see and to hear the 'young man' who had come up from Cambridge University with such testimony to his efficiency. *He* was not of the idle fellows who used to buy stewed prunes of Goody Mulliner, over against Magdalen College—fellows who, in the next century, had their descendants in the gay 'Apollos,' with Prince William of Gloucester at the head of them, and whose distinction was to wear the hair

> 'Unfrizzled, unanointed, and untied;
> No powder seen.'

There was probably never greater laxity in the discipline of Cambridge than during the last half of the last century. Fellows and even the tutors of colleges were rarely seen at the morning service in chapel, and pamphleteers published sharp 'Strictures' thereon. Warburton said of Law, Master of Peterhouse, that he was not half so fit for the mastership as Sancho Panza was for his governorship. Law's *Sleep of the Soul* startled the thinkers and philosophers as well as the indifferentists of his day; and when Hone was tried for blasphemy before Lord Ellenborough, the sharpest stab he inflicted on that irascible judge was conveyed in an allusion to the alleged heterodoxy of his father.

It was then the 'thing' to affect indolence, and the least welcome visitation to Cambridge would have been such a one as that of the British Association. When angles and triangles were defined, a 'Fellow' was thought witty who said, 'Well, what's the good of it?' Students with their tutors talked of stables and kennels; and young gentlemen who boasted that they should not have to live by their learning (they would have starved if they had made the experiment) gave breakfast-parties, in those bad old days, which lasted till the ringing of the dinner-bell. Then were Johnians famed for punning and renowned for slang. A 'Johnian hog' would talk of being a 'constant quantity' at a certain coffee-house, and would coolly tell you that 'the force of his understanding varied inversely as the number of bumpers he took off.' Freshmen were then said to understand Latin better than Sophs; and both were scarcely excelled in power and extent of swearing by those children of the vulture, their own Gyps. There were more angles described on billiard-tables than in college; and young lords took delight in riding horses long distances in very short periods, unaffected by the sarcasm of Fordham, that a monkey could do as much. Meanwhile, however, there were silent workers who were not forgetful of their manhood, nor of what was expected from it; and even 'wooden spoons' took heart of grace and struggled forward, despite the cynical cheering of the leaden *oi polloi*.

There existed an old Tory prejudice against Cambridge. When George II., after sending a troop of horse to Oxford,

> 'Books to Cambridge gave, as well discerning
> That this right loyal body wanted learning,'

as the old Tory epigram ran, Sir William Browne of Peterhouse returned the well-known reply, that

> 'The King to Oxford sent his troop of horse,
> For Tories own no argument but force;
> With equal care to Cambridge books he sent,
> For Whigs allow no force but argument.'

This was neat, but it was not altogether true. If the forthcoming lecturers on political economy will only examine the facts, they will find that in certain matters the logic of interest, and not the force of argument, has too often influenced the University. This presumedly learned and experienced body in 1705 rejected Sir Isaac Newton (who had sat for the University in the Convention Parliament of 1688) as one of its representatives. Of the four candidates who stood for the honour, the great astronomer was the lowest on the poll. At a later period, Mr. Pitt, not in office, sued the University in vain; but when he had the distribution of loaves and fishes in his hand as prime minister, he was elected, whether he would or not. So did the University triumphantly return Lord Henry Petty when in office, and more summarily discard him on his ceasing to hold that office. These are familiar examples of a very old Cambridge policy,—as we may see by an entry in Pepys's Diary for Sunday, the 15th of April 1660, in

which he says: 'To sermon, and then to dinner,
where my Lord (Sandwich) told me that the University of Cambridge had a mind to choose him for
their burgess; which he pleased himself with, to think
that *they do look upon him as a thriving man*, and said
so openly at table.' Since the English Universities
first received the privilege of sending representatives
to Parliament, that privilege was never so abused as
in the above particular cases. The University showed
little more judgment when it chose the Duke of
Grafton for its Chancellor. He was, indeed, the
patron of Gray; but he treated the learned body by
whom he was elected with intolerable neglect. What,
however, could the members have expected from one
who, though a student of Peterhouse, was still an
undergraduate, and who refused the degree of LL.D.
at his creation from his determination not to subscribe
the Thirty-nine Articles?

Browne, whom we have noticed above, was a man
of as stout spirit as solid learning. It was he who,
when coarsely attacked by a critic in a pamphlet, did
not condescend to answer the vilifier, but nailed the
pamphlet itself, like an unclean bird, on his own door.
Gray and West, Garth ('the best good Christian he,
although he know it not') and Jerry Markland, are
all names which will be remembered with respect by
every member of the great congress who may visit
Peterhouse. Gray and West were serious students;
but even they fell into the slang ways and expressions of their time, and while West laughed at mathematics and mathematicians, public disputations,
gaudy days, and 'college impertinencies generally,'

Gray wrote satirically of 'a country inhabited by
things called Doctors and Masters of Arts,—a country flowing with syllogisms and ale.' The fame of
their contemporary, Jerry Markland, has waned; but
he was a potentiality in his day, a critic whose modesty
may be measured by his assertion that there were
many bad lines in the *Æneid* which he would never
have allowed to appear in a poem of his own! Dennis
of Cambridge, that other famous critic, who thought
he had inflicted more injury on France than Marlborough, is now, except by name, little better known
than Markland. The inventor of new stage-thunder
was, however, a member of Caius and Gonville,
whence, according to Dr. Farmer, he was expelled
for 'attempting to stab a man in the dark,'—a story
which is too poorly authenticated to obtain general
acceptance. The great Lord Thurlow, like the Duke
of Grafton whom we have mentioned above—the
one Chancellor of England, the other Chancellor of
the University—left Cambridge without taking a
degree. This was in the last century, when such a
course entailed no particular disgrace, and when
there were 'Masters' as little learned as scholars.
For example, there was the Hon. and Rev. Barton
Wallop, younger brother of the Earl of Portsmouth.
He was made Master of Magdalen, and is described
as having been totally illiterate. Nothing that he
did ever surprised any one, except his dying on the
first day of partridge-shooting in 1781, which was
considered an inadvertence on the part of the reverend
sportsman. So, when Walker, Vice-Master of Trinity,
and a learned and eager florist, was told that a learned

and eager brother-florist had just shot himself, 'Good G-d!' exclaimed the reverend Vice-Master, 'is it possible? Just at the beginning of tulip-time!'

Cambridge, however, possessed more worthy and conscientious Masters than these; among whom we are disposed to place John Cowell of Trinity Hall, who throughout a long residence was never known to be absent from morning prayer at chapel but once in his life. The omission was so striking, that the memory of it was perpetuated, or at least kept up for a considerable period, by a singular custom. The hour for morning prayer was half-past six; but, in remembrance of Cowell's absence, it was decreed that on each anniversary of the occurrence there should be no call to prayer till eight; and the late sleepers blessed the memory and the precedent of Master John Cowell.

It need hardly be said that some of the most learned men and most laborious workers were among the wittiest and merriest in the University. There was none more learned, more seriously given to literary labours, more witty or mirthful, than good quaint Joshua Barnes, who was admitted to Emmanuel in 1671, and whose works are well known and appreciated. He had a rare memory for good stories, and told them well; but in some cases he lacked clear and precise judgment, of which another Cantabrigian wit took advantage, and before Joshua's death prepared this epitaph for him: 'Joshua Barnes, felicis memoriæ, judicium expectans.' But Barnes was not only of happy wit, but of happy invention. The classical scholar married a lady with a dowry, who held that classical books, being written by heathens, were very naughty books. Whereupon Joshua, who wished to read his Homer in peace, composed a little poem in Greek, which he translated to his wife as an ancient work, and which satisfactorily proved that Solomon was the author of the *Iliad.* Mrs. Barnes was delighted; a sensation of which she would have been less conscious if she had held, as the Bishop of Castabala did, that Solomon was as far off from salvation as any of the historical kings recorded in Scripture.

The grave and earnest Bedell is perhaps the great and serene glory of what used to be called in popular local song 'pure Emmanuel.' As a bishop, indeed, the prelate of Kilmore can only be compared with another Cambridge man, Wilson, Bishop of Sodor and Man, who was married to a poor see, and never desired to be divorced from his spiritual spouse. Others look upon Sancroft, one of the Masters of Emmanuel, as its chief celebrity; and much may be said for the bold, honest, and deprived Archbishop of Canterbury. Yet we could have wished that he had left it as poor himself in purse still living as Tillotson did when dead; but out of the revenues the ex-primate enjoyed and bequeathed a considerable fortune to his family.

Emmanuel had a great innovator in the practice of medicine a couple of hundred years ago, in the person of Dr. Croune, who eagerly and hopefully supported the new or the revived practice of the transfusion of blood from the veins of a healthy to those of a sick person, whereby widely useful results were hoped for. The wits adopted the idea satirically, discussing it as warmly as any subject is likely to be discussed in the Association. Some audacious fellows proposed that it should be tried for the purpose of effecting a change in the moral constitution, and they speculated on what might happen if the blood of a Quakeress were transfused into the veins of the Archbishop of Canterbury; not an insignificant joke when it is remembered that the Primate, Gilbert Sheldon, was said to have some inclinations too much like those of the too vivacious Sir Charles Sedley.

Though we have not named the hundredth part of the celebrities of Cambridge, we have said enough to show that next week the philosophers will find themselves in very excellent company. In the halls, King James once disputed; and princes there have sat to be entertained by dramas played by students. From its schools have gone forth the brightest dignitaries of the law, the church, and the senate; and should a member of the British Association look for a greater than these, one above kings, he will find him at Sidney Sussex College, where the name of Oliver Cromwell is still a presence and a power.

But, to our thinking, there is a brighter brotherhood than these in the glorious band of poets who have given more glory to Cambridge than they have derived from it. The father of them all, racy Chaucer, fittingly belongs to both Universities; *his* sons are on both foundations, but Cam can boast of more immortal singers than Isis, as the county can of useful Caxton, to whom all authors are so greatly indebted. In the foreground are Spenser, Milton, Ben Jonson, Beaumont, Fletcher, George Herbert, Francis Quarles, Dryden, Cowley, and Byron. Less prominent, but worthy children of song, are Waller, Marvel, Prior, Butler, Gray and Pomfret, Crashaw and Garth, Elijah Fenton—drolly representing the Dissenter minstrelsy—with Whitehead, the son of a Cambridge baker, contrasting with Mason—a lucky poet with fifteen hundred a year—and Kirke White, the earnest student and the early singer. Oxford, with the exception of Massinger, Addison, and Samuel Johnson, cannot match the foremost men of the Cambridge tuneful record. From either a greater name than the greatest there, Shakespeare, is absent, as if to prove that a poet is indebted directly to Heaven for his inspiration, though, as Jonson acknowledged with respect to his master, Camden, he may be indebted to man for something of his learning. Dodsley's livery covered a tolerable versifier whom instruction would have benefited; but college training would not have given an additional grace to Gay, who began life by measuring out silk for ladies behind a counter; nor would a knowledge of mathematics or of the causes of the precession of the equinoxes have conferred more power on untaught Falconer, the barber's son, whose *Shipwreck* is a picture and a poem, from which Lord Byron, of Cambridge, condescended to borrow with adroitness. The wisdom, the cunning, the might, and the harmony of the poet are of no University, but all from God. In Cambridge philosophy and poetry meet, both vocations divine in their essence, and illustrated nowhere more nobly than they are here in Francis Bacon of Trinity and John Milton of Christ's College. In those two alone lies glory sufficient and to spare for the trysting-place of the members of the British Association. But two other names of distinguished Cambridge men must be added to the crowded roll—those of Porson and Parr. The scholarship of both was accurately defined by the former when he said, 'Parr knows the meaning of every great word, but *I* know the history of it.'

IV.
BATH.
1864.

BATH.

1864.

PASSING over the meeting of the Association at Newcastle in 1863, except in the long and elaborate reports of the scientific proceedings, the *Athenæum* in 1864 followed the members to the city of Bath, where they gathered together for the first time. On the 17th of September the writer of what henceforth came to be considered the 'occasional article' in connection with the gathering, and in some further connection with a book called *Objects of Interest in the City of Bath and its Neighbourhood*, as a sort of text for his comment, remarked:

In Sir Charles Lyell's introductory address, delivered on Wednesday at the meeting of the British Association at Bath, the speaker adverted to the attractiveness of the locality to the student of natural phenomena. It may indeed be said that Bath presents peculiar points of attraction for philosophers generally. Where could they assemble more fittingly than around those thermal springs, which are said to have been first discovered by Prince Bladud, who was himself great as a philosopher and mathematician? That son of Lud Hudibras owed his scholastic greatness to Athens, whence he brought to Briton a stock of learning and a heavy leprosy. His malady reduced him to the condition of a swineherd, and the Prince's pigs, if legend may be credited, were as foully afflicted as himself. The swine, by rolling in the black steaming mud, where the hot springs now boil up, became healed; and the princely swineherd, who could draw an inference, followed the example of his pigs, and became one of the cleanest philosophical princes in all heathendom. Eight hundred and sixty-three years before the Christian era he made the court of his royal sire glad by his recovery. Eighteen hundred and sixty-three years of that era had been told off by Time when the philosophers resolved to meet in the city which had grown up around the springs, the heat and the healing powers of which have not waned since Bladud was made whole. In consequence of that resolution there they are now assembled, hearing, seeing, and talking, enjoying the pleasant hospitality of the mayor and citizens. Sir Charles Lyell ignores Bladud and his swine, disregards the circumstantial story, with its bold positiveness of dates, and begins with the Aquæ Solis of the Romans, whose ruins lie some twenty feet below the level of the city wherein Sir Charles delivered his address.

After the Roman occupation, of which he spoke so well, had passed away (and during which the occupants seem to have been acquainted with and used the fossil coal resembling that now found at Newton), perhaps the most remarkable event which befell Bath was owing to its active and clever monks. The Romans had made it, and the Saxons had kept it, a fashionable and sanatory city. The monks made of it a manufacturing city. Under their auspices the art of weaving woollen cloth was established there soon after its introduction into England, about the year 1333; and it was carried to such perfection during that fourteenth century as to render Bath one of the most considerable places in the west of England for the woollen manufacture. It never lost, however, its fashionable quality. Queen Elizabeth visited the city, and graciously condescended to express her opinion of the place; lifting her nose above the city of the springs, and declaring that it was dirty of aspect and nasty of smell! She recommended the corporation, which was so proud of its healing fountains, to construct a common sewer; and, like a practical woman, she put down a purse full of angels to aid in the construction. The results were beneficial: in 1570 the baths enjoyed a very extensive popularity. The admirable mayor, Mr. Murch, has just completed the work commenced by the admirable queen.

Then settled in Bath those other healers who are 'punctually paid for lengthening out disease;' and marvellously have they flourished in that settlement. In 1628 there was the very flower of physic blooming in the person of Dr. Venner, who wrote a rare old tract to entice sick people to come and be made whole. It began with a truthful assurance and a somewhat alarming injunction to the effect that all sickness was a consequence of sin, and that all sufferers should, before they left home, make peace with God and their consciences. It was right, yet it was not encouraging; but Venner added, 'May that God who is alone able to cure thee lead thee here in safety, and bring thee home again in good health. *Vale!*' In this century there was a strong religious feeling connected—there was, at all events, a strong endeavour made to connect it—with the use of the waters. Towards the close of the century was published a collection of *Prayers for the Use of all Persons who come to the Baths for Cure.* The only singular feature in this creditable little book is that there are two lists of 'ejaculations,' one 'for the rich,' the other 'for the poor.'

Venner pronounced Bath 'more delectable and happier than any other city of the kingdom,' because of the springs and the physicians. There is a touch of self-interest in his counsel to patients not to fancy themselves cured when they seem to be so; and in his recommendation to them to believe that if they are 'of a generous and religious understanding,' they will encourage 'the true helps of physics with the baths.' Even at this early period the touting system was in full swing here. Venner gives a lively sketch of it. 'The thing I would have you take notice of, is how the people of Bath that keep houses of receipt, and their agents—for such they have in every corner of the streets, and also before you come to the gates—press upon you, importuning you to take your lodgings at such and such a house, near to such and such a bath, extolling the baths near which they dwell above all the rest, respecting altogether their own gain, not your good and welfare. And when they have got you into their houses, they will be ready to fit you with a physician, perhaps an empiric or upstart apothecary, magnifying him for the best physician in the town, that will not cross them in removing you to another bath, though the bath near which you are placed be altogether contrary to your infirmities and state of body, or at least not so convenient as some other. And this is also an especial reason why many ofttimes receive rather hurt than good in the use of these baths.' During a long period the Bath medical men waged furious war with each other. At the close of the seventeenth century Dr. Guidott and Dr. Jones were flying at each other 'like French falconers.' Guidott, indeed, took all the points of professional rivals on his single buckler, and thwacked them lustily in return. Of a medical work by old Dr. Jordan he remarks, after brief contempt poured upon it: 'I may some time or other, with due respect, more largely treat of it; and for the present shall here, with good Shem and Japhet, cast a garment over the nakedness of this my father.' These rivals strove to drive each other from the golden ground. They who were driven and compelled to fly shook the dust from their feet as they departed, in testimony against the ungrateful city. One of these, in 1705, was hunted into the outer desert under a charge of drunkenness; and as he turned his face towards Tunbridge, he threatened Bath and the Bath people that he would put a toad into their water, spoil the trade of the city, and bring down the rent of lodgings to half-a-crown a week! If he really attempted to do this, the irate exile did not succeed. The doctors fought for patients, destroyed a large number, made large fortunes, and covered the abbey-walls with tablets, of which musical Dr. Harrington merrily said:

> 'These walls, adorned with monument and bust,
> Show how Bath waters serve to lay the dust.'

In the early part of last century the publication of local Guides, with directions to travellers, indicate that resort to the city was on the increase. One of them, A.D. 1709, gives, among other scraps of information, the 'exact measure of the road from London to Bath, as it was measured by Mr. Tompion, clockmaker, in Fleet-street, London.' This citizen was the very first of his day in his vocation: 'A Tompion, I presume!' is the impertinent remark of the unscrupulous lady in Farquhar's *Inconstant*, as she takes the watch from young Mirabel. The old guide-book to which we are referring also informs travellers that 'to make travelling more agreeable stones are set up at every mile;' and as further useful information, it states that 'travellers from Bath to London must turn to the left at Pickwick Turnpike; and from London to Bath, to the right at Beckhampton.'

When to travel to Bath was an expedition for two days and nights, and not a pleasant trip, as now, of two hours and a few minutes, the journey was a serious matter indeed, though jollity was not lacking. *The* coach at the beginning of last century started from the Saracen's Head, Friday-street. The hour of departure was so early, that travellers generally slept at the old inn the previous night. The proper outfit for a gentleman of the period with an 'inside place' was an 'ultramarine Joseph,' the indispensable 'pocket monitor of Tompion's,' and the probably as indispensable sword, or as it was then called 'silver-hilted rip, of ice-brook temper.' There was a social and not an ungenerous spirit in those days. Parties who spent the night at the Saracen's Head previously to travelling together usually contrived to make themselves known to each other, and to sup together. Ladies were not at all 'squeamish' in falling into this fashion, and generally, in one respect at least, to their profit; for it was the rule of the road that the majority in one sex should pay for the refreshments of the minority in the other, and as more men than women travelled in those days, the latter might journey far at little cost beyond that of locomotion. This Bath coach 'breakfasted' at Colnbrook, famed in those remote times, not for its 'cooks,' but for its exorbitant charges and very short commons. Reading was the appointed place for dinner, and there it seems to have been understood that the host should entertain his guests by waggery, just as the hostess and her maids do in the inn scene in Erasmus. Between Reading and Theale came the afternoon time, when songs were sung, stories were told, the bottle of pure Nantz passed round, and altogether many strange things were said, done, or suggested, that would never be thought of now. At Theale the travellers regaled themselves with cake and ale, for which the house was famous, for no other reason than that it kept such wares for sale. Thus fortified, and the coachman having hoped that the gentlefolk had not hurried themselves, progress was joltingly made to Newbury, the sleeping quarters for the

G

night. But sleep was, of course, the *last* thing resorted to. They who loved a carouse ordered punch, and caroused, drank, and smoked accordingly. Others, if it were summer time, paired off when such pleasant process was practicable, and walked and talked, and made or listened to gallant speeches, with matter-of-course love assurances that were taken for what they were worth, and were not meant to pass for greater value. The second day's journey carried the travellers first to Marlborough to breakfast, which they had well earned by the bumping they had endured and the curses they had ejaculated as they passed over the road of rocks, ridges, and ruts which took them into that town. They required it the more for the perils they might have to encounter between that place and Sandy Lane. The plain abounded in light cavalry, or highwaymen, even in broad daylight. In anticipation of these the gentlemen looked to their silver-hilted rips, hid their watches in their boots, and stowed away their guineas in places where robbers always looked for them. As for the ladies, they exhibited so much ingenuity in concealing their Tompions and gold pieces, that of course the gentlemen talked of rifling them before the highwaymen appeared to take their toll of the road. This peril met, or avoided, the coach tottered uneasily on its way to Aquæ Solis, at scarcely a swifter rate than a couple to three miles an hour; a 'Corporation trot to St. Paul's on Sundays' was popularly said to be 'a fool to it.' This coach, which arrived on the night of the second day, carried no heavy luggage, and ladies who wished to 'make a figure' at Bath generally kept cloistered up in their lodgings till their baggage and finery arrived by the wagon.

Fifty years or so previous to this time, the 'leathern convenience' was hardly considered to be 'the thing.' What does Mrs. Day say in the *Committee*? 'If his honour, Mr. Day, chairman of the honourable committee of sequestration, should know that his wife rode in a stage-coach, he would make the house too hot for some.' In the beginning of the last century, the 'coach' was more extensively patronised, though it carried six insides, and sometimes, as on one of Mrs. Day's eventful journeys, with not less than eleven. Fifty years later, the roads were not at all improved. Even after the bill for the making of turnpike-roads had passed, the route from London to Bath was long celebrated as the worst in all the kingdom.

Arrived in Bath, the traveller found there one personage who was the most absolute of autocrats, the Master of the Ceremonies. *Chapeau bas!* The very memory of that awful and polite despot makes one mentally unbonnet to him. It was once a glorious dynasty, though now it has run to seed. Its founder was a Duke of Beaufort. Its most celebrated Master was that imperious, impudent, gorgeously-dressed, and generous-hearted Beau Nash, who introduced civilisation at Bath as it had once been enforced at Athens, by the abolition of the custom of wearing swords. For the dignity of Master, men intrigued, swore, fought, struggled as other would-be masters for the crowns of the world. The dynasty was of modest origin; it grew into dazzling potentiality,

and only did not die out 'like a snuff' because a
Master is still occasionally dragged up existing from
some old store-cellar, made to do its office, and is
stowed away again. In the early days there were
only the Abbey House and Westgate House for the
reception of pleasure-seekers. There was then neither
ball-room nor card-room. A dance was occasionally
got up on the bowling-green, but rain often drenched
or drove away the dancers. Whereupon a sympathising Duke of Beaufort made over the Town-hall,
not only for dancing, but gambling, and appointed as
superintendent the first of the long-renowned line of
Masters, the gallant and very ceremonious Captain
Webster, Beau Nash's immediate predecessor. Then
was the *Minuet* walked and danced in stately fashion.
A man who stood up to take part in that feat looked
like a man indeed. The nymph was necessarily as
graceful as a goddess. And as admiring crowds of
ladies gazed rapturously, they beat time with their
fans, moved their heads in unison, and languishingly
murmured applause to the men at their sides, who
approvingly and emphatically *swore* that it was good.
In those days, too, gambling was less a diversion
than a high branch of science, the pursuit of which
was to bring profit sooner or later. But the passion
for cards and dice, and the backsliding from the
piety of the old days, when the book of local prayers
put different ejaculations into the mouths of the rich
and of the poor, are well illustrated in the lines
which allude to the result of contemporaneous subscriptions for opening a new card-room and for
providing the expenses of church service:

'The books were opened t'other day,
At all the shops, for church and play.
The church got *six*; Hoyle *sixty-seven!*
How great the odds for Hell 'gainst Heaven!'

The sojourners now at Bath will recognise few of the past century features in the place. They have disappeared, like the old incidents of travel. To-day, the philosophers may communicate through the telegraph-wires with friends at a distance, at a low tariff and in a few minutes. A hundred and fifty years ago, the Bath express letter-office would carry your message to London, at any time, in a day and a night, and charge 2*l*. 1*s*. for the service.

Of course, when 'all the world' was at Bath—in the season—five crowded months out of the twelve, there was great curiosity to know the 'quality,' not knowing whom classed the miserably ignorant with the abominably vulgar. Curll was among the first to gratify this curiosity, which existed both in Bath and all over the kingdom. He sent forth in the year 1710, from his shop, then near St. Dunstan's Church, a poem which had many imitators, but which was surpassed by the immortal *Bath Guide* of that audacious Anstey who slept seven years at Cambridge, and then lost his degree for commencing his speech to the nobs with 'Doctores sine doctrinâ, Magistri artium sine artibus, et Baccalaurei baculo potius quam lauro digni!' Curll's poet had none of the wit and power of the later bard and pungent satirist; but he described his Bath fashionables according to the quaint style of the times. Out of delicacy, the poet gives them all fictitious designations; out of candour or impudence, Curll adds their real names in footnotes; and thus we have a picture in words, something like the picture indeed of the gay and grave people on the Pantiles at Tunbridge. Thus we see 'Julia,' or the Duchess of Norfolk, brilliant with her good-humour, youth, her 'full bloom,' and her majestic carriage. 'Youthful Amoret' is Mrs. Tempest, 'every charm to Nature purely owing.' The calm beauty, Mrs. Villars, is lightly hidden beneath the veil of 'serene Villaria;' her lover, Mr. Cawfield, is 'Auruncius,' 'happy in so true a choice.' Then a couple sweep by who are illustrated in the words,

> 'Tho' in her veins patrician purple flows,
> A *private gentleman* Erminia chose.'

The private gentleman is 'Cleon,' and the happy couple are Mr. and Mrs. Horne. Lord and Lady Falkland have no *sobriquets* at all:

> 'Nor can the camp or court with justice boast
> A braver hero or a brighter toast.'

Lady Shaw is 'pretty Caledonia,' and is 'of humour free;' and Mrs. Noel, as 'noble Zerzia,' in 'grandeur shines,' as a lady with such a name might be expected to do; nor are we surprised to find that she is

> 'Well made and stately as a lofty pine.'

As Mrs. Moody is set down in the guise of 'bright Desdemona,' we conjecture that the squire is given to jealousy, and that the lady does not particularly care for it. We are perplexed, however, with the 'two Mrs. Harcourts,' for whom there would seem to have been but one lord. That there were cruel beauties about the springs we find in 'Corinthia,' Mrs. Levett, who disregards the sighing of poor Captain Derby:

'Tho' wounded by her eyes Hydaspus bleeds,
She knows and sees him with a careless air.'

It is otherwise with 'Phaon and Aspasia,' or Mr. and Mrs. Boyle; for *she* turns to *him* with exquisitely loving languishment, and *he* to *her*, ecstatically blest merely with looking in her eyes. We do not know if Phaon's demonstration affects an *incognita* only known as 'Pastora,'—'Oft forced to colour, yet thou scorn'st to frown.' And in this fashion, or in others not materially differing from it, were the members of the upper ten thousand who resorted to Bath in the first half of the last century depicted for the amusement of all whom it might concern. When Dodsley, in 1766, sent forth Anstey's *New Bath Guide*, the Bath company generally, and the 'B— R— D— family' in particular, were etched as they had never been before, and in a way that could hardly be excelled if Bath had a 'season' and exclusive 'company' still.

All the fair nymphs, married ladies, ardent swains, and more or less jealous or indifferent husbands who patronised Bath, however imperious themselves, were submissive and duteous to that irresistible autocrat the Master of the Ceremonies. Not one of the dames or damsels would have dared to stand up in his presence, to dance a minuet, without her lappets; she might as well have dared to stand up without a reputation. Nor would any of the 'private gentlemen'—that is, commoners—have presumed to take a seat near a peeress. Even Lady Wallace, who was not a peeress, was strongly possessed by a pride she derived from her title. On one occasion a farming squire, who had ten times her husband's fortune, ventured to pass near her in top-boots. With a supremely impertinent affectation of feeling faint, she thanked kind inquirers, and attributed the feeling to the smell of cart-wheels that had just passed her. As eleven o'clock struck the awful Master took out his watch, and at that signal the music ceased, though the *cotillon* may have but just commenced. No dancer would have had the audacity to solicit for a continuation of the dance. A Master of the Ceremonies had been obdurate even when petitioned by Frederick, Prince of Wales. The Princess Amelia had essayed with all her winningness to obtain 'just one more dance,' and the inflexible Master turned from her as hard-hearted as if she had been Potiphar's wife, and he the righteous officer of Pharaoh's household.

When Derrick, who was scarcely a less influential Master than Nash, lay dying in 1769, fierce was the contest for his tinsel crown. Jones promised that if he were elected he would forswear play. Plomer interested the ladies, because in his canvass he had distinguished himself by ' a propriety, decency, and moderation which became a gentleman' who aspired 'to conduct the ceremonies of the *Great Assembly* established in this city. There was a fair faction who resolved to elect Brereton as soon as the lingering Derrick died; and others, fearful that the weal of the kingdom was involved, appealed to the Lord Chamberlain to make election by *fiat*, and save appearances

in the eyes of sons and daughters of good quality.
Had the commonwealth really been at stake, there
could not have been greater heat in and about the
springs. Very good noses were pulled, very fair blood
set boiling, very excellent abuse laid on the fortune-
hunting Irish element, and an outsider chosen 'reigning
monarch' at last. Peace and prosperity were never
afterwards permanently established; for opposition
balls arose, and these bowled down the once erect
pillars which formerly sustained the name and well-
being of the city of vapours.

It was always to be regretted that the authority
of the Master did not extend to the bathers themselves. He who now looks down into the dull, dark,
and simmering waters can have no conception of the
frolic, jollity, riot, dissipation, and indecorum which
once reigned there. There was a regular promenade
in the waters, and the promenaders were of both
sexes. They were in bathing costume, and walked
with the water up to their necks, so that the heads
appeared all floating. While these were frolicking
or flirting, or otherwise amusing themselves, others,
who came for sanitary purposes, were hanging on by
the rings in the wall and sedulously parboiling themselves. The Cross Bath was the famous 'quality'
bath. They were nearly all pleasure-seekers there;
and probably this was as dissipated a place for the
time as could be found in the three kingdoms. Handsome japanned bowls floated before the ladies, laden
with confectionery or other refreshments, or with
oils, essences, and perfumes for their use. Now and
then one of these would float away from its owner,

and her swain would float after it, bring it again before her, and then, turning on his back, would affect to sink to the bottom, out of mere rapture at the opportunity of serving her. The spectators in the gallery looked on, laughed, or applauded till the hour for closing came, and with it half-tub chairs lined with blankets, whose owners plied for fares, and carried home the steaming freight at a sharp trot, and a shilling for the job.

After the bath, the Grove. It would be hardly possible to say which place looks the duller now; but in the olden time both echoed with laughter, and the Grove was brilliant with beauty, fine gentlemen, and nine-pins. The 'tipping all nine for a guinea' was a frequently accomplished feat; and he who effected it was as proud as if he had written the lampoon on somebody which was sure to be hanging on one of the trees, the Pasquin of Bath!

It is not very easy to determine what the behaviour of the congregation at the fashionable Abbey Church was. Dodsley's book on Bath, by the 'Genius Loci,' is evidently not trustworthy; and what others describe is evidently rather the sum of things than what was seen on any one occasion. Considering that Burnet was obliged to have the sides of the pews in the royal chapel raised in order to stop the ogling in service-time between the officers and the maids-of-honour, we may conclude that at the fashionable Abbey there was some carelessness of discipline. It is said that there were often more *billets-doux* passed from one pew to another during morning service than notes to desire the prayers of the congregation—a prevailing custom then among members of a dissenting chapel.

Then the Bath meadows! Can they even be said to exist? No duellist awakes the echoes there with pistols. No Sir Lucius and Acres come to arrange that little matter according to their respective temperaments. Once those meadows were more crowded of an evening than our Mall. It was called a second Hyde Park for coaches, a St. James's Park for pedestrian beaux and belles. There all ages, degrees, and both sexes were on their stage of the world, acting their very best, not always with the best ends in view. Fops tripped at the side of pretty mantua-makers, who listened to the vapid compliments they professed not to heed. Squires, apprentices, bullies, ancient beaux, provincial flirts, and London wenches, who are spoken of as carrying 'tails like countesses,' and showing thereby that then, as now, the *aurata cyclas quæ verrit humum* was worn by one class and imitated by another. *A Character of the Bath*, given by an anonymous writer of the last century, describes it as neither town nor city, yet partaking of both in name. It had a desolate out-of-season time of seven months, when it was a wilderness, and ' bills were as thick for lodgings to be let as there were for houses in the Friary, on the late Act of Parliament for the dissolution of privileges.' The Baths are compared, by one graphic writer, 'to nothing but the Boilers in Fleet-street or old Bedlam, for they have a reeking steam all the year. In a word,' sums up this writer, ''tis a valley of pleasure, yet a sink of iniquity;' and we are told, by an unsavoury simile, that every vice in the metropolis was counterfeited at Bath.

All this has been changed, and neither pleasure nor iniquity now rules supreme in Bath. It fell into the hands of clever old ladies and accomplished old gentlemen, and though in the Piozzi and Whalley period, for instance, there was much frivolity and affectation, there was also much real enjoyment, for the tone of the society was then one of great refinement. The supreme dignity of Bath may be said to have departed when Queen Charlotte drove eastward through its gates. Since then, Royalty has only looked in for a moment, like a visitor to a poor relation. Bath requires no commiseration, for it has many compensations. It is still, in a certain sense, the queen of beautiful cities; beautiful in itself, its environs, its history, and its memories. For the old noise there is modern quiet, dignity, and comfort. For the old spasmodic pleasures, permanent content; and, in many circumstances, the moral differences between the past and the present are as vast and significant and desirable as that between the unclean Bladud, with his unclean swine, wallowing in the mud—with cleanly purpose, it must be confessed—and the princes and followers of philosophy who are now congregated under the shadow of those hills upon which health and beauty are permanently enthroned.

V.
BIRMINGHAM.
1865.

BIRMINGHAM.

1865.

In 1865 the British Association met for the third time at Birmingham, where the members had previously assembled in 1839 and 1849. The writer in the *Athenæum* observed that:

To pass with the members of the British Association from Bath to Birmingham is to undergo a change of stage, scenery, decorations, and, in some degree, of audience. No two places can be less alike. Bath, from time immemorial, has been the tabernacle of roistering fashion or invalid gentility. It was discovered or founded by a king's son with an unpleasant skin-disease, and it has ever since been adopted by those to whom kings' sons and their surroundings are as godly things. The superior people who need not work, will not work, cannot work, or who enjoy well-earned rest and quiet *after* work, have ever been the true denizens of Bath. Idleness, frivolity, pleasure, infirmity, and godliness, all of the undeniably genteel quality, have loved to linger about the terraces, the valley, and the meadowed banks of the Avon.

Birmingham is altogether of another quality. No

king's son gave the ground dignity by curing his leprosy in the waters. When wild in woods the British savage ran, legend says that there were strong-thewed fellows in the district who fashioned rude and highly-offensive weapons. The woods that were their homes, and the iron that was in their vicinity, we are told, soon taught the natives how to use what Nature gave. Those legendary proto-Bromwycham-ites made nails with their fingers, and could drive them into a plank with their knuckles. Tradition fancied them supplying, not 2,000,000,000 of nails annually, as Birmingham nailers can now furnish with ease, but a thousand or two (all wrought, not cut) annually, to Cassivellaun or Theomantius, with spear-staves, javelins, and heavy blades to Cunobelin and his successors down to the time when the royal St. Lucius, first Christian king of Britain, died and left the Roman emperors his heirs. No doubt the early real productions of the iron men were more for use than show. It would have puzzled the original Warwick and Staffordshire nail-makers to have produced any other nail than would have served a man for a little weapon when he lacked a better. The first makers of 'tacks' would have been unable to execute such an order as has been completed in later days, namely, a thousand gold, a thousand silver, and a thousand iron tacks, the whole three thousand weighing exactly three grains.

Setting aside the romance of the manufacture of iron under the Britons, we may assert that it is reeking but healthy labour, and not Royalty with an offensive *impetigo*, that has made Birmingham one of the most remarkable cities in the land. Labour and the sons of labour have done it all; not suddenly, but by slow yet sure degrees. Leland could only say of Birmingham that it was inhabited by 'smiths that use to make knives and all sorts of cutting tools; and many lorimers that make bitts, and a great many nailers.' A later traveller of the sixteenth century, Camden, says that 'most of the inhabitants be smiths.' Fashion, after all, helped the place in which it would not reside. Charles II. brought with him to England the French *mode* of metallic ornaments. Birmingham at once took the lead in supplying them; and the city commenced a career of usefulness and prosperity which has never, save temporarily, suffered abatement. Bath has kept its gentility and lost much of its means. Birmingham has never reached gentility, but has 'made its fortune.' British philosophers may class the two as Edingdon did two sees, when he was offered the primacy and he preferred a bishopric. 'Canterbury,' said he, 'is the higher rank, but Winchester is the better manger.'

Before the period of Charles II. there were very handsome fortunes made in Birmingham, and especially by the nailers and ironmongers. To the masters in those two branches John Saunders, in 1654, addressed a remarkable 'broadsheet,' which was placarded in the streets of the busy city. Saunders was the 'Birmingham prophet;' he boasted of knowing in Warwickshire all that was going on at the moment at Whitehall; he foretold events, candidly pointed out the failures as well as the fulfilments;

and he proposed, as a settlement for all existing difficulties, that Charles II. should be called to the throne, and Cromwell be retained to act as his lieutenant. 'Nail-making,' says the prophet, 'was the trade that God, by an overruling providence, ordained me, your servant in the Lord, John Saunders, to be brought up unto from my youth.' We notice this 'servant in the Lord' because he was the father of 'strikes.' He tells the Birmingham nail-makers and the 'rich and covetous ironmongers' that as they grew rich they forgot God and the poor handicraftsmen who had helped to make them wealthy. 'Give better prices,' he says, '2d. in 12d., to the poor workmen, that they may not have cause to hate you; so shall the nation be served with serviceable wares, and you live more honestly.' He counsels the men, in case of their masters remaining flinty-hearted after continuous labour during summer, autumn, and winter, to cease from work in the spring, to support each other during three or four months, and thereby reduce those cunning Egyptians to certain subjection to the views of their servants. In such wise was the original strike forged in the Birmingham smithy.

Saunders thought Birmingham a growing paradise. Espriella (under which foreign mask Southey wrote of home) denounced it, two centuries later, as worse than limbo or purgatory, where commerce killed or mutilated its hundreds of thousands without condescending to make returns of the numbers so disposed of. In Espriella's eyes Birmingham complexions were made up of oil and dust smoke-dried. 'Every man I meet stinks of train-oil and emery.' Their eyes were burnt red by the fires, and their hair dyed green by the brass-work. The only known use of water was for the supply of steam-engines. The noise was deafening, the filth poisonous to human life; and although the pseudo-Don allows that Birmingham, for astonishing display of human ingenuity, excelled every other place in the world, yet, he says, 'watch-chains, necklaces, and bracelets, buttons, buckles, and snuff-boxes are dearly purchased at the expense of health and morality; and if it be considered how large a proportion of that ingenuity is employed in making what is hurtful as well as what is useless, it must be confessed that human reason has more cause at present for humiliation than for triumph at Birmingham.' This is a good specimen of the old Toryism of Southey, which always fastidiously held its nose at the great unwashed. He could not remember that in Birmingham Baskerville had made printing one of the fine arts, and that Priestley had laid open the arcana of chemical science. He did not know that Boulton and Watt were about to realise the old romance touching steeds that could draw chariots laden with hundreds of men, with a speed which only fiction had ever dreamt of. There is something of the same spirit even in old Hutton, the Birmingham historian. He complains that his fellow-townsfolk will not drink of the once famous chalybeate spring there. If it bubbled over a bed of malt instead of one of mineral, he says, they would fight for it. There is something, too, of a sneer in his remark, that not only buttons but gentlemen have been stamped at Birmingham; that these came into the town ragged orphans, and rode out of it in gilded chariots; that many an estate had been struck out of the Birmingham anvils, many fortunes picked up by light tongs, and that splendid houses had been built by trowels. Altogether Hutton gives more favourable testimony than Espriella. The latter speaks of the Birmingham men as if they were really the descendants of those Ugrians who are said to have landed on our eastern coasts, to have possibly settled in the interior, and to have added the name of 'ogre' to the English language.

By persons of a poetical temperament Birmingham has been called 'queen of the sounding anvil.' More matter-of-fact individuals have adopted the phrase invented by Burke, and Birmingham is with them the 'great toy-shop of Europe.' Both designations are appropriate. Birmingham furnishes a vast amount of indispensable things, whereby life is helped, beautified, disfigured, or destroyed; things to add prettiness to babies, decorate youth, increase household comfort, crush men by battalions, and preserve them when dead. It would exhaust whole alphabets only to tell in alphabetical order all that the philosophers will find the labourers engaged in. We may enumerate a few. The bread-winners of countless homes are there variously employed in making spoons and toys and buttons for children; pins, needles, jewelry, pocket-books, and thimbles for ladies; spurs and watch-chains for gentlemen; and buckles for all who need them. Birmingham not only kindles large fires in her forges and furnaces, but makes the huge bellows that keep up the roar and fierceness of forge and furnace. She also fashions those dainty little sighers of air which fairy fingers may ply, and therewith sustain life in the tiny fireplaces of the most exquisitely diminutive boudoirs. All that comes under the word 'cutlery' Birmingham can supply, though she has rivals at home and abroad. Indeed, what can she not supply, from the humble and useful to the mighty and more useful still? Birmingham produces the finest lightest needles, on the point of any one of which it would puzzle the 10,000 dancing angels who were addicted, according to old legends, to tripping it on needle-points to find footing. Besides these needles, lighter than the gossamer they fly through, there are made here steam-hammers, a blow from one of which would crush a pyramid. Pins such as the fairy godmother of Cinderella might have used to fix the rose upon her godchild's frock, and iron bars such as Polyphemus only could wield, are samples of the 'opposites' produced in this factory for the world's uses. Here are iron chests, in which nations may keep records for ever, defying time, damp, and the pickers and stealers. Yonder are little caskets, in which young girls may keep their first precious homages of love, the first ring given by one not of kin, and the first written words from one dearer than kinsman. As we think of other productions equally useful and interesting, there seems a very chaos of articles, but the most of them are for the furtherance of order and comfort—brass rods and locks, awl-blades, brushes and candlesticks, files, gimlets and japannery, the last so exquisitely finished as to authorise any curious gentleman from Nagasaki to perform the Harikiri, or 'happy despatch.' Then the mind is bewildered at the sight of what is being hourly achieved by the ironfounders and lock-makers, by the opticians and spectacle-makers, by the men who make saws and edge-tools, scales and steelyards, snuffers and steam-engines, the turners, the thread and wick-yarn makers, the makers of all sorts of tools for all sorts of manufacturers, the artists in glass— men who produce forms and patterns which the most accomplished workers of old could not excel; and by the side of these are the humbler artists, who fashion wooden mouse-traps, and traps for rats and foxes. There *was*, till the law stopped that executive branch, a very brisk manufacture of, and sale for, steel traps to catch man, and spring-guns to slay him while he was held fast to be shot at, and which left him a corse, for the keepers or the squire himself to pick up, not without satisfaction, on the following morning.

It was once the fashion to stamp all Birmingham work as 'London made.' With the old-world cockney, capital work was work made in the capital. Birmingham has ceased to provide one article to which she would have been proud to affix her name: we allude to the once famous Birmingham musket, with all appurtenances complete, got up for the market, at 'seven-and-six.' These muskets, we say it in all seriousness, *went off* by shiploads, and generally killed the customers who bought them. For every three or four Brummagem muskets glossy African chiefs sold to the groggy agents of godly Liverpool merchants, to whom they were consigned for that purpose, a 'man and a brother.' The Birmingham manufacturers of those slave-buying guns were highly-respectable men; they brought their daughters up according to Dr. Darwin *On Female Education*, gave 'moral tales' to their sons, kept their wives from London frivolities, paid their taxes, dressed in broadcloth, went to Sunday-morning church now and then, drank their port-wine regularly, and loathed the wretch of a grocer who sanded his sugar and wetted his tobacco before he went to prayers. The Birmingham gunmaker proved his muskets for Africa before they were sent out. Into the barrel the 'trier of guns' did not venture to put a charge of powder; *that* and its consequences were left to the African chiefs who bought them, or to their friends to whom the chiefs sold them. The wiser Birmingham manufacturer filled the barrel with water, and if none percolated through the parts where the barrel was joined the piece was 'warranted.' We hope that amid the discoveries that philosophy or industry may make at this gathering of 1865, may be a couple of the seven-and-sixpenny guns which, in their day, would have bought a couple of better men than their makers. They would be appropriately placed, one at South Kensington, and the other in the museum of the Republic of Liberia.

The sins of the master manufacturers were visited upon, perhaps they were imitated by, the men. All the manufacturing districts were pronounced infamous by the moralists; and Birmingham was honoured with precedence in the rank of infamy. The author of the *History of Whalley* said, in those old days, 'that in great manufactories human corruption, accumulated in large masses, seems to undergo a kind of fermentation, which sublimes into a degree of malignity not to be exceeded out of Hell!' This belongs to the idea that 'God made the country and man made the town,' whereas it is the devil that has marred both. Rural innocence is not more beautiful nor more common than city virtue; the pretty straw-plaiters who work as they walk in our shady lanes, and the prim lace-makers who hardly glance at you from their open windows, can throw no stone at their sisters who toil in Birmingham factories. Very many of these are true, honest, God-fearing girls. If the same contrast be made between the male peasantry and the city bondmen, the same result will be arrived at. The village reading-room, we hope, may be as well attended as the village alehouse. In Birmingham we have heard of factories where one man reads while his fellows work, performing the reader's labour as well as their own. The books read here are of a high class, and it is within our knowledge that the listeners send acute questionings to some of the authors who have a rivet loose in their literary harness.

In much-maligned Birmingham a custom prevailed down to a time within the memory of man, which custom indicated an old affection for the Church. On Easter Monday the Birmingham school-children used to hurry to the older parish church, place their backs against it, as they ranged round the building hand in hand, till the hand of the last comer touched that of the first. Then there was a song, a shout, and a race to the other church, where the same ceremony was jubilantly performed. This was called 'clipping the churches,' and this clipping, or embracing and supporting, was prettily typical of what was due and was paid to the Church by her children. The churches have increased, and the custom has died out. Religion in fine linen keeps the Church, and fustian and velveteen betake themselves to 'chapel.' The only other institution open to them on the weekly festival of Sunday is the tavern. If they were to knock at the door even of a free library, they would find that on the joyous first day of the week the rule is 'Knock, and it shall *not* be opened unto you.' Assuredly there was never such testimony for irreligion against the handicraftsmen of Birmingham as there was against a not far-off Staffordshire village, which may be visited by some of the members of the Association—the village of ' Wotton-under-Weaver, where God comes never !' —one of the most uncomfortable of local proverbs. If, on the other hand, Birmingham has not produced men of extraordinary distinction for piety, it has had, from time to time, some of the tallest and most stalwart smiths in the world. Staffordshire sent thither Walter Parsons, who was so tall that he stood in a hole dug for him in the ground, that he might work at a level with his fellow-workmen. King James I. took him for his porter. Wat was strong enough to take two of the stoutest yeomen of the guard, one under each arm; and his valour and kindly nature were equal to his strength.

Prince Albert took something better from Birmingham than a stout smith for a porter. He beheld the infinite variety of its productions, its incessant activity, the equal ease with which the master-workmen produced, in greater or less time, the perfect samples of their handicraft. Liquid metal took solid form under his eyes; he saw guns cast, and hooks-and-eyes pouring forth like water. He noted perfection in many things, defect perhaps in some; and the Prince took with him from Birmingham the idea of an Industrial Exhibition of All Nations, which put that place especially on its mettle.

At that exhibition Birmingham won honour for many things; for its old metal buttons inclusive. It will be remembered that Moore's Abdallah walked in London,

'The admiration
Of this short-coated population,
This sewed-up race, this buttoned nation.'

At one time Birmingham buckled and buttoned the three kingdoms, and half the world besides requiring such adornment. It furnished every variety of both buckle and button, but its chief staple was the metal button. When shoe-buckles went out the affrighted makers went about in shoestrings, petitioning Parliament to compel people to wear buckles! In like way, the London perruquiers went up to George III. in their own plain hair, to solicit him to bring back the departing fashion of powder and wigs! When the metal button yielded to the mould of wood or horn, covered with silk or some other woven material, the metal-button makers so besieged Parliament by their shrieking entreaties to be saved from ruin that a law was passed which made it illegal for a tailor to sew on to a suit of clothes any button made of cloth, serge, camlet, or any other 'stuff.' Unless this law was swept away by the enactment which recently abolished all laws that had become practically obsolete, this Button Act is still in force; and we believe it to be so. About half a dozen years ago, a tailor named Shirley sued in the Marylebone County Court a customer named King for 9l., the price of a suit of clothes made for the latter. The defendant's counsel asked the tailor of what material the buttons were made; and on being told they were of cloth or silk on horn moulds, he remarked that, by the law made for the protection of the Birmingham button-makers, not only could the tailor not recover, but if the defendant chose to sue for the penalties, the plaintiff would have to pay 40s. for every dozen of such buttons illegally sewed on by him! The judge agreed, and the tailor was nonsuited.

Birmingham now finds employment for nearly six thousand persons, men, women, and children, in metal button-making alone. Perhaps the most singular of all the materials for the manufacture of the button is compressed clay. For the last quarter of a century these have been produced in great quantities. For the first year or two, Minton's Staffordshire porcelain works furnished nearly three-quarters of a million weekly!

All the history of Birmingham lies in such records.

of its works or labour. Feudality does not seem to have either freed or fettered it by charters. It little troubled itself about the outer world except where its interests were concerned. It did, however, send out a battalion of sinewy volunteers to fight on the popular side at Evesham, where the sturdy Warwickshire smiths got their beating and some honour for their pains. In the Wars of the Roses, it worked quietly on, and for any customer. Prince Rupert swept through the city on his fiery way, and left devastation on his track. The Birmingham workers never lifted hammer for the King's side, but their lusty voices roused Charles from his couch at Aston Hall, and their lusty arms perfected fifteen thousand sword-blades for the Parliamentary host. As for Rupert's Birmingham prisoners, they ransomed themselves at prices varying from twopence to a shilling a head!

But the chief event in the city's history is that called the 'great riots' of 1791. Some gentlemen with democratic tendencies dined together, to celebrate the second anniversary of the French Republic. All the rascalry of the town, under the slogan of 'Church and King! and d— all Presbyterians!' took advantage of the opportunity to burn, destroy, and plunder, and they were not actively interfered with by magistracy or clergy till there was little left within the reach of the rioters to destroy. For decency's sake it was necessary to hang a few of the loyal and religious Terrorists, and they were tried to that end. 'If you don't convict those vagabond fellows,' said that learned counsel, Mr. Coke, M.P. for

Nottingham, 'on another anniversary they will not only burn Dr. Priestley's house, but the Doctor himself.' There were many orthodox people in Birmingham who would not have been much shocked at such a rude conclusion to the life of the great Unitarian democrat and philosopher. Three or four 'vagabond fellows,' who had committed every sort of enormity in honour of religion, the throne, and in detestation of the *French Rights of Man*, swung for it. George III. said such enormities could not be allowed; but since they had occurred, he was particularly glad that Priestley's house, library, and manuscripts had perished in the flames. 'It will make him feel the wickedness,' said the logical monarch, 'of the democratic principles he is so fond of propagating.' Pious people thought his orthodoxy might have been recovered if he could have married Hannah More. 'Silly things!' said Hannah; 'they forget that there is a Mrs. Priestley. I wonder they do not marry me to Madan' (a clergyman who advocated polygamy), 'as Mrs. Madan must be more accustomed than Mrs. Priestley to those Eastern usages!'

The controversy that raged after the riots, and which, combined, drove one of the greatest philosophers of his day into life-long exile in America, is not edifying to peruse, save as it illustrates the sayings, doings, manners, and morals of the times. Each party was anxious to shift the blame on some other party's shoulders, and all parties, except the 'Church and King! and d— the Presbyterians!' faction, united somewhat too passionately in denouncing the Birmingham clergy. In the second part of Dr.

Priestley's *Appeal to the Public on the Subject of the Riots in Birmingham* there is an illustration of the writer's previous assertion that the established clergy systematically manifested the utmost discourtesy towards dissenting ministers, and invariably refused to either walk or ride in their company at funerals. As a sample of Birmingham life and charity in the last century, it is not without value. Visitors and residents in that locality may compare it with what now exists there, to the advantage, we hope, of their contemporaries of all denominations. A Birmingham gentleman named Gisborne died. The body was carried to St. Martin's to be buried with the rites of the Church; but Mr. Bourne, a dissenting minister and a friend of the deceased, preceded the coffin. When the reverend rector of St. Martin's, Mr. Dovey, met the corpse at the churchyard-gate, and saw Mr. Bourne in advance of the coffin, he bade him, in rather saucy terms, to go and walk behind. It was the rector's object to walk first and alone; Mr. Bourne's to prevent him. Mr. Dovey endeavoured to outwalk him; but Mr. Bourne, being as nimble as he, kept up with him till, the rector quickening his pace, they both fairly ran for it, till they got to the church-door. Mr. Dovey was so much offended that after the funeral, his pride getting the better of every other consideration, he sent back the hatband and scarf, and even the pins that had been used on the occasion.

Exactly one hundred years have elapsed since Priestley, then 'tutor in languages and belles-lettres in the academy at Warrington,' published the work in which he maintained that every boy's education should be conducted in reference to the profession he would exercise in after-life. The self-evident propriety of such a course was not so manifest to critical perception a century ago as it is now. In September 1765 the philosophers and statisticians among whom he was to take place were not busied with such questions as will be discussed at Birmingham next week. At that time, a third of all children born died under two years of age, and philanthropists were seeking for a remedy for this evil. In that month of the last century critics were busy with Ludlam's report on Harrison's timepiece. The Board of Longitude had requested the former to furnish them with a detailed report on that famous instrument, and Ludlam sent in one which is a model for all philosophers who do not wish to compromise themselves. The substance of it is, that if the instrument should, after long experience, prove to be of great value, the Board of Longitude would probably find it not worthless! Another invention was challenging philosophical attention in September 1765, namely, Dingwall's astronomical tables, calculated to discover the variations of the compass in any latitude. Many philosophers of the last century considered Dingwall's invention as next in importance to the discovery of the longitude. At the same period medical men were engaged in inventing specifics for hydrophobia, and Exeter was proclaiming over the kingdom that her artisans could produce velvet equal in quality to the finest that came from the looms of Genoa!

While philosophical, scientific, mercantile, and

philanthropical minds were engaged throughout the kingdom on these questions (there was no idea *then* of meeting to discuss them), Londoners were, in some respects, doing exactly what their descendants are doing—enjoying, or suffering under, the last hot days of the hottest of summers, and watching the erection of a new Blackfriars Bridge. There was also an aggressive sort of gentility in the City, which was shocked at the vulgarity of Common Councilmen. A reformer suggested that if no citizen was elected to the Common Council who was not worth at least 3000*l*., there would not be such a number of vulgar fellows assembled in the great room at the Half Moon, the place where the Council met. It was in this very month of September 1765 that Garrick was ranked among scientific reformers. When he opened Drury Lane on the 14th with the *Beggars' Opera* and *Polly Honeycombe*, the two lines of metal hoops, with tallow candles in them which used to hang above the heads of the performers, and the brass chandeliers (furnished with similar candles) which used to hang over the front of the stage, and which Birmingham supplied, had disappeared. Critics were in ecstasies at the 'artificial sunlight' with which Garrick was said to have illumined the stage, and scientific men hardly understood how he had accomplished it, till they saw that arrangement of light at the wings which has been, since Garrick's time, so much improved.

Finally, in September 1765, news reached England that Lord Clive had safely arrived at the Cape of Good Hope, on his way to India, on the 23d of the previous January. In certain seasons ships used to get to the Cape by first crossing to Brazil, and to effect this crossing had consumed five months of the year before! In these days Birmingham can supply engines which rule time and space. By their means distances are reduced by the velocity with which they are accomplished. The sailing of a month is the steaming of a week; and the land journey from London to Birmingham, which once required a couple of days, is now a pleasant trip of three hours. If some of the pamphlets which were written in 1834 against the construction of the London and Birmingham Railway had succeeded in their object, Birmingham would not have made the progress which her annals indicate, nor philosophers have glided thither so pleasantly, for the interchange of thought and the glorifying of science.

The next year's meeting was fixed for Nottingham.

VI.
NOTTINGHAM.
1866.

NOTTINGHAM.

1866.

WHEN Herr Nemnich was in course of those travels through England, an account of which he published at Tübingen in 1799, he arrived in sight of the queen of the Midland district, beautiful Nottingham. Having looked at it for a while, he remarked, 'That seems to me the most ancient city that I have yet seen in all England.' There were people well enough up in popular history to tell the traveller that the town was built by that restless, hard-fighting, and town-building son of Alfred, King Edward. Such an assertion would not at all suit the antiquarian eye of Nemnich. Nottingham built 924 years after Christ! 'Nay,' said the traveller, 'it was a town a thousand years *before* Christ. It is a fact, and John Rowse has recorded it.'

School chronological histories, however, continue to make King Edward the founder of that important city, if we may so call it, where, next week, the philosophers of the Isles, and of continents beyond, will be assembled. The Saxon chroniclers, however, afford no authority as to the foundation of such an alleged fact. No doubt in 924 the King and a certain number of clerical and scientific men were abroad in the Nottingham meadows, making plans and giving directions. They were about, not to found a new town, but to add a new half to an old one. On the north side of the river there had been a town, perhaps before Menestheus reigned in Athens, long previous to the first Olympiad or the birth of Romulus. John Rowse at least thinks so; but speculation is useless on the matter. If there be truth in the legend, one would like to know something of the manners and customs of the old and young people; how they lived, how they made love, how they did *not* dress, how they cooked their hips and haws, and what good liquor they swallowed with that primitive diet. Meanwhile, by way of confirmation of the fact of an ancient British city here, its name has come down to us in its British form of 'Tiggocobauc.' Its equivalent is 'House of Caves;' and how well this describes the spot on which the old town and castle stood will not only be seen by the philosophers who inspect 'Mortimer's Hole,' and hear the silly story repeated, that through that House of Caves he found his way to the stately bower of the stern Isabella, but also by those who visit the Church Cemetery, constructed out of the old caves, still popularly called 'the Druids,' a city of the dead, its silent burgesses in the rock stone-girt as at Petra.

When the conquering son of Alfred subdued a revolted city on one side of the river, he created another on the opposite side; an opposition city, partly military, partly commercial, to awe and to stimulate. This he did at Nottingham. He united the two towns by a bridge, making of them one. He settled as many Danes in them as Saxons. Enemies then became friends; we cannot doubt that the old people entered into many a partnership, and the young people followed the example of their parents. The shy Olga learned to raise her soft blue eyes in trusting love upon the straight-limbed Saxon Edwy; and on the broad chest of the Danish Sciold lay the fair head of his young wife Ethelfleda, 'like Hebe in Hercules' arms.' Of such ancestry (with a cross of wholesome Pagan blood) comes the present Nottinghamshire race. The Norman and other admixtures could add nothing to its nobility.

This town will be, for a week, in the hands of the philosophers. It could not be better possessed, for was not the father of the founder of half of it one of the fathers also of British philosophy? Did he not originate our naval power, devise a body of laws, restore learning by restoring Oxford, and make a survey of England which very much helped the authors of Domesday Book?

From the first Pagan chief who looked abroad from his earthworks on the Castle rock down to the reforming era of thirty-four years ago, when the Nottingham rioters burned down the modern edifice, there has been more of bloodshed and sad memories about the old place than of peaceful festival and joyous hopes. King John had a tough fight for it just before he was king. In 1323, indeed, Edward II. held a magnificent Christmas feast there with the nobles of the kingdom, *cum regni proceribus*, and there was not wanting any outward sign or sound of utmost jollity.

The former could be seen in the flaunting banners, the latter heard in the shouts of the revellers by the quieter townsfolk below. But the shadow of death was over the master of the feast, and while he flung himself back in unreserved laughter there were men there who stimulated his mirth, but by whose hands he was to die so terribly, some few years after, in Berkeley Castle.

Even when the Nottingham citizens saw a Parliament, such as Parliaments then were, assemble up at the Castle, and hoped to increase their stock of nobles by the knights and other dignified people who resorted to, lodged in, or passed through the town, there was more grief than gladness came of it. Whatever brilliant but brief flash of commercial prosperity passed over them, gloom and shadow succeeded. Such Parliaments seldom broke up without fleecing the people; and when the traders counted their gains, they had to remember the last Act passed up at the Castle, by virtue of which every fifteenth penny was taken from the *plebs*, and every tenth from all who ranked as citizens in the municipal towns of England.

There was, indeed, once a very joyous-looking assembly beneath the roof of the old Castle; namely, when Richard II. invited his most intimate friends around him, and the town was made glad by the attendant outlay, the feastings, and the riding to and fro. The royal party broke up, and no man heard the slightest insinuation that a new tax had been levied on the people. Merry, however, as they had been up at the Castle, business of a very serious nature had been transacted there. The King there arranged the seizure and the murder of his uncle, Thomas Plantagenet, Duke of Gloucester; that cruel murder, for which Kent, Rutland, Huntingdon, and Somerset won their steps in the peerage, and for superintending which the earl who took his territorial title from Nottingham, Thomas Mowbray, was raised to the rank of Duke of Norfolk. This was in the year 1397, and the duke died two years afterwards, at Venice, of grief, but not for having murdered the prince. The heralds, however, have never lost sight of the descendants of that prince slain by the last Mowbray whose title came from the county of Nottingham. Philosophers themselves may smile sadly at the reflection that these heralds found the representative of Thomas Plantagenet, Duke of Gloucester, in Stephen Penny, the sexton of St. George's burial-ground, Bayswater. Of all genealogical freaks, this, perhaps, is the most curious; the descendant of Edward III. and Philippa of Hainault digging graves for a livelihood!

And this reminds us that when that Edward III. was old, a year or two only before his death, when Alice Ferrers was as saucy and imperious as ever the Du Barry was with Louis XV. and his people, there was carried through Nottingham, up to the Castle, a prisoner at whom the citizens stared in respectful wonder; but they felt much indignation at the woman who was the cause of his captivity. For a stern word uttered to this Alice, Petrus de la Marc, Speaker of the House of Commons, or holding office equivalent to that called so now, was thrown into the keep of Nottingham Castle, where he lingered a couple of years. The Castle, indeed, was seldom without a noble prisoner. Many a stout-hearted abbot who refused to yield the charters of his monastery to the king has pined through long dreary months in the Castle that once dominated the town. Across the meadows, or down upon the busy town itself, the glance of these religious captives was directed, but they seldom saw relief in the distance. Liberty was only to be bought by submission; and that duly observed, the poor man, like the Abbot of Bury, might wend homeward again, over the meadows or through the town, even as it pleased him.

The importance of knowing local history and of being acquainted with the whereabouts of one's dwelling was never better illustrated than when Queen Isabel and Mortimer Earl of March—the alleged wickedness of both of whom must not be accepted without reserve—occupied the Castle. They lay close within, and a number of their enemies lay as close without, anxious to get at them. Queen Isabel ridiculed their efforts, and slept soundly. She had no lack of friends in whom she could trust, but she made assurance doubly sure; and she not only saw, as the chronicler quoted by Dering informs us, that 'the yats of the castel were loken with lokys,' but she sent every night for the 'kayes,' which turned the bars in the locks of those gates, and 'layde them under the chemsel of her beddis hede unto the morrow.' In the mean time young King Edward and Queen Philippa were below, near the market-place; and the members of the Parliament he had assembled in the town had nothing better to do than look up at the Castle, and wonder how they might get at the contumacious people who were therein. Isabel every morning took the keys from under her pillow, rattled them gaily, and as she gave them into the hands of her constable, Sir William Eland, she laughed to scorn all her enemies gathered together in and about Nottingham market-place.

Isabel and Mortimer might have been safe if it had not been for the villany of Eland. The constable was gained by the King's agent, Sir William Montacute. There was no chance, he said, of drawing the keys from beneath Isabel's head; 'but yet I knowe,' said he, 'another weye, by an aleye that stretchith oute of the warde under the earthe into the castell, that goeth into the waste.' This was the passage through the caves in the rock which now goes by the name of *Mortimer's Hole*, with the absurd tradition adopted by Mrs. Colonel Hutchinson attached to it that it was the way by which the gallant (!) Mortimer reached the bower of the light lady Isabel. Of this passage of caves, however, Eland said to Montacute that 'neither Queen Isabel, ne none of her meayne, ne the Mortimer ne none of his company knoweth it not.' Upwards through these caves the party went who surprised the earl and the lady. Shortly after Mortimer was carried down the same passage, and hurried off to the gallows awaiting him in London. Isabel was conveyed away by the road which ultimately brought her to a prison-house in Castle Rising. Edward and his train rode away to Leicester. Nottingham was once more left in quiet, and the citizens explored the passage through the rocks, and merrily laughed as they tried to pronounce the rough old British name of Tiggocobauc.

There were two especial occasions when the streets of the old town were crowded by men who had assembled for sterner purposes than settling questions of philosophy. The first of these occasions was in August 1485. Nottingham was all alive, trembling or rejoicing at the presence of some few thousands of men whom Richard III. had assembled there at his head-quarters. The Silver Boars that bristled on his flags became the 'Blue Pigs' of the taverns—a sign that has not yet become quite extinct. Richard and his men were about to go forth to fight that decisive battle, for which the field was ultimately found within a week at Bosworth, where neither the better cause nor the better man triumphed, if the merits of both are to be judged by the standard of men and morals of the time. On the 16th of August of the above-named year there was no man in Nottingham who was not up and doing, or up and looking at the doings of the more active. Richard's own armourer must have had a difficult task to accomplish, if it be true that his master insisted on wearing the armour he had worn at Tewkesbury. The battle of Tewkesbury was fought fourteen years before that of Bosworth. The young Duke of Gloucester of the former fight was nineteen years of age; Richard III. arming at Nottingham was three-and-thirty. A doublet of the first period might have been easily accommodated to Richard's person by a Nottingham tailor; but an armourer, suddenly called to suit the harness of a boy to the bulk and thews and sinews of a full-grown man, must have had a tougher job of it. But, whatever the suit, Richard rode through the town to the open country, clad like a king and a warrior. The Silver Boar sparkled on his banners. The gazers at his passage through the streets flung up their caps, or held their voices mute, according as their judgments, caprices, or impulses prompted them. They were altogether glad to see him gone.

It may be mentioned, by the way, that by the death in the Tower (if he died in the Tower) of the little Duke of York the town lost its earl, a title which the boy acquired when he was betrothed to the child Anne Mowbray. Once only besides has the earldom of Nottingham belonged to the son of a king, and then the earl was illegitimate. It was among the titles which Henry VIII. conferred on his much-loved son (Henry Fitzroy, Duke of Richmond) by Mistress Blount, who was afterwards Lady Taillebois and then Countess of Lincoln. The title was more worthily bestowed on the Armada admiral, Charles Howard of Effingham. It was borne by three Charles Howards before it passed to the Finches, in the second of whom the earldom of Nottingham became united with the earldom of Winchilsea.

Richard chose Nottingham for his head-quarters because it so pleased him; but when Charles I. set up his standard at Nottingham in 1642, it was because the selfish Royalists of Yorkshire respectfully urged him to be gone, as they did not relish the idea of their county being made the seat of war. How calamitous was the royal progress to Nottingham, Clarendon has told as graphically as the matter can be narrated. On the 25th day of August, two hundred and twenty-four years will have elapsed since the King and his friends declared war against the Parliament on the spot where philosophers and *their* friends will be promoting ends very different from those contemplated by war. 'Upon the 25th day of August,' says Clarendon, 'the standard was erected, about six of the clock in the evening of a very stormy and tempestuous day. The King himself, with a small train, rode to the top of the Castle-hill; Varney, the knight-marshal, who was standard-bearer, carrying the standard, which was then erected in that place, with little other ceremony than the sound of drums and trumpets. Melancholy men observed many ill presages about that time. There was not one regiment of foot yet levied and brought thither, so that the trained bands which the sheriff had drawn together was all the strength the King had for his person and the guard of the standard. There appeared no conflux of men in obedience to the proclamation; the arms and ammunition were not yet come from York; a general sadness covered the whole town, and the King himself appeared more melancholic than he used to be. The standard itself was blown down the same night it had been set up, by a very strong and unruly wind, and could not be fixed again in a day or two till the tempest was allayed. This was the melancholy state of the King's affairs when the standard was set up.'

If we turn now from incidents of war and rebellion to those of peace and order, we may therewith remark that philosophy, which looks with a curious eye at the condition of those who live by agricultural labour, will perhaps be surprised to learn in what relation the Nottinghamshire tenants were towards their lords in the reign, for example, of Henry IV. It was the custom and service of that time that tenants, bond and free, holding a bovate of land, ought to plough and harrow one day in the year for their lord, receiving for their pains threepennyworth of wheaten bread and pease. We must convert the pence into shillings to get at the value of such wage in modern coin. At other times of the year, sowing and weeding were to be done for the lord for similar guerdon; and the tenants made and carried the lord's hay, and reaped and stacked his corn, for which they had, with other good things, fourpence to drink and a pair of white pigeons! But there was something even more of Arcadia (shall we say of Cockayne?) in old Nottinghamshire than this, at the time above indicated. There were thirteen acres in the lord's meadows at Northyng, which were annually mown for him by four-and-twenty tenants. At the end of each day the mowers repaired to the prebendal house to refresh the inward man. The bill of fare, a sort of tenant-labourers' charter, comprised bread, beer, potage, beef, pork, and lamb, for the first course; for the second, broth, pigs, ducks, and either roast lamb or veal. After dinner they sat and drank, with liberty to leave the hall three times, and return as often to drink as much more as they could carry under their girdles. As if this were not enough, a bucket, containing eight flagons and a half of beer, was then borne in joyous procession from the prebendal house, through the town, to the meadows, where various plays were then carried on. At the termination of all, the lord presented each of the tenants with a pair of white gloves; not such flimsy things as form part of modern 'dress,' but gauntlets of stout leather, not one stitch of which would go in a year's dancing with the most romping of Cicelys, nor, indeed, in a year's labour between the handles of a plough, or with bill-hook at hedging, or heavy spade-work in the most clayey of soils. If any doubt this halcyon condition of tenant-labourers, they are referred to a copy of the document, where the customs are narrated at great length, in Dickinson's *Antiquities* (1804). There are certainly no modern instances of such rural good living, unless, indeed, it be in the neighbourhood of Neufchâtel, where Swiss peasants now earn a pound sterling per week, and drink their two bottles of wine daily.

Hundreds of persons who will next week be enjoying the abundant hospitality of their Nottingham hosts will not be surprised to hear that the old magnates of the town had always a fine appreciation of the wants of hungry men and the method of satisfying them. At the opening of King James's reign, when Nottingham got a new Recorder, Sir Henry Pierrepont, the municipality invited him to the Hall to receive a testimonial in public from their hands. When Sir Henry put forward his own to receive it, the officers of the council set before him, not a service of plate, but a loaf of sugar worth 9s., twenty-pennyworth of lemons, a gallon of white and a gallon of claret wine, at little more than half-a-crown the gallon, with a pottle of muscadine and sack, the whole together being of the value of 20s. 8d.! Thus, at the beginning of his office, the Recorder was presented with a congratulatory silver pitcher, whence to quaff his Rhenish and Malvoisy at home; but there was placed before him a significant hint that among the duties of office that of good drinking with the corporation was not to be omitted. Not that they despised the more substantial pleasures of the table, as they delicately suggested in 1604 to the Earl of Shrewsbury, son of him who had had Mary Stuart in his keeping. After thinking what would be the most suitable present for an earl who had an appetite and loved to satisfy it, the Nottingham Council, solemnly assembled, presented him, as the record says, with ' a veal, a mutton, a lamb, a dozen of chickens, two dozen of rabbits, two dozen of pigeons, and four capons.' If the Earl carried away his gift with him, he must have looked like a chapman about to open stall in the market-place; but the probability is that at full noontide he and the donors sat down and consumed the good things together, while Nottingham bells rang merry peals to quicken their blood, stimulate appetite, and help digestion.

It is one of the most remarkable facts in corporation annals that this Nottingham municipality, so liberal in feeding others, half starved itself. For instance, on Michaelmas-day, when the old mayor transferred his power to his successor, there was more of formality than of feasting. The mace lay on a black cloth under a heap of bay-sprigs and rosemary. This was called the *burying of the mace.*

When the new mayor had been duly elected, his predecessor took the old symbol from its fragrant grave, kissed it tenderly, as an abdicating sovereign might do the sceptre which he was loth to resign, and handed it over to the new municipal monarch. After some other ceremonies came the banquet, which was Spartan in its nature. There were numerous guests, but the fare was frugal. Bread-and-cheese satisfied the appetite. Pipes and tobacco were added as hospitable luxuries. Not a word is said of liquid appliances. 'Fruit in season' moderately adorned the board; but of 'jolly good ale and old,' of Rhenish or Malvoisy, even of punch, to which the chaplain himself could not have objected, there is no mention. And yet it is not to be supposed that the 'flowing bowl,' the 'mantling cup,' the 'regal purple stream,' goblets, bumpers, and all the rest of the properties of jollity celebrated in song, were wanting. The Nottingham aldermen surely did not take the pipes from their mouths merely to put Ribston pippins into them!

These men and their fellow-townsmen, whatever they may or may not have drunk, were celebrated for their industry. Nottingham has been in all times noted for its steady, persevering, and successful workers. Labour and the fruits of labour seem to flourish among them spontaneously, like the crocuses that yearly gladden the Nottingham meadows. In spring-time, such of these meadows as have not been invaded by contractors and builders are converted into a seeming lake of violet crocuses. Over the green of the fields Flora throws a mantle of the freshest and most delicious hue. The consequent delight influences more senses than one. There is a charm for the eye, and a charm for the ear in the songs of the birds that hang enchanted above the magic carpet; and there is another charm besides, for at every footstep made among the flowers a sweet incense arises from the crushed petals, sweet as the air wafted from the Spice Islands over the sea. Nottingham thus becomes truly Flower Town, the English Florence, for young and old go forth to collect and carry away the precious treasure of the fields—a treasure which springs spontaneously nowhere else save on the spreading Inches of Perth. With the young it is a period of high festival. They plunge through the sea of petals, gathering heaps of odorous beauty as they pass. *She* is queen who finds a white crocus among her violet-hued sisters; but all return laden with sweets to the town, joyous beneath their double burden, and rich in the twofold fragrance of youth and of flowers.

Let us add of the Park here that, in the proper sense of the word, that of Nottingham so called has had no existence for many centuries. Even in Charles I.'s time, when the Castle itself was nothing more than a prison in ruins, and the older castle of Isabel and Mortimer was crumbling in more ancient ruin above it, there was neither deer nor tree in Nottingham Park. There were one or two half-withered trees, indeed, and one of these was planted, so ran the story, by Richard before he marched out of Nottingham, on his way to Leicester. When the Commonwealth soldiers occupied the Castle ruins, they looked curiously at this tree, which from root to top was twisted violently awry, and had not a straight twig or branch in it. 'Ay, ay!' said the Parliament troopers, 'it's as crooked as he who planted it;' and King Richard's tree was speedily felled to feed the Castle fires.

But to return to the history of Nottingham, we have to observe that the useful had precedence of the ornamental. Nottingham made stockings before it made lace; but it was a gentleman who invented the stocking-frame, and an ordinary Nottingham stocking-weaver who first made bobbin-net by so adapting his frame as to make it produce the imitation of lace after it had woven the reality of stockings. Soon after the Rev. William Lea invented the stocking-frame, at the end of the sixteenth century, the old trunk hose slipped away from the limbs of our ancestors. Nearly two hundred years later—that is to say, in 1770—Hammond, a weaver, was sitting at one of Lea's old-fashioned frames, and as he plied his task his thoughts dwelt on the expensive pillow-lace made of flax thread, by aid of fingers and bobbins; and he thought of the old Italian lace made by the needle, of the costly productions of Brussels, Alençon, and Valenciennes; of Honiton lace made like the Italian, and of Buckingham lace, which more nearly resembled the commoner point d'Alençon. The result of Hammond's thought was the far-famed bobbin-net. The Nottingham weaver, it would be more correct to say, rather made the first attempt than fully succeeded in the manufacture. The final success was achieved when Mr. Heathcote invented the bobbin-frame, whence machine-made lace obtained the name of *bobbin-net*, and made Nottingham famous even in the bazaars of Eastern Ind. It is still the centre of the cotton-hosiery and bobbin-net trade.

Those trades have, like all others, been subject to great fluctuations. Out of the misery and consequent calamities wrought by those who could not bear it Nottingham and the shire generally issued just half a century ago (1816), after a struggle of five years. It began in 1811, by an outbreak of the hungry framework-knitters, who could not exist on the small wages to which they were reduced. Under an imaginary General Ludd they issued by night, their faces variously disguised, and, appearing where they were least expected, would smash into fragments five or six dozen of a manufacturer's valuable frames before dawn. The ruin wrought, they scattered, were not to be tracked; met again at night, armed with swords and muskets, and in detached bodies carried on their work of destruction in several directions, but never where the weary military and the vexed magistracy were waiting for them. Factories were regularly stormed and defended, blood flowed profusely, life was sacrificed, soldiers and weavers came into collision, and prisoners were made of the latter, but no severity of punishment could deter those who were free from carrying on the work of devastation. They not only destroyed frames, but burned the stacks of those farmers who served in the yeomanry against them; and they broke into the farmhouses and carried off money and provisions. The ruin was widespread, and at one time nearly half the then

population of Nottingham was receiving parish relief.
The work of destruction did not cease even when
Parliament decreed *death* as the penalty of breaking
a lace- or stocking-frame. The destroyers only withheld their hands when they discovered that by chopping up and burning frames they were destroying
the means by which they might live; and that as
the damage had to be made good out of a countyrate, the manufacturers would go comparatively uninjured, while the poor-rate was likely to be all the
less when the county-rate was abnormally increased.
At the end of the five years' fray they had cause to
remember that the Wise Men of Gotham were natives
of Nottinghamshire, in which that place, renowned
for the peculiarity of its philosophy, is to be found.
The rioters, in short, resembled their Irish prototypes,
who, made angry by the failure of a local bank,
avenged themselves by burning piles of its notes in
front of the door from which those promises to pay
had once been issued!

There is something, however, to be said for those
ruthless Luddites. They were not only ill-fed, but
worse taught. Then, and long after then, Richard
Carlile and his partner in iniquity, the Rev. Robert
Taylor, made a little British Association of their own,
with its head-quarters in Nottingham. The philosophy they pretended to teach was atheism without
disguise. Carlile was the devil's servant and was
not at all ashamed of his master; but the Rev. Robert
Taylor, who was in the same service, wore openly the
livery of Christ! One of their most active and efficient opponents was the late Rev. Joseph Gilbert,

then an Independent minister in Nottingham. How well qualified that Christian gentleman and scholar was to overthrow such adversaries may be seen in his remarkable work on the Christian Atonement. If any visitor at the coming meeting of the British Association should find a copy left in Nottingham (it is a scarce book), he will do well to avail himself of the opportunity thereby offered.

The Castle of to-day is only the relic of the mansion built on a small portion of the site of the old edifice by the first Duke of Newcastle, in Charles II.'s time. He gave a six weeks' housewarming, and never opened his house again. This building was destroyed by fire in the election riots of 1832, which deed was denounced by 'Anne Taylor of Ongar,' as she will be affectionately remembered, in stinging verse. The Robin Hood Rifles occupy a nook of the old place; and this they owe to the patriotism of the Nottingham ladies, who successfully exerted themselves to obtain the Castle kitchen, and convert it into a drill-room. In the caves beneath, from which the British town is named, visitors may search for, and we very much hope may find, the story of Christ and His twelve apostles, scratched on the walls by the nails of a captive northern king named David. However this may be, there is one spectacle of delight which they may enjoy whenever philosophy and hospitality leave them a little leisure. The Trent still describes its gentle curve towards Wilford. It is still a breadth of silver on its gleaming passage to Clifton and its groves. There are still the rich valley and picturesque woodland drawing the eye towards distant Derbyshire;

and as Thornton quaintly and truthfully adds, 'a vast space is seen between Buddington Hills and Colwick, in which Belvoir Castle appears majestical.' The town itself yielded Kirke White from a butcher's-shop to earnest poetry, and thence Bailey flashed his promise of a poet, and William Howitt there belonged to literature while he was yet a chemist and druggist. Nottingham had the last of the English minstrels who made and sang his own songs in David Love, and the last of town fools in the person of 'General Ben.' But as we are dealing with philosophy, and not with folly, let us conclude by noting that Nottingham has given Dr. J. H. Gilbert to agricultural chemistry; boasts of Mr. Josiah Gilbert and Mr. Churchill as the discoverers of the Dolomite Mountains, for the benefit of English travellers; and confers, with reasonable pride, the brightest crown that mine can furnish on the brow of the great metallurgist, Dr. Percy. And, à propos to crowns, let us conclude with a reference to skulls. The skull which Byron preserved, in shape and use as a cup, at Newstead, in the neighbourhood of Nottingham, has been buried by its present scrupulous owner! Philosophy may no longer speculate on the wisdom, nor jollity calculate on the measure of wine, that was once held within that old mansion of the brain. But they will find other matter for speculation in the Sections, and other subject for discussion in the hospitable homes of ancient Tiggocobauc.

VII.
DUNDEE.
1867.

DUNDEE.

1867.

THE annual manifesto of the British Association is making an unusual stir among the ninety thousand honest bodies whose home is on the Tay—that river which caused the weary Romans when they first came in sight of it to shout '*Ecce Tiber!*'

There was a little coyness on the part of a few when Dundee was named for the meeting of 1867, under the presidency of the Duke of Buccleuch. The stringent orthodoxy of some very well-meaning persons was considerably shocked by the electric power of Mr. Grove's inaugural address at Nottingham. 'Continuity' was a burden to their minds, and they would fain have kept the philosophers at a distance; but good sense and generous feeling have prevailed, and the town has its arms open to its guests. Come they by land or by water, they will be welcome. In the second town of Scotland for commercial importance—amid the linen factories and the ironworks, which have uninterruptedly flourished since the Stuarts ceased to trouble the land—the Association will open its thirty-seventh session on the 4th of September. It is well they should meet in

Dundee before the great change takes place which was foretold by a learned man some forty years ago!

That Scottish philosopher, Dr. M'Culloch, who had a fine eye for beauty and none at all for clean linen, was probably the last of the 'hangers-on' in great families. He was at home with the ducal Murrays in Athol, as Gay was with the Queensberrys, and he repaid the hospitality in a graceful way, by writing an admirable volume on the scenery of Dunkeld and Blair in Athol. From that volume the visitors at Dundee may learn that the city in which they are foregathering exists only by chance, and is merely temporary! Its destiny is to become by and by, from a seaport, a quiet inland town!

When philosophers turn from lecturing to excursionising, and explore the river at the mouth of which Dundee stands for the present, they will be struck by the terraces of gravel and sand high above either bank of the Tay, a hundred feet higher than its modern bed, the deposit of the river as the Romans beheld it. 'The terraces,' says Dr. M'Culloch, 'which still exist are the remains of a solid plain or strath, through which the stream once wandered laterally, just as it wanders still, and all that is wanting has travelled downwards to form the Carse of Gowrie, as more will yet reach the same spot, to make Dundee hereafter what Perth now is; converting sea into land. Had Perth existed when the Tay ran high in the hills, and when the place of Dunkeld was deep buried in the earth, it would have been what Dundee now is, a maritime town.' Meanwhile, visitors will confess that there is no empty boast in the Scottish assertion that forth from the ancient town spreads one of the richest and most varied landscapes in Scotland, though it may not be, as was once claimed for it, 'quite Italian, and such as Claude often painted.'

'Donum Dei,' or 'Dei Donum,' the legend on the borough seal, has nothing to do with the old name of the town, *Taodunum*. Dunkeld was '*the* fort of the Celts' on the Tay; Dundee (or Taodunum) was '*the* fort on the Tay.' The name has slipped into the burden of a French song; it is at least suggested that some archers of the Scottish Guard in France, singing a song about 'the fair of Dundee,' introduced the well-known chorus which the French pronounce as '*La faridondaine, la faridondé!*' The words 'Bonny Dundee' themselves fairly interpret the 'Alectum,' which the Romans called the town, borrowing the Celtic *Ail-lec*, which is yet applied to it by a few 'old stagers,' and which signifies *pleasant*.

Perth and Dundee have been as jealous of each other from time immemorial as any two of the turbulent Italian cities of the Middle Ages, each of which was better contented that both should be ruined than that the other should be a little in advance of it in dignity and prosperity. Dr. Robert Chambers is about to show, we believe, that icebergs were no unfrequent visitors on the Tay in early periods, and this circumstance may have established a coolness between the two people. The truth, however, is that pride was at the bottom of it all. Exactly three hundred years ago Dundee was shedding tears, uttering oaths, was rampant with indignation and depressed by the humiliating circumstances to which it was subjected. In 1567 the Regent Murray summoned a Parliament. The getting together such an assembly of august rulers and advisers was a sight which gave the spectators wherewith to talk about for a lifetime. Who has not heard of the 'Riding of the Estates'? All the members of the burghs caracolled to their task in wonderful procession. Now in this equestrian procession (amid accompaniment of drum, trumpet, blunderbuss, and thunder) Edinburgh, by her representatives duly hoisted into saddle, took the lead. Nobody doubted her right of precedency, but there was a fierce fight in 1567 for second place. The dispute lay between Perth and Dundee. Each claimed it long before the day of meeting; and when the representatives solemnly rode out of their respective towns to the trysting-place, they were enjoined to remember local honour, and to uphold the dignity of what they represented by taking such a position in the 'Riding of the Estates' as should show the world that if Edinburgh had precedence of all besides, Perth or Dundee, as the case might be, was certainly second; and second to none other. On the day of meeting, the mounted representatives, with an ensign-bearer, galloped into the market-place, and Perth and Dundee battled for the second place of honour. So delightful a circumstance as a serious fight on the causeway was not so rare but that the populace should hilariously join therein. The handsenyie (which was 'ensign' under the adverse handling of Scottish orthography) of Dundee was held aloft by

William Rysie, and such a tumult was the consequence that it came to be doubtful whether the equestrians would ever ride to Parliament at all. Things looked so serious that the Regent himself interfered, but the onslaught was not suppressed without difficulty. In the scrutiny that followed, Dundee seems to have been divested of her precedency over Perth, though her representatives were acknowledged to have borne themselves worthily; but Dundee raged and would not be consoled at the loss of her dignity in the eyes of a mere Master of the Ceremonies.

If, however, urban precedency is to be reckoned by amount of contributions made to the state treasury, Dundee should have ranked before Perth. The latter town furnished in taxes at the above period 985l. annually, while Dundee contributed nearly twice as much, namely, 1729l. If this was 'punds Scot,' it was nothing to boast of; if 'pounds sterling,' it represents a very flourishing condition of the latter town three centuries ago. It is uncertain what the population amounted to at that period. When a census was taken in 1782 the numbers were given under religious heads. For instance, Kirk, 12,903; Dissenters (but of Presbyterian organisation), 1752; Episcopalians, 903; and with them a class who described themselves 'of no religion,' amounting to 104. Which class contributed proportionally the greatest number of criminals is not stated; but of the prison which held them Dundee was proud, and all Scotland beside was envious. It was the boast of honest men and the despair of felons that it was the strongest prison in all Scotland. There was no getting out of it by 'breaking.' A toad might as easily break from the centre of the stone in which it has been immured for centuries. A sense of security pervaded both felons and their keepers. The latter locked up their prisoners at eight o'clock every night, and repaired to their lodgings in town, returning to their involuntary guests at six in the morning! In the interval no attempt at evasion was made; for it would have been useless, and merely spoilt the rest of him who made it. So thieves and jailers lived on easy terms with each other, though the former must have often sung sadly the song of Sterne's starling,. 'I can't get out.'

The most famous of the assaults made upon Dundee, the most complete in its success, and one which is supposed to address itself most to our sympathies, is the famous one under General Monk, when the town and all it possessed, with a score of rich ships in the harbour, fell into the power of the captors, and when, after the slaughter was over, and a business account of things was taken, the handsome sum of 60*l.* fell to the share of every common soldier! But there is a comic side to this story which rather chills and overshadows our sympathies. Previous to the siege a vast number of refugees from the country parts flocked into the town, and among those now shut up in it were very many godly ministers of most hilarious habits and unquenchable thirst. They probably drank late; for their first business on awaking was to renew drinking. They sat down at nine, and drank till noon, always with the garrison. Such as

had not fallen asleep before fell into it then, and took
their siesta, till wakefulness and thirst brought them
again to the business of their lives. There was a
little Scotch lad, who, being *but* a lad, was allowed
ingress and egress, and to play about the place as he
listed. The boy observed the habits of the topers
and slumberers, and it led him to imitate the rascality
of Monteith towards Wallace. He went and told
what he had seen to Monk. What followed we know.
Monk burst into the town, and gave the sleepers a
waking different from that to which they had been
accustomed, and sent them to quench their thirst in
the final sleep.

There is matter for a ballad in this incident, and
similar material is to be found in details of the feuds
of Crawford, Glamis, Strathmore, and Panmure, who
lived in times when a man with a social foe was content to 'stand all his life in a soldier's posture.' Social
joy sometimes afforded a subject, as in the case of
Maud Lindsay, daughter of the Earl of Crawford
(whose family maintained a regal pomp at their house
in Dundee), when, in the beginning of the fifteenth
century, Maud married with the fifth Earl of Douglas.
Tradition still keeps up the memory of a wedding
which, in gorgeousness and jollity of celebration,
perhaps never had its equal in all Christendom. In
later times Scottish nobles held no such state. They
celebrated in other fashion their marriages. In the
early part of the last century another daughter of this
house of Crawford (her father was the sixteenth earl)
married with Patrick Lindsay. The bridegroom was
described as 'heir male of the grand old house of

L

Lindsay of the Byres;' but he was also 'an upholsterer in the Parliament Close of Edinburgh,' yet so well-to-do as to be Dean of Guild for that city.

Dundee offers a more sober subject for a ballad in one of its many witch-burnings. Grizzel Jeffray was the widow of a Dundee maltman, whose only son, a sea-captain, was far away with his ship. The solitary woman sat weeping alike for the dead and the living, from whose companionship she was debarred. So, ever mourning, Grizzel was taken and condemned for a witch; and as the flames shot above her, while she stood bound to the stake in front of the Sea Gate of Dundee, her son's ship came up the Firth. When the young captain learned the significance of that terrible scene on shore he wandered seaward again, and—according to the legend—was never heard of more.

No ballad-monger has more misrepresented fact than tradition has misrepresented Graham of Claverhouse, Viscount Dundee. Many of the sins of an obscurer Graham have been lifted to the shoulders of Claverhouse, and been kept tightly there, by his enemies. So it was with the two Penns. As far, at all events, as regards the town of Dundee, ' Bloody Clavers' is a designation not accepted there. One of his first acts, as Constable of Dundee, when he found many thieves under sentence of death, was to petition the Council to save their lives. It would be fitter, he said, that their crimes ' should be punished arbitrarily than by death.' And the Council heeded Claverhouse's recommendation to mercy, and gave him leave to whip or banish thieves as he ' saw cause.'

But the widow of Dundee affords a better subject for a ballad than any of the instances here produced. A year after Killiecrankie, Livingstone, Viscount Kilsyth, in the garden of Colzium House, Stirlingshire, whispered at the fair widow's ear, found a way to her heart, and put a ring on her finger bearing the motto, 'Zoors onnly and Euer,' which was meant to be English for '*Yours only and ever.*' This Jacobite couple wedded, and in a few years had to leave the country. The lady had previously (in 1694) dropped the ring from her finger in the garden of Colzium, and by no research could it be discovered. This betokened ill-luck, realised in the banishment; and full of fresh apprehension of evil, the banished household set up a new home at Rotterdam. Episcopalian as the lady was, she there heard the famous Robert Fleming preach—that prophet who in 1701 foretold a humbling of the French monarchy in 1794. On one occasion, when Lady Kilsyth was present, Fleming is said to have alluded to an impression he vainly strove against, that, before many hours, a calamity would fall upon some member then in the congregation. Shortly after the widow of Dundee, her infant son, and the nurse were crushed to death by the fall of the roof of the house in which they were seated. Mother and child were privately buried in Kilsyth Church; and some old men may yet be living who, when young children, looked on the two bodies, as they lay in one coffin, which was opened some ninety years after its interment. Not many years subsequently a man, digging soil in Colzium garden, turned up a ring with a motto on it as above described:

it was the token of love which Kilsyth, above a hundred years before, had given to the widow of Dundee when he was a-wooing, and the loss of which had filled the lady with superstitious fear. Can ballad-writers be in want of a subject while this story is unsung?

The painter may find his account quite as readily as the poet in some of the incidents connected with Dundee. Of all the gatherings in and about the town, none is of more powerful interest, more picturesque in detail, or more illustrative of the time and people than those of which that especially heroic reformer, George Wishart, was the summoner. Of the various assemblages which Wishart addressed, at peril of his life whenever he spoke, none was so solemn or so significant as the one of 1544, when the plague was sweeping the town. The imagination may easily bring him again to where that fearless, humble, honest apostle stood on the East Gate. The mass of people below him were divided, the infected from the disinfected. The former lay, or stood, or reclined, without the gate; they who were as yet whole, or who had been smitten, but were again clean, clustered together beneath the eaves of the houses, or in silent yet eager groups on the causeway—folk of all ages and degrees, their eyes straining at the preacher on the gate, their ears drinking in every word that fell from his lips into their hearts, and no sound upon the air but that of the inspired voice, with an occasional sob of anguish, or a sharp short cry of gladness, or a murmur of acquiescence sent up from those eager earnest listeners in testimony of the unweariedness with which they hung upon the utterances of the preacher.

Frequently, as long as the pestilence raged, Wishart, after passing from one stricken family to another, affording them such consolation as he had to give, preached from the same eminence at the Eastern Gate. On the last occasion of his proclaiming the justice and mercy of God from that magnificent pulpit, he gave with unusual solemnity his blessing to the people who were on either side the gate, the sick on one side and on the other the free. As Wishart was descending he was met by a wildly enthusiastic priest, Sir John Wrighton, who rushed at him to settle all controversy by shedding the blood of the reformer. The people, marking the purpose of the assassin, uttered a howl of execration, and, losing all sense of distinction, the plague-spotted mingling with the clean, they flung themselves on the would-be murderer, but only to find that vengeance was denied to them. For Wishart took his assailant in his arms, and held him there in sanctuary till the popular rage had subsided, when, because he wished it, those earnest Dundee folk opened their serried lines, and left passage for the abashed fanatic to go on his way unmolested. Never was there child with heart more tender, never soldier with heart more bold, than this hero of the Reformation. In the hour of his dreadful death at the stake he abated no jot of his habitual courtesy, nor of his fortitude. Cardinal Beaton, lying on velvet cushions, looked down from the walls of St. Andrews on his victim; and Wishart, just before he died, exclaimed, 'He who from yonder high place looketh down upon us with such pride shall within few days lie in the same as ignominiously as now he is seen proudly to rest himself.' And because of this prophecy, Wishart (whom men of all communions might esteem) has been accused of having been privy to the plot which soon after culminated in the Cardinal's murder. Dundee honoured itself as well as Wishart, when, abolishing the other gates of the town, the people preserved the East Gate in honour of the old missionary.

An enterprising seafaring native of Dundee, named Crichton, sailed in the last century to seek for fortune in the East Indian seas. He was in a tight ship, freighted with all sorts of stores, and Dundee thread and Osnaburghs were down in the bill of lading. The terror of those seas in those days was Angria, the active and ferocious pirate, into whose hands Crichton and his ship fell, after a tough fight of a day long. At the close of it the pirate was too hungry to trust himself with having the man before him who had so nearly brought him to grief; nor did he think that Crichton was in much of a condition to answer his queries. Accordingly he ordered dinner for two in separate cabins, and he commanded Crichton to attend him as soon as he had 'got his skin full!' At the appointed time the two foemen met, and the 'materials' were on the table between them. When each had mixed his draught as he best liked it, Angria in fair English questioned Captain Crichton. 'Ay, ay!' said the pirate, 'so you're a Dundee man;' and then he examined him as to the town and people and environs in a way which made Crichton stare; but as he replied with readiness and correctness, Angria exclaimed, 'Weel, I see ye are just what ye describe yersel'; and deil hae my saul if I hurt a hair o' your head; for ye see, Capt'n Crichton, I'm a Dundee man mysel', an' I ken what's corract betuxt fellow-townsmen!'

The Dundee captain was as much astounded as *his* fellow-townsman was who found a Scot at the head of a tribe of Bactrians. Marshal-General Keith had a similar surprise in 1793. He had concluded, on the part of Russia, his conference with the Grand Vizier respecting a treaty of peace, at which an interpreter facilitated a mutual understanding. When the two great men were about to separate, Keith was astonished to hear the Vizier remark that he was 'unco' happy' to meet such a distinguished personage. 'Dinna be surprised, mon,' he added; 'I'm o' the same country wi' yoursel.' I min' weel seeing you an' yer brither, when boys, passin' by to the school at Kirkcaldy; my fauther, sir, was bellman o' Kirkcaldy!'

Turning from personal to political incidents, it will be found that as a rule, when loyalty to Jacobitism was treason to Brunswick, those towns and cities shouted more lustily for King George (on formal occasions, when the eyes of Hanoverians rested scrutinisingly upon them) than they ever did for King James, except when they found their hearts as open as their throats, and no enemy at hand to censure their utterance. Aberdeen, Brechin, and Dundee were famous or infamous, according to circumstances, for their heart's love for the Stuart and their lip-service for the 'wee wee German lairdie.' On occasions of public rejoicings, such as royal birthdays, the illuminations, bonfires, bell-ringing, and the like were always most brilliant, noisy, and demonstrative in the cities where Jacobitism abounded. There the Hanoverian party exerted themselves to establish their loyalty, and Jacobites united with them out of fear of the authorities. It is creditable, however, to Dundee, where the Jacobites were as two to one to the Hanoverians, that on anniversaries when political demonstrations were to be made there were friends of the Stuart who, if they could not drink to the king over the water at the market-cross, would not disgrace their principles by toasting King George in the public causeway or anywhere else. But when they refrained from a show of loyalty to the king *de facto*, they did it at their peril, at least at the peril of being fined. For example, when Dundee celebrated the birthday of George Prince of Wales in 1716, which was done at an outlay of much light, liquor, and laughter born of the mountain dew, the report in the *Scots Courant* is that 'everybody looked cheerful, and vied who should outdo the other in rejoicing, except some few of our Jacobite neighbours, who, being like owls, loved darkness; but *care will be taken that they spared not their money by being singular*.' If they would not stand a pint stoup in honour of great George, they were evidently to smart for it! Perhaps economy had somewhat to do with their abstinence; they reasonably objected to being called upon to draw the strings of their purses and to rejoice in the accession of a king who was not *their* king. When the monarch and the heir apparent, after fierce quarrel and long unseemly sulkiness, were ostensibly reconciled, the Scottish cities got dutifully drunk with joy; and such Cavalier cities as Dundee and Aberdeen were expected to get as drunk as the rest, because the German lairdie and his heir had agreed to what they meant to avoid, namely, let bygones be bygones.

The old political spirit of Dundee asserted itself by its Whig Club leading the way in 1790 to congratulate the National Assembly of France on the establishment of constitutional monarchy in that country. Such a document may now be read with a smile and a sigh. It is so droll, and yet so grave; abounding with simplicity, yet full of earnestness; full of matter to interest the world at large, with much to gratify the pride of Dundee in particular. Humble, however, in self-appreciation, it almost begs pardon for supposing that the National Assembly will deign to listen to the congratulations of the members of an obscure club. Yet they cannot forego expressing their approbation at France having turned from giving bad example of life to the world to making herself a political model for the universe to follow. It is intimated that the French king will henceforth be nearly as excellent a personage as his brother of England, who, according to the Dundee Whigs, was an object 'almost of adoration.' Unwisely venturing on prophecy, they foretell that Louis XVI. had 'added lustre to the House of Bourbon, and riveted the crown of France on the heads of his posterity.' This address is of unreasonable length, but the authors of it assure the Assembly that they had intended to be more concise, and were sorry they had failed.

Great was the enthusiasm in Dundee when the reply to this address reached the ancient town. It was signed by one of those men of contemporary note whose names are not subsequently recorded in the pages of history—Treilhard, President of the Assembly. The answer overflowed with civility and smart sayings; but it chiefly insisted on the fact that an era of universal peace and good-will had arrived, and that the throne of Louis XVI. was firmly established in the hearts of his people, who, imitating their English brethren, regarded him as *almost* worthy of being worshipped!

The Dundee Whig Club made the town keep holiday in honour of this polite reply of M. Treilhard (who voted for the King's death soon after, became an active Republican, and died with the Cross of the Legion of Honour on his breast which he received at the hands of Napoleon). They mounted the French national cockade, paraded the town, and sat down to a dinner which was followed by a couple of dozen toasts of the most humorously mixed nature. 'May liberty always be accompanied by religious toleration!' happily embraced all sects; but the 'Immortal memory of King William' was not likely to gratify the 'Papists;' and by the time the company had drunk to the 'Revival of ancient liberty in Rome,' there was a license in Dundee which would have shocked the finer sense of the Conscript Fathers!

The noisy partisans of those days sleep in the old cemeteries of Dundee, which no sojourner should omit to visit. There is as much food there for philosophical speculation as in any of the Sections; as much even of amusement, at least, as at the *conversazioni*, where life swarms and tongues wag. It is an old story how flattering epitaphs teach us that only *good* people die. The Ephori prohibited epitaphs altogether, because they described everybody as irreproachable, and such lying it became a wise magistracy to suppress. Some such power might have been sagely exercised in Dundee, for most of the dead there seem by their epitaphs to have been once of the very cream of the cream. Every man is a little above the angels, and every woman higher still. Better than this, however, are the eccentricities of the tombstone literature and sentimentalism. Here is Margery Forester, who proudly erects what she calls a 'Mausoleus monument of marble' to an incomparable husband, who had never done her an ill turn till the day he left her a widow. If we were to hear of a 'singular wife' or a 'singular matron' in the South, we should conclude that the lady had what ladies seldom have—a few troublesome whims and caprices not known to her sisters. In the Dundee churchyard no such conclusion must be come to. Every 'singular' wife or matron who sleeps there was simply but once married; and there are so many of them that a local registrar might be well employed on a brief 'paper,' the object of which should be to inquire whether this singularity arose from lack of opportunity to put another face upon it.

One famous stone has disappeared, or at all events the inscription on it; and this, considering the sta-

tistics of population once inscribed thereon, is to be
deplored. Statisticians who take interest in such
matters will seek in vain for the solemn authority of
that tombstone which tourists whose memories can
run half a century back, and who used to begin their
tour by a formidable tossing in a little sailing-smack
from London to Dundee, will remember for the
astounding information which it imparted. When
disbelievers destroyed the record, wiser people had
already made a note of it, and, trustworthy or not, it
was to this effect: 'Hier lyis ane honest man, Walter
Gourlay, maltman and burgess of Dundee, qvha
decessit' (which was elegant Scotch for 'who died')
'in 28 day of April, 1628, of the aige of 46 zeires,
with his twenty bairnis.' A man of forty-six, with
nearly half the number of children, is a thing for
philosophic celibacy to raise its shoulders at; but that
the children should all have died along with their
sire will seem odd to statists and philosophers. The
tradition is to that effect; but did the inscription
above Walter Gourlay assert as much? and if it did,
what corroborative proof was to be obtained? Well,
it was once to be found on the same stone. Gourlay
and his score of children left a widow and mother
sole relic of a household of two-and-twenty persons!
However she may have sorrowed when living soli-
tarily, she seems to have died with hilarious readiness, if we may judge from the tone of the record
which was placed above her and the old companions
of her home. Using, as was the custom once in
Scotland, her maiden name instead of her married
one, the widow, joyously laying down her widow-

hood, thus let all wayfarers know that she was sleeping the long sleep by the side of her husband and among their children : 'Epyte Pie. Here lie I. My twenty bairnies. My Good Man. And I.' Here is as good evidence as can be procured at the 'grave of a household,' which has as much poetical sentiment in it as that which inspired the Muse of Mrs. Hemans.

These matters belong to the old world, and we may add that, as elsewhere, so at Dundee, the old-world air and habit have passed away. Her merchants do not breakfast as of yore at the ale-houses. 'Dundee thread' is not asked for as it used to be by notable sempstresses in every corner of the three kingdoms. 'Osnaburghs' have more completely passed away than 'Russia ducks.' Old women are not to be seen moving to kirk with a Bible under one arm, and a folding-stool for a seat under the other. Godly constables no longer sanctify or desecrate the Sabbath by seizing all loiterers on the causeway or in the meadows, and clapping them in the lockhouse if they could only succeed in dragging them thither. At the close of the last century, the ladies of Dundee *fashed* the gentlemen by continuing to wear wigs! Whether false hair still takes the look there of what it is not, who shall dare to say? Of one thing we *may* be certain—that the old hospitality and the old light-heartsomeness of Dundee will be found by the British Association as profuse and attractive as ever; ay, and its light-heeledness also, if the younger philosophers care to dance with the daughters of *Taodunum*. In love for treading a measure, Dundee surpassed all

Scotland. It showed the way to others by being the first to found an 'assembly-room;' and it imported such a teacher of dancing as would have astonished Coulon or Frédéric Marc Antoine Venua! Wonderful man was that stalwart German, Noseman! Such a name, whether his own or not, became him; for the huge Teuton loved brandy, and his nose hung out the signal of his love. Such a giant teaching a minuet was like an elephant playing on the tabor. The very sense of his stature and threatening look induce us to retire, as it were, from before this ponderous dancing-master with a certain reverential readiness, but not without whispering, as we take leave, that on beginning to learn the minuet it would have been well for you to add a little cognac to the fee, and that on being perfected in that graceful series of movements, and qualified to go through them with the most stately She that might condescend to test your gracefulness, you were expected to give a pound of Bohea to old Noseman's female servant! Reflections on this social arrangement suggest themselves, but we leave them to be pursued in the town where Noseman began with brandy and ended with Bohea. Suffice it to say here, that if we compare the minuet and the sages of the last century with the quadrille and the philosophy of this, we shall find that if we have lost all the 'poetry of motion,' we have greatly gained, not only in knowledge, but in wisdom.

VIII.
NORWICH.
1868.

NORWICH.

1868.

Though England is rich in beautiful and interesting cities, there is not one which, for certain features of beauty and matters of interest, can excel the city of Norwich. Travellers from the sacred East, looking on it, are reminded of the holiest of cities. Its gardens and foliage have been famous for centuries. Sea, river, and land yield it rich tribute, and Norfolk men generally have always been as remarkable as the pleasant places in which their lives have been cast. They were ever famous for boldness. When the Conqueror gave to his follower, Warren, the lands of Sharnbourn of Sharnbourn, the latter went to law with the Norman king, and got the best of the suit. People lifted their hands, wondering at his audacity; but when they heard that Sharnbourn was a 'Norfolk man' their wonder ceased; for a Norfolk man would stand up fearlessly for his right, though king or kaiser were against him.

Fancy need not far strain itself to see in the more quaint and antique streets and houses of the picturesque city the stout-hearted men of old. They were of the race which rescued our drowned lands from the sea, and made the soil yield another sort of gold than that of Pactolus. The piety and the charity of the place are symbolised in the numerous churches and the well-endowed hospitals. Warriors, philosophers, traders, and manufacturers have, in their turn, shed a lustre on this city. Beauty too, it was once said, had in this county a native home; and Beauty's daughters still abound. They are as stately and graceful as the swans, which still flourish, more stately and graceful on the waters near Norwich than elsewhere. That these swans are the best of their kind may be gathered from the fact that a swan from Norwich is yearly presented to the Pope as a tribute of respect from a devoted son of the Church of Rome.

In the old capital of Norfolk the members of the British Association will begin to assemble on Wednesday, the 19th inst. If there be in the world of spirits one of the long-departed who is likely to be more glad than another at the assembling of wise men on the above day at Norwich, that one is certainly Sir Thomas Browne. That physician, antiquary, philosopher, and joyous spirit was a Norwich man, despite his having been born in London. He was but one-and-thirty years old when he settled in the ancient city in 1636; and that city was almost exclusively his home till 1682. If he might be permitted to revisit his beloved Norwich during the coming proceedings, one would expect to see him in his King Charles hair, beard, and mantle, more lively than his own Marquis of Dorset, who, buried in 1530, was uncered in 1608, and looked as fresh, as fair, and as pleasant as when affection was preparing him for the tomb by garlanding him with flowers.

Sir Thomas would be happily at home with the grave yet cheery sages who will come together next week. Credulous himself, he would have his little good-natured laugh at the credulity of others. Can you not fancy his short curls shaking dissent, as the uncouth names of barbaric kings are mentioned as having reigned there and thereabout? *He* has no belief in the legend which talks of Julius Cæsar having a pretty cousin, named Blanche, of all names in the world, and giving her away in marriage, after being duly asked in church, to a son of King Lud. Can you not catch the learned knight's very words addressed to any fellow-antiquary who would give to Cæsar the glory of having built that old castle? 'Sir,' said Sir Thomas, 'its Gothic form of structure abridgeth such antiquity.' Does any one express regret that the name of the builder is lost to fame, Sir Thomas straightway plays with the gold chain which Charles II. gave him when he was knighted, and again he saith: 'Circumstances might determine. Good folk have not ever the worst of it for being forgot. The Canaanitish woman is better off than Herodias, and the penitent thief hath more honour than Pilate.'

The ever-fresh and joyous Norwich physician presents an example to be followed by his brother-inquirers. He was ready to believe any matter,—upon proof; and he was careful not to deny merely because proof was lacking. 'Truly, it may be so; but it cometh not to me.' Even on some solemn question of religion this great man would say, of himself he could not conceive it; but since the Church said so and so, he was ready to avow that her wisdom was of a better quality than his understanding.

Probably, as Browne would smile at many things he might hear in the Sections, the learned men there would laugh outright; perhaps irreverently *pooh-pooh* many, ay thousands, of the subjects he would like to try them with. They would not care to discuss whether painters were right or wrong in making the cross which was the most gloriously burdened higher than the other two at the Crucifixion. Does the aspen tremble because the cross was made of it? Sir Thomas would be hardly content with the reply that no aspen ever grew in the far-off land. When he puts forth his hand, and bids the philosophers tell him by the lines whether he was born by night or by day, modern philosophy itself might be excused for shrugging its shoulders; but the older sage would flush with transient impatience, and ask that younger philosophy if it had ever read Cardan. Should Sir Thomas fall among the doctors *par excellence*, he would certainly astonish them by asking if the children of the English plantations in America were subject to the new and common, but ill-understood, infirmity of his day—the rickets. On the other hand, the members would agree with him that Absalom could not well have been hanged by his hair, if he had worn a helmet; and that Judas *did* hang himself, or perhaps *didn't!* Learned in modern, as in ancient, languages, the old physician could pleasantly show how Nero said '*Après nous le déluge!*' before Madame de Pompadour, though not exactly in the same words. In short, with thousands of ancient subjects would he amuse the modern sages; but we think if he attempted to read a paper on his well-known idea of the Lion and the Unicorn, even *his* unperturbed spirit would be awed by the determined cries of '*Order, order!*'

It may be safely asserted that, quick as the old Norwich antiquary was at imagining, the last thing he would guess would be the manner in which the Association had got down to his favourite city. What queries he would ask! Had they eaten cakes in Wood-street before starting? Were the Wood-street cakes the delicious things they used to be? What sort of horses could they get now at the George in Lombard-street? 'I suppose, sir, you slept the first night at Chelmsford? A pleasant county, Essex! A horseman who leaves Chelmsford at four may breakfast at Colchester by eight or nine; and if he make good speed he shall dine at Ipswich, and get his bed at Thwait, if he be not afraid of the Pye-road. Yes, it's very safe riding; and the famous carved road-post on that route, with its brave figures of horse, man, and woman, and its globe with four hands, one pointing towards Norwich, is sure to keep the traveller in the right path. And *you*, sir, did you pull rein at Swale? The White Hart is the handsomest inn and has the noblest sign-post in England. I warrant you did, and that you never saw a more stately white hart hanging from wreaths, with Actæon and Diana, Charon and Cerberus; and also wondrously carved in wood! That sight would leave you plenty to think of on the remainder of your ride into this city.' Sir Thomas, however astonished, would soon be interested in the new ways of travel which bring Norwich nearer to London than Chelmsford was in *his* days; and if he could only inform the Association, in return, as to what had become of those once famous carvings which together made up 'the noblest sign-post in England,' he would earn the thanks of the meeting.

We will say nothing of those early Britons of the district, in whose huts the children addressed each sire as *Dad*, the then fashionable word which is now vulgarised into Papa. The Roman eagles, of course, were here, or in the neighbourhood; for

'Caistor was a city when Norwich was none,
And Norwich was built of Caistor's stone.'

Then came the Saxon, thane and thrall; and, next, the heavy-handed Dane; and, last, the Norman, with final amalgamation. But there was one race that came hither, and which deserves to be as well spoken of as any of the others, perhaps better—the Dutch. For they came not with slings nor with stones; nor argued in armed phalanxes, nor settled a question with battle-axes, nor made it clearer by incendiarism, nor crushed men into the earth, and boasted of all being at peace. The Dutch entered Norwich almost as suppliants, but they brought rich gifts with them, —industry and ingenuity, taste and invention, conception and execution. They came with their silks and threads and worsteds and implements; and then camlets and bombazines were manufactured to charm East Anglia, enrich the Dutch, and give impulse to the

Norfolk people to do the like. They want a little fresh impulse now, to restore the flourishing condition of their textile manufactures. Such manufactures were once the glory and fortune of the county. Beauty arrayed herself in bravery that *was* cheap and was *not* nasty. *Perpetuana* lasted for ever; and an East Anglian lass was as proud of her *Stand-afar-off* as any Ma'mselle on the Boulevards is of her *Pincez-moi-cela*.

Dutchman, Fleming, Walloon, Frenchman, and Englishman have all worked hard for the profit of Norwich and of themselves. The cruelty of the Duke of Alva enriched the county with many able foreign workmen; and a want of success at Manchester took Barrow to Norwich, where he introduced his manufactures. At his death, in 1813, he would have been happy to have had for an epitaph, 'Here lies he who invented the shawl.'

If such industrial benefactors of the place are worthy of more grateful memories than the men who are supposed to hold more brilliant positions in its history, so the resident nobility have more claim to our notice than those sovereigns who rode down to keep Christmas there, to scare the monastery with reckless royal followers, or to leave a host half ruined with the cost of keeping his lord the King. Now of local nobility there was no family that could compete with that of the Duke of Norfolk. He kept state in his ducal palace at Norwich almost as lavishly as, and perhaps more joyously than, the Plantagenets at Westminster, or the Tudors or Stuarts at Whitehall. In the old days, when that Duke was unavoidably absent, 'Christmas' was not forgotten at Norwich; and that means a keeping of the feast which lasted from the eve of the day to the festival of the Kings. When the poor Duke who died crazed at Padua in 1677 was sojourning in Italy in 1663-4, the brother who was to succeed him, but then plain 'Mr. Howard,' albeit so near the peerage, kept the old season for the absent Duke with a splendour, profusion, and jollity that had not been surpassed since, about two centuries earlier, the first Howard had put his hand on the dukedom by wedding the heiress of the Mowbrays. The host built a hall for the dancers in which Comus himself might have been enthroned. The tapestry could not be excelled in any imperial chamber in the world, and silver was the meanest material of the commonest objects there. But there was that also there which no other country could have matched,—English beauty, so abounding, so dazzling, so intoxicating, that all beholders confessed the glorious presence with such overflowing gallantry that the tradition has come down to our times, and brought upon its wings the name of many a fair one who dealt life or death with her eyes on that famous occasion of Christmas at Norwich. Then, the especial gallantry of the noble host is to be observed. He had a carriage built which cost him 500*l.*, to say nothing of the appurtenances; and in this chariot of love the beauties were conveyed to the ball—fourteen at a time! It says something for the sweet tempers of those Norwich nymphs that they could thus pack into a sort of omnibus,—a gorgeous state vehicle indeed!—and be borne over the rough streets of the East Anglian capital in perfect good-humour, laughing with, and not at, each other, and with no more than a light little shriek, as some sudden jolt shook those living flowers, as it were, a little rudely. And so to the arena, where gallants received them in their arms, and danced with them every night (save Sundays) for a fortnight!

In those earlier times the common people often hungered and thirsted while the greater folk feasted; but on that occasion of Christmas there was general revel, and if universal Norwich was not drunk it was not for want of abundance of liquor. There was the butt of beer in the lower halls and in the streets, after unrestricted consumption of gigantic pasties made up of cartloads of materials. At this time, however, and for long after, Norwich might be the gayest of episcopal cities, but the county was in anything but a satisfactory condition. Men with hearts in their bosoms as well as brains in their heads were beginning to look for a remedy for the disease—for the condition might be so called. And the agitation of thought struck out that spark of light by which men groped, till, in the following century, the 'Norfolk system' was the admiration of the wise and a thing hated by blockheads. Any one who has a taste for the facts and literature of agriculture should read the history of the 'Norfolk system.' It is as full of interest as *Robinson Crusoe*. That system introduced the rotation of crops, if we may so speak. In five successive years the same land was made to yield five different crops, each of which was the richer for the previous variety. Many good and wise men devoted themselves to turning a county, which once seemed to belong only to rabbits and paupers, into a paradise. By this devotion fortunes were decupled in one generation. If one crop in perfection was 'Norfolk barley,' another was more perfect still, 'Norfolk turnips.' In presence of these, Norfolk dumplings were only indifferent things; but the barley and the turnips and the Southdown sheep that flourished on the land and its produce were matters that might have made Gargantua ecstatic. One of the Norfolk land-holders, Lord Townshend, went down to the grave with an increase of dignity that was worth more than the marquisate that fell to his descendant. In memory of what he had done grateful men pointed to him living, and affectionately alluded to him when dead, not as the 'gewd ol' lord,' but emphatically as '*Turnip* Townshend.' Marcus Tullius *Cicero* was nothing to it.

Men had never seen such turnips as that lord, and lords who followed him, raised on the soil. The hoe was so merrily at work among the growing bulbs, pulling them out by scores, that an ignorant person might have thought turnip was a weed to be destroyed. But for every one hoed up its nearest neighbours grew five times as large as they would have done otherwise. A strolling actor on circuit, *conveying* a turnip under his coat, found it sufficient for his dinner. Then, with the turnips, soon grew mutton to match. Mr. Coke had some difficulty in persuading farmers that he knew all about sheep, but he came to as great honour as Turnip Townshend. A county farmer proposed a resolution at an agricultural meeting, which was carried *nem. con.*, and which said, 'Why doant us do as Mister Coke o' Holkham do do? If we'd only do as Mister Coke o' Holkham do do, we'd all do better than we do do!' Honest East Anglians, they were proud at last of Mr. Coke; and he was proud of his sheep. He was, indeed, *so* proud of them that he once had them all brought together for the inspection of the great Hungarian sheep-breeder, Prince Esterhazy. 'Have you as many sheep as you see there, Prince?' asked Mr. Coke; and he did not relish the answer. 'Coke,' said the Magyar, 'I have got more *shepherds!*' After all, this reply was a begging of the question.

Then the barley! Norfolk barley, Norfolk malt! A Norwicher would snap his fingers in scorn at the idea of any other county beating his own in these matters, or in the barley-brew for which Norfolk was also once famous. There was a proverbial 'Dr. Wright of Norwich, who always stopped the bottle.' It may have been because he cared less for the wine of his day than for the fine exhilarating beer which then was the pride of every Norfolk man, from the Wash to the Ouse, from Lynn to Yarmouth. What is still meant by a *Norwicher?* He is a man who, taking first pull at a tankard, does not draw breath till he has swallowed three-fourths, and then reluctantly yields the rest to his partner. But that partner will take first turn at the second tankard, and show himself a *Norwicher* by keeping his nose in it till three-quarters of the delicious draught has passed his lips, and in luxurious slowness has flowed over his grateful palate. Thirsty souls! there was no resisting it. Half a dozen old Norwichers, after a bout of this sort, would become as hilarious and would dance as uproariously as half a dozen Egyptians, full of the barley-wine of Memphis, keeping wild revel in the courts of the Pharaohs!

Indeed, there has always been a tendency in Norwich towards jollity. In the latter days of Charles II., the city was so full of taverns that the mayor would license no more of them. The excisemen and the brewers called his worship *puritanical traitor;* and they made so much noise about it, that the mayor was summoned to London to render explanation to the King. Charles did not dislike good fellows, and he did not know why there should not be plenty of them in Norwich. 'Sir, there is more than enough of them,' said the mayor. 'These good fellows abuse privilege, become deboshed rascals, and beggar their families. They have increased our poor-rates by 800*l.* a year.' Charles saw that such a circumstance was likely to diminish the general good-fellowship, and the King sent him back to Norwich with hearty commendations. As for the taverns there, the topers were packed in them almost as closely together as Norfolk biffins.

There had long been men even then who thought that to make their fellow-men think might be as amusing as leaving them to drink. Accordingly, and taking an interest in all that concerns periodical literature, we are glad to record that Norfolk produced one of the earliest of the editors of the weekly sheet. Nathaniel Butter plied his busy calling for nearly the first half of the seventeenth century in

London. There were no news-boys then, but the 'Mercury Women' cried and vended the *Forayne Occurrents!* and similar sheets in the street. Butter of Norwich was probably the first editor or printer (it was all the same then) who assumed the form of *we* in addressing his readers. It is worthy of remark that the Jansenist writers on the Continent followed this fashion out of humility. It was offensive to Jansenist austerity for a writer to speak directly of himself. The first person plural, or the third singular, was more accordant with that austerity. It excited the disapproval of Pascal. 'L'usage,' he said, 'de supprimer le *moi*, que l'austérité Janseniste a introduit, me paraît plus propre à embarrasser le style qu'à montrer la modestie de l'auteur.' Pascal says that the Jansenists *introduced* the new form. They had found it in England.

In Norwich itself the utmost simplicity marked the local newspapers down to a late period. In Queen Anne's days the *Norwich Postman* thus intelligibly advertised its tariff: 'Price one penny; *but* a halfpenny not refused.' Perhaps this was a trap to catch pride in, like that of the Norwich haircutter, who on being asked by a cockney whom he had just polled what he had to pay, replied, 'Gentlemen give me sixpence, other people threepence.' 'I'm *other people*,' said the wary Londoner, who laid down his threepence and walked away. It was in a Norwich paper that a chandler advertised for a journeyman *who had had the smallpox!* This was not such a joke as it has seemed to many persons. The Danes themselves were never such a scourge in East Anglia as the smallpox once was in Norwich. To receive in a house an inmate who *had* survived an attack was in a certain degree a warrant that infection would be neither introduced nor propagated by him.

Of the old episcopal glory of Norwich there survive only the glorious memories. It is hard to say where the old bishops were lodged in higher state, in Norwich or in London. Some indications of the ancient state are to be found in the first-named city; none at all in the latter. The cathedral speaks for itself, but the visitor may overlook what is worth notice, namely, an example of the *rebus* carried to its utmost application, in illustration of Bishop Walter Lyhart (1446-72). The prelate's *rebus* occurs again and again. It consists of a *hart lying down* in what is supposed to be *water*.

Of the fourteenth-century bishops of Norwich Bateman and Le Spencer were perhaps the most remarkable. Bateman cared not for the great King Edward himself. The bishop loved his deer, but so did Lord Morley, who, having none of his own, used to steal the bishop's, and was caught in the fact at last. Nothing would satisfy the prelate but that Morley should perform public penance for the felony, all baron as he was, in Norwich Cathedral. The noble deer-stealer appealed to the King, and Edward tried to soften the prelate, but Bateman was inexorable. The baron was not ashamed to steal the bishop's deer, but he was obliged to confess that he was, nevertheless; and the ceremony was done in the presence of the highly-edified Norfolkers, who must have grinned in hilarious sympathy when they heard the great Lord Morley acknowledge that he had been caught *flagrante delicto*, and was very sorry for it!

Bishop Le Spencer was, perhaps, a more remarkable man than Bateman. He was surnamed the 'warrior' or 'fighting bishop,' and he took many a Norwich man, not to say Norfolk man, with him when he went to uphold Urban VI. against Clement, who was favoured by the French. This pontifical brigade was so popular that the London rascalry, or beggars, being no longer able to pretend that they had been in the Crusades, turned out all over the country as maimed Norwich men who had fought with noble Le Spencer. The catching one of these fellows, particularly within the episcopal district, was a great delight to the captors. They had him at once to the justice for form and to the pillory for punishment. He stood there with a whetstone round his neck, the badge of a liar. It is creditable to the truthfulness of the times that the employment of whetstones for this purpose had no appreciable effect on the price of the article.

The Norwich Chapter was as independent as its diocesans. It had small regard even for a royal *congé d'élire*, which is a permission to do a thing according to somebody else's liking. The Chapter preferred to follow its own. When Archbishop Wakering died in 1425, Henry VI. sent down a *congé* to elect the son of the Norwich Alderman Wursted; but the Chapter took its own course, elected William Alnewick, and kept him in his post, in spite of the young King and his Council. The old city had then a reputation for religious strictness. But matters went not so well subsequently; for in the sixteenth century the livings in the diocese of Norwich were sold as openly as goods and chattels; and in the century that followed the Norwich people were first kept from church through lack of preachers, and were afterwards driven to it by compulsion. In 1647 Atkins, the Mayor of Norwich, ran away to London, where he offered himself for sheriff. On being questioned, he gave several reasons for leaving his provincial post; but the chief was that there was so little preaching in that city. Subsequently the citizens got more than enough of it. They went, not unwillingly, to prayer, but they could not stand the long sermons. After an hour of it they used to leave the preacher and hurry out of church. Never did the Norwichers resent impost so sulkily as when the municipality passed a law in 1661 that every man *should* go perforce to church, and *must* stop to hear the sermon. They went, but they forgot to take the little revenge of their ancestors of Elizabeth's time, who (conforming by legal pressure) used to stuff their ears with wool before setting out to church, that they might hear nothing of what was going on after they got there. This city folk, however, who loved not long sermons, always loved music. In 1642 they were up in arms for the preservation of their organs, as resolute to defend them as some were to uphold the King and others to sustain the Parliament. Their successors of the eighteenth century cared less for orthodoxy than *they* did for their organs. This course was so aggravated towards the close of the century that Bishop Horne, while deploring the growing disbelief in the Trinity, took a grave way of refuting it by giving a 'slap' at Cambridge University. The mathematicians, he said scornfully, argue that 3 can't be 1 in divinity, because it is not so in arithmetic; and then he must have made some of the parsons of the Norwich diocese open their eyes, by gravely telling them that this was not a question of quantity, but quality.

Horne's successor, Sutton, who died Archbishop of Canterbury, was hardly wiser when he went up from Norwich to preach the famous fast-sermon before the Lords in 1794. It was a time when the nation had to be goaded into liking our foolish and sanguinary war with France; and accordingly the prelate, with wonderful simplicity, told the august assembly that the principal object of our war with that country was for the defence of the Protestant religion; that the political and mythological systems of France were intermixed, and that we must necessarily be interested in the struggle to defend our system against the French, inasmuch as that in early times the worship of the true God was often made to depend on the issue of a battle. If the Cambridge men in the Norwich diocese had smiled at Horne's slap at the mathematicians, the Oxford men in the same diocese must have been tickled by Sutton's logic. They might well ask if he had not started the patriotic idea that Heaven had prophesied the destruction of France in its denunciations against *Mount Seir!*

Sutton was the prelate who had the once celebrated 'bout' with a lawyer of Norwich named

White. The lawyer, failing in his vocation, sought to be ordained then and there. The prelate refused, despite the lawyer's persistent reiteration. Mr. White set forth, as his special qualifications for the ministry, that his moral character was good, and so was his reading. With this Parthian dart, carrying double implication on it, against the Norwich clergy (who were not worse than their neighbours), the latter retired from a battle in which his diocesan had by far the best of it.

White may remind our readers of those Norwich Christians in whom Wesley saw so little of Christianity, and towards whom he himself manifested so little Christian charity. Between Whitefield and Wesley, or rather between their Norwich followers, there was some danger of a wrong touch being given to the ark. The memories of that old but lively history call up a smile now. Whitefield, professing to ignore distinctions, boasted that the 'polite and great' of Norwich went to hear him. Wesley, who inculcated charity in all things, was so incensed by the people there, that he wrote of Cudworth (who was as 'broad' as the great latitudinarian divine of that name) as being a 'brute beast;' and Wesley said of the Norwich religionists generally that they were the most weather-cockish, the most ignorant, the most self-conceited, self-willed, fickle, intractable, disorderly, disjointed society in the three kingdoms ! Further, the apostle stigmatised them as 'bullocks unaccustomed to the yoke,' bears and lions; he confessed there were some lambs of grace among them, but even they needed taming; for the Norwich 'lambs' (said John Wesley) 'roar like lions.' Wesley abandoned the Norwich Tabernacle to the Rev. John Hook, one of whose grandsons was the too celebrated Theodore Hook, and the other was the equally vivacious James, chaplain to the Prince of Wales, Dean of Worcester, writer of plays and novels, and father of the present grave and popular Dean of Chichester. See what strange matter may be traced back to the old turbulent Tabernacle at Norwich! The rough character attributed to even the 'serious' men of Norwich by Wesley was, in truth, a very old characteristic; but it was often joined with a merry sort of humour. Take, for instance, two incidents. In 1272 the citizens so far disagreed with the local clergy and monks that they wound up their argument by burning not only the cathedral, but the monastery. The usual excommunication and heavy fines followed, and the ringleaders were executed. To this day there are two opposite accounts of the merits of this quarrel, and it is not clear whether the prior did not as much deserve hanging as any of the citizens. The second incident has 1795 for its period. A large meeting took place in St. Andrew's Hall, to denounce Pitt and Lord Grenville's Treason and Sedition Bill. The people denounced it so unreservedly that the leaders got into serious trouble; but they gaily said the old say about treason never being treason, &c., and they gravely defended sedition. Into what authority they looked is not to be conjectured, but they asserted that sedition was derived from *seorsum eundo*, a dividing of the people to ascertain their numbers. The *seditiosus*, they said, was only the divider, and *therefore* sedition in face of government was no more criminal than heresy in face of religion. The fellow who tried this argument had the making of a special pleader in him, but he had evidently not read Cicero.

Nearly midway between these periods we have that great insurrectionary movement of 1549, the most serious, obstinate, and nearly successful development of which was made at Norwich. It was against the enclosure of commons, the oppressive taxation of the lower classes, and the new church service. We are wont to speak of the bold chief of this outburst as Kett the Tanner, but he was also lord of three manors, and was not far from achieving all at which he aimed. The Norwich tanner was as merry a fellow as he was a bold one; as courteous as he was ruthless. When Parker, beneath the oak in sight of the city, preached to Kett and his followers against the purpose they had in view, he stood on a platform, through the interstices of which Kett's spearmen kept him dancing by gently pricking his feet with their weapons. Otherwise he was treated with very great civility. His audience had the quality which Wesley afterwards discerned in his Norwich lamb-lions. When Kett's men had pricked the future Archbishop of Canterbury, listened to arguments they scorned, and dismissed him under safeguard, they quenched their thirst at the camp 'ellas,' as it would still be called, and quaffed their 'ell' that they might not be 'frorn' by the chilly dews that would hang about even on a July night. From that terrible Norwich uprising we owe the institution of Lords-Lieutenant, whose office, since

Kett the Tanner's day, is to inquire of treason, misprision of treason, insurrection, and riots, with authority to levy men and lead them against the enemies of the reigning sovereign.

In less than a century—in 1656—Norwich was nearly as much moved by Will Wayneford the Comber as it had been by Kett the Tanner. Kett wanted to restore old systems; Wayneford sought to establish new. The comber was for overthrowing old thrones and old altars, and would have no king but Jesus. In the old hall of the episcopal palace, wherein the Fifth Monarchy devotees (the alleged throne of whose assumed king—priest and magistrate —was in heaven) had assembled, Wayneford put up a prayer, in which he asked among other things that the Lord would be pleased to throw down all earthly power and rule and authority. 'Consume them, O Lord,' said the comber, 'that they may be no more alive on the earth. Set up the kingdom of Thy Son, that we may be all taught of God.' The scaffold annals of Norwich might fill a volume, from Kett, whom stern necessity *would* hang, down to Rush, who had a little box in his house to receive contributions for the conversion of the Jews, and who slaughtered his fellow Christians with the fury of a Malay running a-muck. The year we have named above, 1656, was the one in the summer of which, when Wayneford was shaking Norwich, Evelyn designed a journey that way, but was overcome by the heat and the dust, and stopped short at Ipswich. East Anglia was then agitated by the Quakers, some of whom he saw in prison at Ipswich.

'A new fanatic sect,' he says, 'of dangerous principles, who show no respect to any man, magistrate or other, and seem a melancholy proud sort of people, and exceedingly ignorant.' The social condition of the Norwich Quakers was as grievous as that of their Suffolk brethren. When James II. came to the throne there were seventy Quakers in loathsome captivity in Norwich alone; but just before his downfall he conferred on forty Friends the freedom of that city.

East Anglia owes something of its prosperity to the Quakers who were thus persecuted. Many of them were manufacturers, the persecution of whom fell partly on the workpeople, whose labours were suspended by the closing of the factories. The county can boast of many honoured names of these benefactors. To this day none is more honoured than those of Gurney and his sister, Elizabeth Fry. They were at the head of the philanthropists of their time, as others of their really noble house were at the head of the princely merchants of their day. Before their time, indeed, Gresham of Norfolk had made his name famous, as it continues among philanthropic merchants. It would be hard to find a better lawyer than Norfolk Coke, the Chief Justice; and though the old Windhams of the true blood have left a brilliant reputation in the county for eloquence and chivalry, even they must yield the palm to Nelson, the eloquent significance of whose signals stirred the hearts of his men, and who died such death as is desired by heroes. In his own heart Nelson never forgot his native county; and when in

1797 he sent the sword surrendered to him by the Spanish admiral to the municipality of Norwich, it was out of love for a county that was in its turn proud of the noblest of her sons. The Spanish Muse treated her Norfolk adversary with less than poetical justice. A popular bard subsequently represented the English hero as running away at Trafalgar. Don Jose Mor de Fuentes says in a contemporary poem, 'Huye el Breton' (*the Briton flies!*)—as if the Norfolk hero had cared more for 'the floating ensigns of Cisneros' than Sharnbourn of Sharnbourn had cared for the Norman himself.

Even from these brief hints, our friends who are going to Norwich will see that the city is a pleasant and an interesting place.

IX.
EXETER.
1869.

EXETER.

1869.

Part I. Local History.

In one of the comfortable inns of the ancient city of Exeter, where every traveller will find a welcome, and also a bill, we find lying on a side-table a book thus entitled: '*The History of the City of Exeter.* By the Rev. G. Oliver, D.D. With a short Memoir of the Author and an Appendix of Documents and Illustrations. Exeter, Roberts; London, Longmans.' Having looked it through, we think it over, and then compare it with other histories of the same place.

'Exeter is ancient and stinks!' was a description of the western city by Southey, in the journal of his visit in 1799. At the period of his visit, Admiral Mitchell had captured the Franco-Dutch fleet, and Exeter was doing its little best with its joy-bells. 'One church with two bells went ding-dong; another had but one, and could only ding.' Southey's judgment on the old cathedral was, that it looked finest when you could only see half of it. He was then a Liberal, and something more; and he denounces Exeter as a 'bigoted place' for this reason—'there are persons here who always call the Americans the rebels!' At a dash, he pictures the ancient town upon the waters—Caer Isk—as consisting of one great street and many dirty lanes. He does not allude to the British name of the city, but he unwittingly justifies it by remarking that, 'as you cross the bridge, you look down upon a town below you intersected by water in a strange way.' Whether he was acquainted or not with the antiquity of the canal, we are not able to say; but his eye, acute to mark beauty, was struck by its shores, so 'completely naturalised,' as he depicts them, 'and most beautifully clothed with flowers.'

In a few words well applied like these Southey conveys graphic pictures to the minds of his readers; and we regret that the late Dr. Oliver did not resemble him in this respect. From the pen of this learned Roman Catholic ecclesiastic—a man whom his fellow-townsmen of every denomination respected, and who had sympathies with every one of his loving neighbours—we looked for more satisfactory work than is here produced. The book is heavy without being learned; but in every page we encounter proofs of the kindly heart and the liberal soul of the writer.

Of the internal history of Exeter this volume contains little; and yet no man was better acquainted with it than Dr. Oliver, who was appointed to the Exeter mission after his ordination in 1806, and continued in the city till his death in the spring of 1862. He loved to go over the traditions and the records of the old natives; and bolder men never stopped the tide of conquest to turn it in their own favour. Even the Jutes and Angles were unable to carry the war successfully beyond the Exe. They obtained one half of the city, but the stout-hearted natives held the other. Throughout this, as in other countries, however, the memory of the Anglo-Saxon occupation is so strong, that 'names unknown to the present owners of property remain sacred in the memory of the surrounding peasantry, and of the labourer that tills the soil. I have more than once walked, ridden, or rowed, as land and stream required, round the bounds of Anglo-Saxon estates, and have learnt with astonishment that the names recorded in their charters were still used by the wood-cutter or shepherd of the neighbourhood.'

Less pleasant is the memory of the savage Danes, at whose hands Exeter suffered the more severely because of the 'pluck' of its inhabitants. Dr. Oliver accounts for the immense amount of the coinage of our unready King Ethelred, preserved in the Museum at Stockholm, by considering it as part of the sums he paid to the Dane as ransom-money. Little wonder is it that after the Danes had given place to the Saxon King Edward, and that Confessor-King slept his long sleep, the lesson read in Exeter Cathedral on that day of his festival alluded to the national delight, and the national love for the heir of the Saxon line and the restorer of the ancient liberty. Exeter, nevertheless, had a weary time of it under the Normans; but during the wars of the Barons 'perhaps no town suffered less.' The fact is that the good folks there were much addicted to commercial pursuits, and while other men were fighting, they, in significant phrase, 'stuck to business.'

They clove as closely to loyalty, and would not give up the legal cause of York against Lancaster till long after the union of the Roses gave legality to the conjoined two. Of sovereigns sojourning in the city there are many records; none is of more interest than that of Katherine of Arragon, who was lodged in a house next door to the church of St. Mary Major, the horrible creaking of whose weathercock prevented the princess from sleeping, and the authorities accordingly, not thinking of oiling it, caused it to be taken down. In later days, when a princess of Bonaparte's family was lodged next to a church in Italy, the imperious lady caused the church itself to be taken down; the smell of the incense, she said, made her sick, and the noise of the organ gave her a headache.

The Exonians were more thoughtful touching their trade in wool than about the comfort of royal personages rendered sleepless by their weathercocks. If their famous 'Exeter cloths' kept up a reputation and profit to themselves all over Europe, they cared little how the world wagged. That Exeter should wag—that is, *grow* in importance—was a fixed idea with them; and that canal whose banks of flowers so delighted Southey was commenced by them so long ago as 1539, and remains, according to tradition, 'the earliest instance of inland navigation in this country.' While the citizens gave themselves a canal, Queen Elizabeth distinguished the city by a motto it still bears proudly, 'Semper fidelis'—*always faithful!*

But observe what comes of a blue-stocking queen honouring Saxon folk with a Latin device. Even at this day it is not understood. The motto is inscribed beneath the city arms, the supporters to which are 'two Pegasuses *argent*, their manes and hoofs *or*.' We are told of a countryman showing these supporters to a stranger, and observing, 'These be the two race-horses that rinned upon Haldon wi' names of 'em put under, *Scamper and Phillis*.'

We have noticed the prosperity of the trade of Exeter; but it begat peril. What do you think of 'fifteen sail of Turks' in the English Channel in the middle of the seventeenth century snapping up our merchantmen? Ships with Exeter produce for abroad could hardly show their cutwaters beyond Topsham without being attacked, plundered, sunk, and the crews carried into captivity. The very harbours in the south-west were infested by Moslem pirates, who often entered the town armed, creating thereby the greatest panic. The loss to Exeter in ships, money, and men was enormous; at length sailors refused to go afloat at all in these merchantmen, saying 'they had rather starve at home than be brought under the tyrannous and Moorish subjection of those Mohammedans.' Sermons were preached that funds might be raised to redeem the captives from slavery, and in 1623 'the constables were ordered to make returns of all who are in Turkish captivitie, and what their friends will give to bring them home.' The same century had, however, its joys as well as sorrows; and well might all thirsty citizens, wearied with the wars of the Commonwealth, in which Exeter had her part, hail the restoration of Charles II., when order was given, on making proclamation of that monarch's return, 'that Mr. Marshal do cause three hogsheads of good claret wine to be put into the cisterns of the three conduits, to be drunk out to his Majesty's health.' It is unpleasant to find that where there was 'good claret' given away there was little attention paid to the sanitary condition of the inhabitants. In the seventeenth century, the filth, indecency, and abomination in the streets, in and about the churches, and even in the cathedral and cloisters, defy description. Dr. Kellett, an old writer, describes as 'a *wicked wonder*, with grief and indignation of heart, that whereas the city of Exeter is, by its natural situation, one of the sweetest cities of England, yet, by the ill-use of many, is one of the nastyest and noysommest cities in the land.' So wrote Dr. Kellett in 1641. 'Exeter is ancient and stinks,' wrote Dr. Southey in 1799.

The castle of Exeter, founded by Athelstan, and dismantled in the reign of Edward VI., is so complete in its history that the most audacious of guides would not dare to ascribe its building to Julius Cæsar, nor its destruction to Oliver Cromwell. In the days of the Commonwealth it was a 'gaping ruin;' for in its time it had seen as hard service as any castle in England, was often besieged and as often defended by men of great bravery and fiercely unyielding tempers.

Our old kings do not appear to have kept their state in this their once royal castle. Some of the Earls and Dukes of Exeter, however, lived there occasionally in great splendour. Among the latter, the Hollands, the first duke of which family was uterine brother of Richard II., are especially remarkable. The first of these dukes lived really 'like a prince' in Exeter Castle; but neither he, nor his son, nor his grandson, the last of the dukes of that family, was enabled to sustain his ducal splendour for a long period. The first of them, when plotting to overthrow the King, who had usurped the place of the duke's half-brother Richard, was adroitly seized in Essex by the Dowager Countess of Hereford, the mother-in-law of Henry IV., whose interests were so thoroughly understood by this vivacious old lady that she took upon herself to order his execution; and the duke was beheaded accordingly. Some splendour was attached to the dukedom when it was restored to his son, by giving him precedence over all other dukes after York. The third and last of the Hollands was that famous Lancastrian fugitive, after the battle of Hexham, whom De Comines saw in Flanders, barefooted, running after the Duke of Burgundy's train, and begging for God's sake for bread! And yet the wife of this Duke of Exeter, who died a beggar in the Netherlands, was that proud vixen Anne, sister of Richard III. The wealthy widow re-married with Sir Thomas St. Leger, who fought against her brother, and was beheaded by that brother's order in the courtyard of Exeter Castle.

The ordinary prison, a sort of pit, in this castle was one of the most horrible of those gloomy strongholds. Henry More describes it, in the year 1604, as a place in which eighty men and women were confined for various crimes. A wooden palisade divided the male from the female prisoners; but this was so loose and broken in various places that not merely hands or head, but half the body, could be forced through the opening. The prisoners were so heavily and cruelly ironed that, though they could sit and lie down, they were unable to move about. 'Duobus ex eo numero,' says More, 'fiebat potestas obeundi locum cum situlis ad requisita naturæ.' For the liberty of walking for a short time in a very close and filthy court a fee of twopence was demanded. Contrast this prison misery with the present luxury, and you have the two vicious extremes of penal organisation.

The Guildhall had its stronghold like the castle, 'for the safe keeping of such as shall at any time be *commended to the ward of the mayor* for the time being;' as pretty an euphemism of the sixteenth century for being in custody as the most popular of dramatists could have devised. If there was daintiness of phrase, there was, however, not much nicety in practice. We find that on the 19th of December 1561, one Richard Sweete, a sort of Exeter Giovanni in his way, was consigned to 'a strait prison in the pit of the Guildhall for forty days' solitary confinement, there to be fed on Wednesday and Friday on bread and water. There he continued till the 12th of January, when the mayor, on his repentance, ordered his release.' His worship, perhaps, thought that under a queen regnant devotion to the ladies was not to be construed too harshly. Among the

very officials of the corporation, however, we meet
with individuals too much addicted, not to loving
their neighbour as themselves, but to loving their
neighbour's wife more than their own. Thus, in
1612, one Thomas Toker is dismissed from the office
of sword-bearer 'for his incontinens lyvinge with the
late wief of Stephen Toker, deceased.' In the same
year he was arraigned and convicted before the
judges of assize for the murder of his wife, and was
executed at Heavitree. He must have married another wife (probably his paramour) immediately after
the murder, as appears by her application to the
chamber, as his widow, for the restoration of his
goods forfeited by his attainder. There was a very
loose morality observed, at this time, in higher
classes than that to which the Exeter sword-bearer
belonged; and while Toker was swinging at Heavitree for infringing the sixth after breaking the seventh
commandment, Sir Pecksnel Brocas was standing in
a white sheet at St. Paul's Cross, with a stick in his
hand, doing penance for the infraction of a commandment which Toker had followed up by murder. The
mention of this naughty sword-bearer enables us to
add that the city swords are the actual weapons
presented by Edward IV. and Henry VII., according to Sir Samuel Meyrick; but the blades and the
scabbards have undergone such repairing and renewing that it would be hard to say how much of them
is original. So with the cap of maintenance, presented
by Henry VII., it is said that 'the original cap, made
of black felt, is still inside the (outer) velvet one;'
but as it is subsequently said that another delinquent

sword-bearer stole the old cap and converted it to his own profane use, and that a new one was made in 1652, the originality of the cap is as doubtful as that of the swords.

If nothing can be brought against the Puritans with respect to damaging the castle, it is not so with regard to the cathedral; but these charges (except one of their bricking up the arches, and, by thus dividing the chancel from the nave, converting one church into two) Dr. Oliver pronounces to be greatly magnified. The doctor's impartial spirit throughout forms the chief charm of his book. He and Dr. Lingard were men whose existence is almost ignored by the ultra party, at least, of their own communion, of whom they should have been the pride, as they might justifiably have been accounted the glory. Their impartiality brought down upon them this penalty; and while laud and honour are rendered to the ferocious Cahills of the day, a silent contempt is awarded to the purer and nobler writers we have named. The better spirit to which we have alluded is manifested here at every given opportunity. Do king and churchmen cheat, Dr. Oliver remarks that 'the want of good faith, the disregard of plighted promises and solemn oaths, was lamentably characteristic of the Middle Ages.' Does the Pope himself confer on monarchs what it was not his to give, Dr. Oliver stigmatises either party with equal severity. He brands the pontiff who gives as sharply as he does the monarch who receives. Again, do kings require Exonian prelates to denounce the exercise of the temporal power of the Pope in this kingdom, before such kings could put bishops in possession of their sees, Dr. Oliver says 'it was a reasonable and expedient measure, distinctly marking the boundaries between the ecclesiastical and civil powers.' As for punishing men for their religious sentiments, he declares such a course to be 'a departure from the genius and spirit of the Founder of Christianity,' serving only to 'provoke and embitter fanaticism,' and not to be reconciled with sound policy and humanity. When Exeter feels the consequences of 'the detestable advice of Queen Mary's Cabinet in favour of persecution,' the author acknowledges his 'indignation;' but adds, truly enough, that 'the universal system of intolerance' was the system of whichever party happened to be uppermost. Even James II., in whom Dr. Lingard himself finds little to censure, does not escape the impartial Dr. Oliver. 'What,' he asks, 'could be more obnoxious and illegal than his intrusion of Roman Catholics into the offices of the Universities and his encroaching on the rights of the Church established by law?' But let us close this pleasant local history and go abroad into the city.

PART II. A RETROSPECT.

'BEWARE of the man who has read but one book,' is one of many very foolish proverbs. The quality of that man's knowledge and the weapons it may afford him for argument depend entirely on the truthfulness of the author. Now authors, as the visitors to Exeter and the students of Devonshire history will find, have not left the curious inquirer to one book. The catalogue of works illustrating Devonshire history and topography is a large volume in itself. If a man's life were long enough to enable him to read all these productions, he would lack leisure for digesting them. He would, indeed, have the chance of getting at something besides the chronicle of this 'land of deep valleys.' A large subject is, for example, opened in Mr. Wilson's *View of the Universe, including the History of Bideford*.

Then all the scholars, philosophers, and others who are neither, who will be assembled next week in the fair and ancient city of Exeter, might have one question alone to occupy them, and no satisfactory way of settling it after all. For who *could* reconcile the etymological irreconcilabilities, if we may so call them, connected with the score of alleged derivations of the names of the county and of the city? Every man has his favourite puzzle, which he picks to pieces and refits with an air of comic satisfaction. Some of the most accomplished hands at these difficult exercises come very near to the solution, and yet contrive to muddle it. They are like the retired Londoner who, hearing 'John Parry' mentioned, blandly remarked, 'I know! John Parry is a musician who plays at some place in town on a German Reed!'

If Westcote's quaint book on Devonshire in 1630 had not been all that his pains and patience could seriously make it, one might now be excused, perhaps, for taking it for sly satirical history. How wonderfully he flounders in the very slough of confusion, as he learnedly and unlearnedly discusses the meanings hidden in the otherwise unintelligible names of places! With what an air of relief he comes to the conclusion that De Avonshire, or the shire of rivers, is at least as true a meaning as any other! And how marvellously does he stumble and splash and scramble through the old British marshes to find meanings, which need not be looked for, for *Exeter!* And how droll he looks as he emerges with a couple which will not at all adapt themselves to his purposes! *Iskia* is an elder-tree, he says, *argal* 'Exeter.' Or, 'look here,' he seems to exclaim, ' take this other fact. *Hisc* was the name for the reeds which Northmen used for thatching.' So Exeter, it is suggested, may be the City of Reeds! He might as well have tried to find a trace of the name in the apples and the cider for which the county *is* famous. But the elder-tree is as strange to the city as the ilex was to Marnhead till Mr. Balle imported it from America. As for the thatching-reeds, they were as rare about the Exe as the Scandinavians who used them beyond sea. *Exe* is only one of the many old words for 'water.' Westcote in his fitting British names to English meanings illustrates the remark of Voltaire, to the effect that etymologists are people with whom vowels go for little and consonants for nothing at all!

Other county writers have stumbled in other ways. Indeed, there was a time when a fatality seemed to connect itself with writers who took Devonshire for a subject. Pole and Risdon left their works incomplete. Milles, Chapple, and Badcock died, we believe, in the midst of their labours. This fatality so influenced Polwhele that he determined to bring out his work in separate volumes as soon as each was finished. He did it, he remarked, to save time; and he got so confused in his own over-hastiness that his second volume outstripped him in hurry, and contrived to appear before the first! At a later period the Rev. Mr. Moore wrote a county history, and by forgetting to enrich it with an index rendered it all but useless to the 'curious inquirer.'

Still the country is open and beautiful, easy of access, and so full of old memorials that excursionists from Exeter will find that they can scarcely turn their faces in any direction without striking the trail of races long since passed away. About Dartmoor, the way of life of the old Britons—how they dwelt, where they tarried, how they wended, the bridges they built, the roads they made, and the graves in which they rest—may be seen, or may be faintly traced. Up this very Exe the swarthy Phœnicians brought their well-freighted vessels, and in place of the foreign gear took back the British tin. The refuse ore of the smelting-houses of the Phœnicians who lived and worked on the soil is not unfrequently turned up to connect the present with the past. The language even of the old nations sometimes presents itself in the names of localities, but losing to the vulgar ear the significance the names once bore to all.

The memory of the Dane is like the blood of the invader, not yet washed out of the Teignmouth cliffs, down which it ran, a red libation to Fate. He who stands by the Hubblestone, and muses on the defeat at Appledore, is a sort of contemporary with two epochs; particularly if he has faith in the local story, that there sleeps the once dreaded Hubba, the hoop of gold encircling his luxurious locks, and his stalwart hand on the treasure which is also said to be lying at his side. Antiquaries may be audacious enough to look into the secrets of this rock-sepulchre of a hero. They may then track a road which is the pathway of heroes: that road from Brunedune to Axminster, along which Athelstan struggled with and smote the Norseman. At the latter place, noted now for giving a name to such carpets as Athelstan's foot never pressed, the valiant soldier joyously buried five kings and six thousand foemen, and tearfully laid in the ground his own Bishop of Sherborne, whose presence in the fight was more pleasant to Athelstan than was that of the priestly warrior Walker to King William at the battle of the Boyne.

Like the historian who thought it worth while to state how recently snipe had been shot in Conduit-street, or where Conduit-street stood, we may record that the ancient and respectable squacco was shot in Devonshire long after the last bustard had been brought down on Salisbury Plain. If we were to say that the Exeter mail was exposed to the sudden attack of a hungry lion on the road as late as 1816, we should seem to imply that the route to London had its wild African incidents. We simplify the matter by adding that this lion had escaped from a menagerie near Salisbury. When the guard fired at it to save the passengers, its owner, with a fine sense of the fitness of things, offered him and others 500*l.* if they would desist. The passengers were worth nothing to the lion's owner, but the lion was worth a good deal; and moreover, as he justly remarked, if the beast was shot the holes in the skin would render it almost valueless.

As connecting the present Exeter with the past, there is no more potent link than the cathedral, dedicated to St. Peter. It took four hundred years to build after its first stone was laid, in the year 1050. This fact gave the city preëminence, but Exeter has not been without a rival for supremacy in the county. It has always been of first-rate importance, but there was a time when one other Devonshire city at least looked down upon its trading prosperity as vulgar. Drewsteignton, the 'Druids' Teign Town'—a town of priests on the Teign—is said to have once prided itself on its ecclesiastical superiority. It ranked, in its own estimation, above secular towns, just as the *genteel* people of cathedral cities who live in the 'Close' rank themselves above the 'persons' who live in the suburbs or in the market-place. Exeter, however, had at one period that excellence of cleanliness which is next to godliness. 'Since Nature is the scavenger thereof,' said Fuller, in the seventeenth century,

'Exeter is a very cleanly city.' It either lost its scavenger, which it could hardly do since it remained on its hill-side, or men's ideas as to what was or was *not* clean changed. 'Exeter,' said Southey, in the last year of the last century, 'is ancient and stinks.'

The government of Exeter was once of a twofold quality. The corporation ruled the city, but not the Close, which was under the jurisdiction of the clergy. In disturbed times the temporal power took the upper hand, and on one occasion, at least, with excellent effect. In Edward VI.'s time Exeter was saved from rebel capture by the unity of the local rule. In quieter times the old division had force again, or rather weakness; and it is singular to hear of the complaints made in the reign of Charles I. of the inconveniences arising from two distinct magisterial jurisdictions. The Close actually became a sanctuary for any villain who chose to resort to it. Things were worse when the cathedral clergy were absent at their benefices. A universal and more or less ragged rascalry made temporary home in the Close, and could not be removed. The inhabitants had a well-founded fear that some day or other this mass of villany, of which might be said, as Dryden's Dorax says,

'Each of 'em a host,
A million strong of vermin every villain,'

would possess themselves of the city, and enjoy it as gentlemen of their quality would like to do.

It was at this period that Devonshire had a great reputation for the manufacture of what was called *Spanish* cloth. Free trade was not then understood, for the Exeter merchants could not export any cloth so called that was not made in the county, nor could they buy any such cloth but in the market of Exeter! Into the question of the miscellaneous manufactures of Exeter we need not enter. Its liveliest time, perhaps, was when it produced 3000*l.* worth of serges weekly. Its prosperity had both native and foreign enemies. When the city refused to pay a toll levied on its ships by the feudal earl who was lord of both banks, he resorted to the simple process of toppling his trees down into the river, which formed bars that impeded navigation for years. He stopped the goose from laying because she would not give him all the golden eggs the earl demanded! The coast-lords, too, were wont to be as obstinate touching their right to the 'providential wrecks' cast upon their coast. The Barbary rovers were hardly more cruel when they daringly ran up some of the rivers, looted a farmstead, carried off the hinds as slaves, and the pretty Devonshire lasses for the harems, and left subjects for touching sermons to be preached in behalf of the funds for delivering Christian souls from captivity in Tunis, Algiers, or Morocco. If the Devonshire lasses became reconciled to being sultanas, the hinds who were repurchased were not in a very joyous condition after returning home. The press-gang kept the whole coast in terror. It is still remembered that at one period the press was so hot that no herrings could be got into Exeter for a whole fortnight.

 Probably, but for difficulties presented by the roads—by bad roads, or by the want of any roads at all—the important city of Exeter saw less of the face of Royalty than would otherwise have been vouchsafed to it. Nevertheless, the visits of Royalty to the capital, or to some favoured part of the county, have been not unfrequent. Perhaps the most remarkable was that of Edward the Confessor. It certainly made as much noise as any other princely visitation. When the King arrived the gates were closed, and the porter was too sound asleep to be easily roused. In attendance on Edward was Edulf, son of Ordgar, Earl of Devon. He was a gigantic young fellow, with a giant's strength, and none of that usually amiable individual's patience. In wrath at the King being kept waiting, Edulf tore the ironwork from off the gates with his hands, broke it across his knee, forced open the gates themselves with his foot, and, to give the King room enough to enter, set his back against the city-wall, and pushed therewith a yard or two into the road within. An earl's son with such thews and sinews should have wedded with some one of those old Burgundian princesses, who, in training their wall-fruit, used to hammer the nails into the bricks with their knuckles! To pronounce the baptismal names of those delicate creatures would have made the jaws of a Devonian lover ache for a month; for the Devon mouth best shaped itself to soft syllables. The old intonation of West Saxon kings has not yet quite died away from the lips of the West Saxon peasantry.

Royalty was once much interested in the silver-mines of Combe Marten, but it never condescended to visit them. Their existence must have been pleasant to Edward I.; for the greatest of the Plantagenets joyfully saw arrive at the Tower the Combe Marten silver, which made the hearts of his coiners as glad as his own. This Devonshire silver effectually aided Henry V. in carrying on his more brilliant than profitable war with France. This drain was the slow death of the mine. It was closed and reopened again and again; but Hope herself would have battened it down for ever, as the proprietors did in 1848, when the produce would not half pay for the work. There was no use in raising sixpences at ninepence apiece.

The mines were not profitable for working when Richard III. was in the county, which he left hurriedly on hearing that the castle of Exeter was called *Rougemont.* He was, however, not a man to be frightened at a name, as he showed at Bosworth. Queen Elizabeth saw more of the men than of the county. 'The gentlemen of Devon,' she said, 'are all born courtiers, with a becoming confidence;' every word of which is justified by her own experience of the frank devotion of gallant Walter Raleigh.

Of all the royal incidents connected with Exeter, perhaps the most remarkable is the birth therein of a king's daughter—one who has certainly not slipped out of history. Exeter once possessed a famous Dominican convent, which, with property thereunto belonging, fell to the share of the Russell family. They turned the conventual edifice into a family mansion, which they called Bedford House. It stood on a part of the site subsequently occupied by 'Bedford Crescent.' When Henrietta Maria was under peculiar difficulties in 1644, and sought a home in Exeter, the corporation assigned Bedford House to her as a residence, and a couple of hundred pounds to meet all exigencies, including the expected birth of a child. The child was, in due time, christened 'Henrietta Anne,' in the cathedral, with much state. It is just possible that Charles I. may have once looked upon the last of his children, as he was in Exeter, for a hurried moment or two, in July of that year.

This Exeter princess was subsequently smuggled hence, and ultimately out of the kingdom, by Lady Morton. The lady was disguised as a beggar, the child passed for her son Peter—disguises that were not thrown off till the fugitives reached the other side of the Channel, when a coach and six carried them both to Paris. The little Exeter lady has left a name in history. She was the Henriette d'Angleterre of French memoirs, the nymph of many swains, the wife of the Duke of Orleans, the victim of a poisoned glass of chicory-water, and the subject of one of the finest funeral orations of Bossuet.

The Commonwealth knocked at Exeter gates as loudly as young Edulf of the tough sinews. Loyal or royal, tradition says that when the city was famished larks, by thousands, flew and fell into it from the open quarter towards the sea; 'the Cause of Causes,' as it was piously said, 'providing a feast for many poor people.'

Devonshire saw Henrietta Anne's brother, Charles II., skilfully dodging his pursuers. Sidford is worth visiting, with chronicle in hand, were it only to see the place where he was so nearly trapped and whence he so cleverly escaped. As for later kings, William III. paid homage to the beauty of the Devonshire coast. Queen Caroline, the wife of George II., loved the Devonshire wheatears. If she could not have got through her agents a dainty dish of these birds to set before the King, and take her full share of, she was almost capable of appearing in Exeter market itself, and buying up the whole supply. She loved them, as Quin loved the mullet; and she would say to the official who took her orders for dinner, that she cared for nothing in particular except it might be the 'English *ortolans*,' as Caroline called the wheatears, which were bought for her at the market-stalls of Exeter. Her grandson, George III., after inspecting ships, ate his boiled mutton and turnips (a dish for a king, if a king of cooks have the cooking of it) at Saltram, where, for a whole working-day week, he was the guest of Lord Boringdon; and even loyal people did not scramble for the cherry-stones his Majesty left at dessert. When this King lay dead at Windsor his son, the Duke of Kent, lay dead also in a Devonshire house, Woodbrooke Glen, near Sidmouth.

Two very distinguished foreigners may be cited as having a natural longing to find a home in Devonshire. When the great Duke of Medina Sidonia first beheld Mount Edgcumbe, he protested that whenever Spain got what she coveted, possession of England, Mount Edgcumbe should be his (the Duke's) summer residence. Spirited and hospitable Torquay, which fanciful people call the Montpellier of England, which it is not in any one respect, attracted the gaze of

Napoleon from the deck of the Bellerophon. 'It reminds me,' said the fallen warrior, 'of Porto Ferrajo. It would well suit me to live there.' So we may fancy a modest country parson gazing at the Italian palace of the Bishop of Exeter—Bishopstow, above Torquay—and thinking it would be a marvellously pleasant place to play the prelate in. Let us assure him that there are far more agreeable illustrations of episcopal life than this. Let him go over to Paignton. If he can be touched by sentiment, if his pulses can be stirred by heroism, if he have head to understand and heart to feel all that Miles Coverdale was, he will not look on what remains of the walls and towers of that bishop's residence at Paignton without a feeling of reverential affection for the gentle scholar who went to dwell there in 1551, and left it, for exile, in 1553. Eighteen years before had appeared his translation of the Scriptures—the first English Bible that had ever been printed.

Devonshire is proud of the old ex-Augustinian who became Protestant Bishop of the see of Exeter. Coverdale, though a Yorkshireman, should rank among the Devonshire worthies: not that the county lacks native sons who give her glory, and receive from her the homage of love and honour. To name them all, with record of their deeds, would lead us very far beyond our limits. The county might have just cause for pride if it had no other sons to boast of than half a dozen who were the foremost men of their respective times : Raleigh, soldier, sage, scholar, courtier, true-hearted Englishman; gallant Richard Granville, his friend and fitting companion in learn-

P

ing or in arms; Drake, who not only burnt the King of Spain's beard, but foretold the golden fortune of California; Marlborough, whose name stirs a thousand echoes, and will stir them joyously for a thousand years to come, wherever *virtus*, as of old, is synonym for manly valour. There are, no doubt, loftier poets than Gay; but Gay, as a poetic fabulist, with 'manners gentle and affections mild,' is at the head of all English weavers of stories which illustrate certain morals. If Haydon be not the first of historical painters, there are men still left in Plymouth who remember how, just sixty years since, the 'Dentatus' of the old bookseller's ill-fated son gave promise of his becoming so. But in Art Devonshire possesses a son whose equal would be far to seek. Once, England hoped that Dobson had founded a native school which need not fear comparison with Vandyke; and Vandyke was frank enough to think and generous enough to hope so too. But the Londoner died, and the brilliantly-flashed promise died with him. Artists of *some* power came after Dobson, but none of *great* power till Reynolds began to draw on the walls and beams of the Plympton Grammar School. He thus opened with promise a career which had culminated in glory when he died, full of years and honour, in 1793. A pilgrimage to Plympton, and to Plymouth, where Reynolds first painted, will probably be within the itinerary of many of the visitors to Exeter. Nothing could be more appropriate, not so much because in both places are to be seen some samples of the first efforts of a great genius, but rather because it is exactly one hundred years since

Reynolds delivered his first lecture as first President of the Royal Academy. The once *tyro* of Plympton was then the great master of his art. At that period there had not yet come to London, from Bath, that Suffolk painter whose noble and well-preserved works are perhaps beginning to be more highly appreciated than those of Reynolds—namely, Gainsborough. But this is an idea which is not current among the fellow-countymen of Sir Joshua.

In speaking of the county celebrities, there is one at least who can hardly reckon among the worthies, —one who was notorious rather than great. It is about a hundred and twenty years ago since Johanna Southcote was born, but there are many persons alive who remember having seen that obese prophetess in their youthful days. Whatever Johanna may have been when she was a Devonian lass, in Exeter or other markets in the county, she was unpleasant and unsavoury of aspect when she was, at more than threescore years of age, about (so she said) to give birth to the promised Shiloh, in St. George's Fields! Nothing is so humiliating to human credulity as the fact that this unlettered woman persuaded a hundred thousand followers that she was the woman of the Revelations. Her West-country intellects had, indeed, their sharp side, for Johanna might have bought a pleasant Devonshire homestead with the money she made by selling 'seals,' which were passports to purchasers, assuring them safe admittance through the gates of salvation, without let or hindrance! Her insane writings were accepted as inspired sense on the part of her dupes, who looked with the ecstasy of awe on Johanna's dropsical body, and believed that it was the temporary tabernacle of the promised Shiloh. The preparations for the miraculous coming on earth of the heavenly child-prince were as wonderful as any part of the subject. Greatest wonder of all is that when dropsy killed, in 1814, the would-be new Queen of Heaven, the faith of her followers was not quenched. Even yet the bearded Southcotians, though in diminished numbers, are unshaken in their belief that Johanna and the babe will come together and shame a generally unbelieving world.

Johanna's own county did not yield her so many supporters as to furnish exception to what has been said concerning the little honour paid to prophets at home. A certain belief in the supernatural, perhaps, survived as long in Devonshire as elsewhere. Legends are still told, though it is possible that the tellers do not believe in them, of crabbed fiends and tricksy fairies; of men who have raised the devil, and have been made to rue it, as men engaged in such work generally do; and of the pixies, which, it may be, are still considered with compassion as the souls of unchristened children, who would fain get to heaven if they could. The last three women who were burnt as witches were Devonshire women. They were burnt at Bideford in 1682.

Next to witches, those people pass for the most knowing who wrap their wisdom up oracularly, and drop it about in proverbs. The county furnishes an unusual number of wise saws, but all of them are not intelligible. Explanations fail to show satisfactorily why 'a Plymouth cloak' means a stick for defence. If Exeter had a proud rival in Drewsteignton, so also had she another, with respect to antiquity of origin, in Crediton, of which the popular lore says, 'Kerdon was a market-town when Exeter was a fuzzy down.' This sort of boasting was common to the county, for another saying tells us that 'When Plymouth was a fuzzy down, Plympton was a borough town.' As for 'Lidford law,' it was a law common to Jedburgh and Abingdon, and is not now uncommon in Colorado, where hanging is said to precede inquiry. Crediton boasted of excellence in spinning, as is shown in the saying, 'As fine as Kerton yarn.' The prosperity of a Devon merchant of Lancastrian days is illustrated by the proverb 'It bloweth fair to Hawley's Hoe.' The pride of race is to be traced in the district:

'Crockers, Crewys, and Coplestone,
When the Conqueror came were all at home.'

And how races might or might not, would or would not, wed is hinted at in the quatrain—

'First cousins may marry;
Second cousins can't.
Third cousins will marry;
Fourth cousins won't.'

Cousins or not, if a husband was not master in his household, he was not 'a man to move Mort-stone.' The Dart was so fatal a river that the Devonians individualised it as 'Dart ev'ry year claims a heart.' Some wise man of the Exe probably hit upon the scrap of truth wrapt up in this adage: 'The afterthought is good for nought, except it be to catch blind horses wi'.' All the Devon wind does not blow so fair as at Hawley's Hoe, if it be true that 'the people are poor at Hatherleigh Moor, and so they have been for ever and ever.' But even the Moor might be made to grow something profitable by the process of '*De'nshiring*,' that is, to pare off the top turf, burn it, and apply the ashes for manure. Of weather proverbs there is, of course, no lack. 'Widdicombe hills pick their geese' when it snows; and Maxton folk literally look out for squalls 'when Heytor rock wears a hood.' Finally, while Devonshire men are alive they are said to 'live under hatches,' wet weather being more common in the county than dry; and when a man is dead and buried, it is euphuistically said of him, 'He lieth by the wall.' In the proverbs which smack of superstition there is still full belief in many parts of Devonshire. A man who is subject to fits collects a penny each from as many single women as the sufferer is years old. With the money he buys a metal ring, which he wears in the full belief that while it is on his finger the fits will not return. The very belief *may* do some good. Mr. Pepys borrowed Mr. Batten's hare's foot with the joint to it, to cure the attacks of which he was the victim. 'It is a strange thing,' he says, ' how fancy works; for I no sooner handled his foot but I became very well, and so continue.' With such a precedent, we may be the less surprised at the Dittisham publican who, being unable to check a mortality among his pigs, cut out the heart of one, stuck it with pins, roasted it to a cinder, and was persuaded that no witch within the county could harm any more of his porkers. As a sign how old superstitions linger in the beautiful shire, it is only necessary to state that the other day a Devonshire charmer tried (without success) to save the life of a scalded child, who was brought to him for that purpose, by thrice murmuring over it, ' There was two angels come from the north, one of them being fire and one being frost. In, frost! out, fire!' He had learnt the charm from an old labourer near Exeter; *that* accounted for the failure! A man may tell a woman the charm, a woman may tell a man; but if a woman tell a woman, or a man tell a man, the charmer thought ' it would not do no good at all!'—which is very probable. Devonshire, by burning witches in 1682, did not burn out all belief in the potentiality of the supernatural.

Let us now glance at those rather distinguished personages, some of whom have, to use a common phrase, hooked themselves on to Devonshire, without always belonging to it. The county has given titles to other than its Devon-born sons. Devonshire has furnished more men with local titles to peerages than any other shire in England; saving, perhaps, Yorkshire. There were Earls of Devon, of the De Redvers family, from the reign of Henry I. down to 1293; but many of them were styled Earls of Exeter, in which city they kept their state and exercised their power a good deal at the cost of those who beheld the one and felt the other. Following them came the imperial Courtenays, whose illustrious descent forms the subject of the most brilliant chapter in Gibbon; but it is said that the blood of the De Redvers was mingled also with that of Eastern emperors. Two of the Courtenays paid the penalty of greatness. When that brave young bachelor, Earl Thomas, was beheaded in 1461, Edward IV. put his head up at York, in place of that of Edward's father. One other earl suffered death at the block in 1539; and the line seemed to have failed in his son, who died in 1556. But in 1830, William, Viscount Devon, proved himself nearest heir male, though not by bodily descent, to the last earl, and the ancient honours are at this moment worn by his cousin, William Courtenay.

With Earls of Devon there have been first Earls, then Dukes, of Devonshire. In 1618, William, the first Baron Cavendish of Hardwick, was raised to the earldom. His great-grandson William was the first duke, in 1694. He was the duke who excited Evelyn's astonishment by losing 1600l. at Newmarket. Lords now reckon losses by thousands and are not appalled. This duke, moreover, was the eccentric lover of Miss Campion the vocalist. Their history enlivens all operatic chronicles. Of this line there was one who died abroad, and one who was born abroad. The corpse of the former was brought home, but it was treated with so little respect by the suspicious Custom House officers that they probed it through and through with their rods. 'As like as not,' they said, 'the duke might be stuffed with lace.' The late duke—one whom 'H. B.' and Bulwer have alike immortalised, in different but masterly styles of caricature, and who distinguished himself to his personal and to his county's honour in the famous embassy to St. Petersburg—was born in Paris, and this led to his being nearly drawn within the grasp of the law of conscription! The most singular member of this line of dukes was undoubtedly the one who married Lady Georgiana Spencer. He was all apathy; she buoyant with life, and brilliant in her way of enjoying it. The duke was indeed a great scholar, but therewith he could see as little beyond his nose as Modus, who it will be remembered was a great scholar too.

The De Redvers live only in name, but Courtenays and Cavendishes still add lustre to Devonshire peerages. The chief city of the county has been as brilliantly represented by its earls and marquises and dukes. The Hollands, with all their Plantagenet blood and alliances, were a luckless race. The last of them became a fugitive, after the battle of Hexham. De Comines says that he saw this Lancastrian refugee in Flanders, running after the Duke of Burgundy's train, and begging 'For God's sake, bread!' The duke died while in this degraded condition. After Exeter had given the title of Marquis to two of the Courtenays, and had been without peerage dignity, conferred or acquired, since 1556, Thomas Cecil, the second Baron of Burghley, was created Earl of Exeter in 1605. This was, we believe, the first instance of a man being made earl of a city when another man was earl of the county, of which that city was the capital. From 1303 to 1306 the earldom of Devon was held by Charles Blount, Lord Mountjoy, to whom Penelope Rich, the sister of Essex, stooped to be mistress. Blount passed away without legitimate issue; but the Cecils have abided, succeeding each other in the male

line, with the earldom raised to a marquisate since
1801. The line, however, was once hard to find.
Of all the lords of Exeter, poetry and romance
have had most to do with Henry Cecil, the first
marquis of that house. Thomas Cecil, the first Earl
of Exeter, is in the front of every page of history of
his time; but the romancers in prose and verse have
alone taken possession of the marquis. How often
are we told that under a feigned name he wedded a
lowly maiden, took her to Burghley, proclaimed her
lady thereof, and killed her by the sudden shock of
such intelligence! The prose record of this Marquis
of Exeter may be told in a very few words. When
Mr. Henry Cecil, he married the beautiful Emma
Vernon. He lost his money by gambling. He got
rid of his wife, after fifteen years of wedlock, by a
divorce. In June 1791, directly after this catastrophe, he found an asylum at Bolas in Shropshire,
where it is said he assumed the name of Jones, and
where in October of that year he married, it must be
supposed under his real name, Sarah Hoggins, a
modest fair young girl, who is not to be prejudiced
by her cacophonous appellation. She was the
daughter of the farmer with whom Cecil had lodged.
Already two children were born, it is reported, of
this marriage (but if so they must have died early),
when in 1793 a search after the hidden heir of the
then dying Earl of Exeter resulted in his discovery
at Bolas. The earl died, his nephew succeeded, and
his wife was carried by him to Burghley, unconscious
of her now being a countess. The announcement did
not kill her. She survived it, at all events, for four

years, and was the mother of two sons and a daughter, when she died in 1797, at the age of about twenty-four, and of something like *ennui*, and a consciousness, it is said, of want of qualification for the station which she occupied. Her lord was not an inconsolable widower. He married, for the third time, with Elizabeth, daughter of Peter Burrell, sister of the first Lord Gwydyr, and relict of the Duke of Hamilton. The Shropshire farmer's daughter was a most estimable lady. Through *her* daughter, who married the Hon. Mr. Pierrepoint, whose only daughter became the wife of the late Lord Charles Wellesley, the Shropshire blood of the stout yeoman Hoggins flows in the veins of the future Duke of Wellington. Reality, after all, is as wonderful as romance.

Accident too, or what men call such, has much to do with these matters. If Mr. John Russell had not been at Weymouth in 1506, when the Archduke Philip of Austria put in there in a storm, and received sundry good services from the former gentleman, who alone could converse with the foreign prince, the abbey of Tavistock and the marquisate of the same Devonshire locality would have probably passed, with other good things, into some other family. The earldom of Plymouth was created to give dignity to Charles Fitzroy, son of Catherine Pegg and Charles II. He died a soldier's death at the siege of Tangiers. His merry widow, a daughter of the Duke of Leeds, married the Rev. Philip Bisse, who had kissed her in the dark in the gallery at Whitehall, mistaking her for a maid of honour. This pleasant audacity obtained for him a wife, and, in course of time, the bishoprics of St. David's and Hereford—sees which were once occupied by Theophilus Field, the brother of Nathaniel Field, the actor of Shakespeare's time. The Devonshire earldom, now extinct, went to the Hickman Windsors, one of whose ancestors, Lord Windsor, when dying at Liége, said that though his body would lie there, he would have his heart placed by the side of his father under their chapel at Bradenham, 'in token that I am a true Englishman.' The earldom of Dartmouth was fairly earned by loyal service. Honest Jack Legge, whom Charles I. so loved, would take nothing in return from Charles II.; but the Legges continued faithful and active, and first a barony, then an earldom, of Dartmouth were their reward; and the dignities still remain in a family whose history is full of incidents so strange that imagination could hardly build up stranger. Torrington gave the title of Viscount to Byng, another champion of the seas, whose heirs may be proud of their ancestor. The Edgcumbes, Earls of Mount Edgcumbe, are of the soil, true Devonians from very early times, and seem—what indeed they are—part and parcel of the shire. So was the first Lord Ashburton, Dunning the lawyer, who made his native Devonshire village proud by selecting it for his local title when he was raised to the peerage. The Barings, in which family the title now survives, are connected with Dunning by blood relationship. The barony of Boringdon, which has, so to speak, blown into the earldom of Morley, is another Devonshire title enjoyed by Devonshire people, the Parkers being originally of North Molton, gentlemen and lawyers, at a remote period. It must be allowed that the little town of Bideford, politics suiting, had cause to be glad that as a barony it figured among the titles of the Earl of Bath, the son of that Sir Beville Granville who was killed in the fight at Lansdowne, and almost the only, if not *the* only, man really trusted by Charles II. and Monk to bring about the Restoration. Teignmouth gave its name to grace the title earned by Sir John Shore in India. When he and Lord Moira, that other Indian Governor-General, met, what reminiscences they must both have had of the time when they sat side by side in the modest school at Hackney, studying book-keeping by single and double entry! If Teignmouth rejoiced, the little village of Sidbury must have been astonished when Jack Fitzgibbon, the notorious Irish Earl of Clare and Lord Chancellor, was created an English peer by the title of Baron Fitzgibbon of Sidbury. Earldom and barony are extinct through the death of the sole male heir on the field of Balaklava. When Mr. Rolle (whose father had refused an earldom) was made a baron by George II., the Devonshire village of Stevenstone was gratified by his being called Baron Rolle of Stevenstone; for there the family had settled at the time of the Reformation, when George Rolle, having made a fortune as a London merchant, bought largely of abbey lands, and set up for a gentleman in the county of Devon. This barony is also extinct. The pretty village of Sidmouth gives title to the viscountship of the Addingtons; otherwise there is no connection between them. The first viscount was the son of a Reading physician, and was brought up to the law, by abandoning which for statesmanship he may have missed the Woolsack, but he succeeded Pitt as Prime Minister. He first entered Parliament in 1784, when he was twenty-seven years old. In five years he became Speaker; and he is the only example of the House having raised so young a member to that office. When, after twelve years' service, he left the chair, Mr. Addington stood on the floor of the House still a commoner. It was not till 1805 that the Sidmouth bell-ringers rang out their congratulations at the honour paid them by the new viscount—a man who refused a pension, an earldom, and the Garter. One other Devonshire locality remains to be named in connection with the peerage. The gallant Admiral Pellew, who bombarded Algiers and abolished the slavery of Christians in that dey-ship, was raised to the peerage as Viscount Exmouth. He, however, had no personal connection with the place, being a Kentish man, and member of a Cornish family.

Of the sixty bishops of the see of Exeter, none, except it be a Courtenay, has been especially connected with the county. We reckon from the time when Leofric settled the two sees of Devonshire and Cornwall at Exeter in 1050. We meet with several who refused to accept this bishopric. Warlewast resigned it in 1127, after holding it twenty years, and when he felt himself incapable of any longer performing its duties. Stapleton had held it nineteen years when he was beheaded by a London mob in 1326. He *trimmed* in his politics, and the highly scandalised Cockneys murdered the fine old man in Cheapside. Voysey resigned the see in 1551, after possessing it six-and-thirty years—two years less than it has been held by the present prelate, Dr. Phillpotts. Voysey, however, was restored in 1553, and he died the year after. Miles Coverdale, who had been driven from the see at the earlier period, refused to return to it when it was offered to him after the death of Mary. He lived privately till he died at the age of eighty. Bishops Stafford and Neville were also Chancellors of England. Neville was the first Bishop of Exeter who was translated to York (1465). The others were Lamplugh in 1688 and Blackburn in 1724. The cathedral is considered as the work of the designer, Bishop Quiril (1280-91). One of his successors, Grandison (1327-69), must have had all the supposed refinement of the Grandison character; for in designing the screen, he chastened his florid ideas so as not to injure the simple grandeur of Quiril's edifice. We are not surprised to find Bishop Courtenay (1478-87) as the first Englishman to do homage to Henry VII. at Rheims. Alley, who was bishop from 1560 to 1570, had a grandson in the Irish Church, who died in 1763; the two thus bringing the reigns of Elizabeth and George III. together. The grandson was rector of Donoughmore for nearly three-quarters of a century. He had thirty-three children, by two wives, and he died (so it is chronicled) at the age of 110! He was long remembered as the rector who would never take tithe of a poor man's garden.

Among other Exeter diocesans of the seventeenth century are to be named Seth Ward, afterwards of Salisbury, and Sir Jonathan Trelawney, Bart. (translated to Winchester in 1707), who, while he swore in his character of baronet, hoped to be saved by virtue of his office as bishop! Another sort of man and prelate was to be found in Offspring Blackhall (1708-1716). A Tory in politics, he was able as a scholar, pious, and not inefficient in controversy with Toland or Hoadley. He had more charity than Lavington (1746-62), who, in his *Enthusiasm of Methodists and Papists Compared*, took occasion to say that Methodist fanaticism resembled that of the Ancient Mysteries, and that the Ancient Mysteries were an abomination from the beginning.

In the year 1796, Bishop Buller of Exeter preached one of many fast-sermons that were preached in that year, and it excited more notice perhaps than any other. It was delivered before the Lords Spiritual and Temporal in Westminster Abbey, and it had a remarkably strong flavour of politics in it, scattered with the improvident profusion of wrong-headedness. There was the Admiral Nelson doctrine in it of the duty of hating our enemies, but this was put in an episcopal and not in a naval commanderish way. The French, said the bishop, had apostatised from the national faith as well as from the national loyalty, and had become abominable as infidels and republicans. Some critics in his own diocesan city expressed surprise that their very Protestant bishop should hold up people to general abhorrence for giving up ' French Christianity *nursed* in the lap of the Scarlet Lady of Babylon.' There was much gentle joking in Devonshire Rural Deaneries at so staunch a Protestant prelate being angry with the French for breaking with Rome. The old sermon was talked of till, at the end of ten years, another excited the attention of the diocese. The latter was preached in 1806 by Bishop Fisher. It advocated liberty of conscience, but underneath the advocacy lurked opposition to a repeal of the Test Act, hatred of Calvinism, and horror of all idea of Catholic Emancipation! From this, it may be easily seen that Devonshire was kept a little behind the world at the beginning of this century. The people, however, longed to go ahead. How they manifested the longing is amusingly shown by a cry in high places. Tradesmen and even the honest yeomen, it was wonderingly said, send their boys and girls to grammar and boarding schools! Every one below was struggling to get up at least to the level of the men above him. The Exeter and Tiverton schools were all the rage. Why, mechanics were beginning to study the elements of Latin, and yeomen's daughters were known to be learning French! It was evidently thought they would find out something more than the language; and even in the north-west parts of Devon, where good cheer and rudeness of character were not different from what they had been in Charles I.'s days, there was an impression that this new-fangled scholarism was a very sad matter indeed.

Men of an earlier period were not so alarmed at the idea of the poorest Devonshire folk being taught. There was a grammar-school in Exeter as early as 1322, founded by Bishop Grandison, a man of scholarly and refined tastes, who also founded the old grammar-school at Ottery St. Mary. In the sixteenth century were established the school at Ashburton, whence notable scholars have proceeded; that at Bideford, where, in the next century, Hebrew was taught, with Greek and Latin; the school at Plymouth, for the teaching of youth in grammatical knowledge; and, at the end of the century, that once famous school at Tiverton, which its founder, Peter Blundell, declared should be 'a free grammar-school for ever, and not a school for exaction.' Visitors may inquire how the matter stands now. In the next, the seventeenth, century were founded the grammar-schools of Barnstaple, where Jewel mused over his exercises, Gay wished his task-time over, and ready Aaron Hill would write a theme for any dunce for a bite of an apple; of Chudleigh, which, getting into Chancery, has got a good deal away from the groove in which its founder set it; of Dartmouth, where 'the art of navigation' was one of the especial arts for coast lads to be taught; of Hele's school at Exeter, for the particular bringing up of sons of tradesmen, innkeepers, and warehousemen; of Honiton, of Kingsbridge, of North Tawton, for the sons of yeomen, a class which later was thought unworthy of being cared for as to grammar; of Plympton, not unknown to fame derived from some of its pupils; of South Molton; of Tavistock, which has ungratefully forgotten the name of its founder; and of Totnes, which was subsequently endowed by 'Pious Uses Hele,' and which gave tastes to Edward Lye, which made him known as Lye the antiquary. Of the last century is the school at Uffculme. They are all more or less endowed, have scholarships to stimulate the emulation of pupils, and will be found generally worthy the notice of members of the Association.

But there have been other teachers in Exeter, and the county generally, besides those in the pulpits and the schools—namely, those connected with the press.

At the commencement of the last century, Exeter began to long for a fuller account of both London and county news than it could get by news-letters and untrustworthy carriers. In 1715 the *Salisbury Postman* became a medium for sending news westward by undertaking to despatch several copies 'as far as Exeter.' The paper was then a new one, but 'containing the whole week's news,' as it says, 'it can't be afforded under twopence.' Exeter liked the thing so well that it soon had three *Mercurys* of its own—the *Exeter*, *Protestant*, and *Royal Mercurys*, the last being also called the *Postmaster;* and it is sometimes quoted as the *Loyal Mercury*. Unluckily, they all got into the troubled waters of affliction. The Devonshire taxpayers had much curiosity touching the sayings and doings of the Lords and Commons. News-letters in manuscript brought just enough parliamentary intelligence to an Exeter coffee-house or two to make the man or squire of much importance when he carried it home. Thence it spread to other homes, more or less incorrectly; and to satisfy the growing desire for this especial sort of knowledge, the *Mercurys* began to copy from the news-letters the sayings in 'P—t,' as Parliament was mysteriously signified, of certain 'L—ds' and 'M—rs,' which Lords and Members were often made to speak under Greek and Latin names. Now, even to repeat, much more to write, and most of all to print and circulate, the utterances of august wisdom in either House was an offence and abomination in the eyes of that awful legislature. The audacity of Exeter must be repressed. Messengers with warrants went down to that city to arrest the printers. There was a dodging and evading and pursuing, but at last the victims were pounced upon, and in due time were set before the terrible assembly. There, neither boldness nor justification availed them. On the other hand, the Senate was more angry than cruel. The plea of ignorance of offending, lack of money, cost of household, and largeness of families touched the bosoms of the judges. The offenders went down on their knees and acknowledged that they had been rude and naughty knaves; after which they were bidden to betake themselves home, and be honester men in future! We need only add here, that the Exeter press has since then been a credit to literature. There is no true brother of the craft who does not think with respect of Robert Truman, who founded the *Exeter Flying Post*, and edited it with zeal, courage, and ability for more than forty years.

To that city in the west, learned and also holiday pilgrims will, in a day or two, be wending; and we may say to them, in the cheerful spirit of Justiniano to his fellows in Webster's old play—the spirit being more applicable than all the words—' Take water; keep aloof from the shore; on with your masks; up with your sails, and *Westward Ho!*'

X.
LEICESTER.
1870.

LEICESTER.

1870.

THE ROYAL ARCHÆOLOGICAL INSTITUTE OF GREAT BRITAIN.

THERE are some societies that are like some men: their lines are cast in pleasant places. There is not a pleasanter county or a pleasanter county-town in England than Leicestershire and its capital; Romance and Reality seem there to go hand in hand. The meadows are as verdant as the Vale of Tempe. The oxen that graze in them are as fat as the bulls of Bashan. The shepherds may not very closely resemble the familiar 'pastor Corydon,' but the sheep are sheep that Landseer might be gladdened to look upon and Verboekhoven worship while he sketched them. A man may have Cuyps and Paul Potters in Leicestershire for nothing, for the mere trouble of opening his eyes and enjoying what is before them. There are herds in picturesque groups, and there are flocks wanting only Watteau's pink ribbons and daintily-gauzed shepherdesses to make them—what nothing else could make them—ridiculous. There is an atmosphere of poetry about the sheep, and therewith material ideas of well-roasted saddles and currant-jelly! Sidney

Cooper himself might look upon the oxen, and be pardoned for the rich suggestions they convey of brown sirloins and horse-radish. The beautiful and the useful are combined in Leicester and its shire. There is a womanly beauty abounding there that might make any reasonable man distracted. There was a rude and hungry time, indeed, when it was said that if you shook a Leicestershire woman by the petticoat you might hear the beans rattle in her throat. 'Nous avons changé tout cela!' When one thinks that the archæologists are gathering in such a place and among such objects, it is impossible not to see that their lines are cast in pleasant places,—pleasant and perilous; for even archæologists may be forced to acknowledge another beauty than that which they reverence in old pots, pans, coins, and ruins. They may be in ecstasy in presence of castle or grange or abbey mantled with ivy; but let them beware of the Leicestershire 'teretis puellæ longam renodantis comam.'

The programme of the Royal Archæological Institute shows the anxiety of the managers that the visitors shall see everything in and about the town. It, however, begins with an error. It announces the opening of the reception-rooms for '*Monday, July* 22*d.*' Business will seriously commence on Tuesday the 26th, with addresses, sight-seeing, and the reading of papers. Leicester Abbey is the great feature for Wednesday. On Thursday the Society go boldly over the border of the county, after exploring various ancient spots within it. They will visit Tamworth and Tuxbury. The vicinity adds to the temptation,.

and the archæologists will wisely avail themselves of the opportunity. The excursion for Friday will be to Kirby Muxloe Castle. There are half a dozen for Saturday, including Bradgate, so associated with old griefs and old glories, and Beaumanor Park, where a living master will show himself worth a dozen defunct earls and their stories. Mr. Herrick will entertain the Society, not with a lecture, but a luncheon. Sunday is not named in the programme, probably for sufficient reason, but Monday, August 1, will take those who have remained thus long in Leicester to Melton Mowbray and Oakham. After all the pleasant excursions have been run through, and no more of the light and luxurious work has to be done, there will be a meeting on Tuesday, 'for reading memoirs of interest for which time may have been insufficient.' For such reading we do not anticipate many listeners. The voice of the reader will be less potential than the whistle of the steam-engine.

For archæologists who are as much influenced by sentiment as by science the county can offer few things more tempting than the trip to Bradgate, the ancient manor and residence of the Earls of Leicester. But it is not on *their* account that Bradgate is attractive. It has higher and more tender associations. *There* were born the three sisters, Jane, Catherine, and Mary Grey, whose destinies were so varied, and in different degrees so sad. Jane was that Queen for an hour, who paid with her life for wearing the greatness that was thrust upon her. Catherine was that prisoner in the Tower, whence she could not escape to liberty, but whither love went, despite

Elizabeth and all her locksmiths. Mary, youngest sister of the short-lived Queen Jane, had no heart for any lord in Leicestershire. She gave, however, food for a nine days' gossip in the county, when she, who might have chosen from among a score of noble suitors, chose to wed, and found quiet, safety, and happiness in doing so, with plain Master Martin Keys, or Kayes,—a serjeant-porter, of whom some one saucily said, 'He is a Judge of Court indeed; but of dice only, and not of law.' Had Lady Mary murdered a noble husband, as Dame Smith did Sir Walter near Leicester Grange, she could not have excited more surprise than she did by wedding with an obscure one like Master Martin.

The town itself might profitably occupy the members of the Institute throughout the whole time of the meeting, if they chose to confine themselves within such limits. There is something there for every class of archæologist. Groups may stand round the ancient Roman milestone, and may discuss the meaning of the ancient name of the city—Ratæ. With regard to the origin of the name it now bears, we trust that King Lear will be deposed, and never have a friend to attempt his restoration. *Lear's Cester* is as puerile in connection with *Leicester*, as the famous descent of *gherkin* from *King Jeremiah*. The Saxons saw the local beauty, and took from it a happy name—the Camp in the Meadows. The local names have doubtless undergone considerable change. The Sancta Via has been vulgarised into *Sanvy*, Gallowsgate has been refined into *Goltre*. The 'Janua' has been utterly forgotten in its modernised form of *Jewry* Wall, with legends to fit 'Jewry,' and mislead Fellows of the *Soc. Antiq.* looking for the 'Janua.' This fragment of Roman work, which adjoins St. Nicholas's Church, is at present being propped up with brickwork.

But it was never intended that the meadows which glorify Leicester should be forgotten. The Romans themselves must have been sensible of their refreshing and fragrant beauty. Why did they call the station there Ratæ? Will no archæologist be bold enough next week to discover, assert, or suggest that *Ratæ* should be *Prata*? There is not much difference, and the latter would be acceptable to the Romanticists among antiquarians. The Saxons, perhaps, adopted that reading. They, at all events, did honour to the spot to which fortune, fate, and that Saxon persistency which makes both fate and fortune, brought them. The Camp in the Meadows was followed by a church similarly named. The monks were not to be outdone in poetical feeling by the pagan Saxons; and their abbey, church, and monastery had but one name, St. Mary de Pratis— St. Mary of the Meadows. They who tarried therein when the sweetest bells in England, those of St. Margaret, rang out silver-toned messages at eventide, had a double pleasure. Each listener may have confessed the double joy, by murmuring, 'Festus in Pratis.'

The fine old church of St. Nicholas and the Guildhall are each of them worthy of note. In the old days, the two churches of St. Mary and St. Margaret were what may be termed, without offence, the 'spectacular' churches of Leicester. There was one especial solemnity—a Whitsuntide procession of pilgrims from St. Mary's to St. Margaret's—at which a singular ceremony was observed. Among the oblations laid on the altar were two pairs of gloves, one for the Deity, the other for St. Thomas of India! To the profane succeeded the comic ceremonies. Among the latter is to be named the alleged original manner of electing a mayor for Leicester. The candidates for the dignity sat in a semicircle, each with a hat full of beans in his lap. A sow was then introduced, and the first man whose hat full of Leicestershire beans was emptied by the sow was raised to the coveted and awful dignity of mayor. This is the legend, but we fancy that something like it has been told to bring Mr. Mayors of other municipalities into contempt. The Leicester mayor had no exceptional privileges to excite envy. If men are to be envied for their power, few men have been more enviable than the Earls of Leicester, some of whom within the county were greater than the king within his realm.

The title of Earl of Leicester is one of the oldest and noblest in the peerage. It has been borne by some of the most remarkable among Englishmen since the creation of the dignity in 1103. It was enjoyed in succession by a handsome, a hunchbacked, or a white-handed De Bellomont. During a hundred years and one, four heirs of that noble house were Earls of Leicester. The title and lands then went, as so many have done, with the sole heiress, to the foremost man of his day, the Simon de Montfort whose son and successor was a sort of Cromwell in his way. The title was forfeited before De Montfort lay dead on the field at Evesham. The dignity, with the Castle of Leicester, and all the other honours and possessions of Simon, were made over to Edmund, the second son of Henry III. Four princely Plantagenets had borne the proud title when Henry Plantagenet, Duke of Lancaster, Earl of Derby, of Lincoln, and of Leicester, died, leaving two daughters for his heirs, of whom one, Maud, died childless; the other, Blanche, married John of Gaunt, who got with her the castle and honour of Leicester; but the title of the Earl of Leicester was not what is called attendant upon that tenure.

The father of Blanche died in 1361. Two hundred and two years elapsed before our peerage knew of another Earl of Leicester, that brilliant Robert Dudley, the favourite of Elizabeth, the brother of Guilford (the passionate boy-husband of Lady Jane Grey), and brother also of Ambrose Dudley, Earl of Warwick, who started Frobisher on his first North-West Passage. Those Dudleys, with all their faults, were really noble fellows. They will not be thought lightly of by the archæologists when it is remembered that their father, the luckless John Dudley, was a scholar and the friend of scholars, and that the most ancient books in the library at Lambeth once belonged to the Earl Robert whom Queen Elizabeth loved after her queenly fashion. And again the title went away with an heiress. Robert Dudley's sole sister, Mary, married Viscount Lisle, Baron Sydney of Penshurst, and the Queen, Elizabeth, conferred on the bridegroom the title which had been so splendidly borne by the bride's brother. The son and heir of this couple held some Lammas land close to the metropolis, for which he paid a poor 3*l.* yearly. He got leave to build upon and near it. Forthwith our soldiers lost fields that were to them what Wormwood Scrubs are to the volunteers of the present day. Leicester Fields became encumbered with bricks and mortar, and upon them rose the Square, Lisle-street, Sydney-alley, &c., which perpetuate the memory of a family to which belonged knightly Philip, the popular Algernon, the handsome Henry, and that wayward Dorothy whom Waller has celebrated as 'Sacharissa.'

After the death of the last Sydney, in 1743, the ancient earldom was made over to a stranger, Coke, Lord Lovel, at whose demise, in 1759, the title became extinct. It was revived in 1784, in the person of George Townshend, who took precedence of his father Viscount Townshend till the viscount was made a marquis! Here, however, was a man whose memory archæologists may fairly cherish. The blood of De Montfort, through a female line, was in him. He knew more of heraldry than old Gwillim, and all the heralds together could not surpass him in genealogical lore. The earldom of Leicester was held by the Townshends till 1855, when it ceased, though an heir general succeeded to the marquisate. Nevertheless there had been a second Earl of Leicester since 1837. For nearly twenty years there were two Earls of Leicester—Coke of Norfolk, and the peer who was Marquis Townshend and Earl of Leicester. It has been erroneously said that both held the same title by grant of the Crown. The titles were not the same. The Marquis of Townshend was 'Earl of the county of Leicester.' Coke of Norfolk was created 'Earl of Leicester of Holkham, county of Norfolk.' Therefore his son, the present Earl, has nothing to do with the castle and honour of Leicester, which were once enjoyed by the Bellomonts, De Montforts, Plantagenets, Dudleys, Sydneys, and Townshends. Mr. Coke's ancestor—Coke, Lord Lovel—was Earl of the county of Leicester; but Mr. Coke himself was created, as we have said, Earl of Leicester of Holkham, and had none of the blood of the old Leicester earls in his veins. We do not say this in disparagement of his own.

We may notice in passing that, if Walter Scott's Countess of Leicester be but an apocryphal personage, as far as she is called 'Countess,' there are others, whose dust now lies within the city-walls, who were of repute in their day. But these ladies are nothing compared with the most perfect woman in the world, of whom Leicestershire preserves what is mortal at Hinckley. The lady was a Mistress Mary Seagrave, and this testimony is inscribed on her tomb: 'Many daughters have done virtuously, but *thou excellest them all!*' We should be inclined to prefer, at least for her works, that ever-to-be-reverenced Mrs. Orton, who made Leicestershire famous by her invention of Stilton cheese. Like a clever woman, she learned the secret from Cooper Thornhill, the landlord of the Bell at Stilton. Like an acute woman, she persuaded people that the delicious cheese could be made only from the milk of cows that fed in one close—her own—in the parish of Little Dalby. For a quarter of a century Mrs. Orton made Stilton cheese and much money. About the middle of last century two or three other persons took up the work. The whole secret lay in mixing with the new milk as much cream as it would bear. This gave the cheese its peculiar richness. Extreme care and unremitting attendance did the rest, and *now* Stilton cheese is made everywhere but at Stilton, where indeed it was never made, except in the way of amateur farming by the landlord of the Bell. The produce was not known to the county-town press, or the latter might have given it a 'lift.' The local paper at that time was in rather a singular condition.

In the middle of last century the Leicester newspaper press—or rather the Leicester newspaper, for there was no press—was in an equally droll and embarrassed position. The paper was written in the town. The copy was sent to London to be printed. The paper set in type was returned by coach. It took two days to 'go up,' as many to print, and two more to get back, by which time the latest news was a week old. One would suppose that matter would have so accumulated that room for insertion would be scarce. Room was superabundant; matter was scarce. It was so scarce that during one dry season the editor adopted a sort of *feuilleton* to fill up with. It was a serial, but not anything like a modern sensational story. It was simply the Bible in regular chapters, and the editor had got to the end of the tenth chapter of Exodus before further news than about what Moses had said unto Pharaoh turned up for the amusement of the

Leicestershire subscribers. That primitive paper was the *Leicester Journal*. The *Herald* belonged to the last decade of years of the eighteenth century. When Sir Richard Phillips was a flourishing bookseller in town, one of his happiest memories was his having stopped in Leicester when on his way to London, and having there founded the *Herald*, which became one of the signs of his progress towards his well-fought for and his well-won fortune and distinctions. The *Chronicle* dates from 1810.

The local press dealing with local history does not ignore Briton, Roman, Dane, Saxon, or Norman. Later times have quite as romantic illustrations. The siege of Leicester in 1645 is as dear a theme to those who live on the spot as that of Londonderry is to the dwellers within the walls of the ancient Daire Calgaich, the 'oak wood of Galgacus.' But a dearer theme used to be that of Richard and Bosworth Field, and the Blue Boar in Leicester in which Richard passed the night, and the huge bed in which he slept, and which beholders religiously believed was the camp-bed which that active monarch carried about with him whithersoever he went! More than one writer has 'leaped over the traces,' and bolted in a mad sort of enthusiasm after this melodramatic personage. It was reserved to one of the many historians of Leicester to be madder than all the rest. Throsby, in his fanaticism of adoration, lovingly familiar, calls Richard 'King Dick.' Referring to the bridge near the Blackfriars, he is almost delirious with delight. 'The arches of this bridge,' he exclaims, ' which span the ancient river Soar, should

R

be ever memorable as the passage (of one of the bravest kings that ever swayed a sceptre) to the field of battle and his death, arrayed in martial glory, panting for fame and victory.' This Leicestershire historian never tires of the theme. He roars at it, like Mr. Bradley in an old Coburg drama. In his 'Select Views' of the county he touches on the battle: 'Bosworth's fight,' he says, 'lost one of the greatest heroes England ever produced his crown and life, and levelled his conqueror and successor with the lowest of the human race. Unlettered peasants, butchers, and chimney-sweepers have killed their fellows in a conflict; but none of them insulted the bodies of the helpless slain. That alone was left for the Earl of Richmond and his followers.' These be 'prave 'ords;' braver could not have been uttered in Wensleydale when the news of Richard's death reached the house in the North where he was loved when living, and where Richard's memory with his charities survived till long after his death.

Perhaps something yet may turn up from the muniment chest at Beaumanor in reference to Richard in Leicestershire. The matter will be worth remembering at Mr. Herrick's, if his luncheon do not drive it out of the heads of his guests. At the close of the last century there were chests there, crammed with papers more or less important, which had not been examined for a hundred years. So ran the story. Many of the papers have since been made public; but it is possible that a few may remain that would repay research; and we commend the subject to the Beaumanor guests next Saturday.

We close the programme of the coming meeting with increased respect for a county so full of such present beauty and ancient memories as Leicestershire. It is full too of pleasant contrasts. Barton in the Beans seems to the yeomen what Ashby-de-la-Zouch and its chivalry were to knights and ladies. Old Latimer kept a farm there, with a hundred sheep, half a dozen servants, and a score and a half of kine which his wife milked herself. Their son, the martyr, fed other lambs. All Christians may reverence the memory of this Leicestershire hero, if it were only for his desire at the Reformation that two abbeys in every diocese should be preserved for the maintenance of learned men out of their revenues. Ashby itself was not merely the stage for knights; it was the cradle of that English Seneca, John Hall, who survived to see episcopacy abolished, but not to see it restored. At Brooksby was born that most accomplished courtier of his age, Villiers, Duke of Buckingham. But to enumerate all the Leicestershire celebrities is altogether beyond our limits. They are numerous, not to say numberless, from Lady Jane Grey to little Miss Linwood, who worked her effigies in worsted work that looked marvellously like what it really was, and made our grandmothers half worship that Queen of the Needle. The heroes may be said to date from the days of the kingdom of Mercia, and Leicester is not sterile of such productions yet. There is a tablet in the chapel in Belvoir-street to the memory of Robert Hall, who was long minister of the chapel. Nor has the county lacked chroniclers, from the time of the Carmelite, Belgrave, who wrote six centuries and a half ago, down to the last handbook for the uses of archæologists and strangers generally. These works are from the ponderous folios of the Nicholses and others down to pamphlets of chronological events. They are from histories in half a dozen volumes to a mere broadsheet with its pennyworth of tradition. Of the six-volume history Walpole said in his off-hand way: 'It seems to be superficial, but the author is young and talks modestly, which, if it will not serve instead of merit, makes one at least hope he will improve, and not grow insolent on age and more knowledge.' The most convenient and trustworthy history of Leicester is by Mr. J. Thompson, which was reviewed in the *Athenæum*, No. 1194.

Leicestershire since that period has not added much that is new to its history. It still has the broadest beans, the heaviest sheep, the largest horses, the longest staple of wool in England; web-fabrics and shoes are the products of the town. The Avon, the Soar, the Wreke, the Anker, and the Welland are pleasant among rivers. The castle, abbey, gates, and many other things which added to its state or its security have not crumbled away out of memory, whatever they may have become in fact. Leicester has many memories of which it may be proud; a few of which it may be sad. It has only one of which it may be ashamed. At the parliament held at Leicester in the reign of Henry V. was enacted the famous law for the burning of heretics.

XI.
LIVERPOOL.
1870.

LIVERPOOL.

1870.

FROM Exeter last year to Liverpool this is a great change for the British Association. It is from the cloisters to the mart; from silence and past memories to the noise of tongues and active present occurrences. Liverpool is, in a certain sense, old; but it is only from the last century that it dates its dignity of being the *second eye* of Lancashire.

It is one of the advantages of Liverpool that it has a name for the derivation of which there are a dozen, perhaps a score, of suggestions. Conversation and controversy are thus rendered more easy. Men have quarrelled over the meaning of this name, and antagonistic correspondents of learned journals have fought for their several ideas with an amenity that has borne some close resemblance to ill-temper. We suppose it may have occurred to a few of these gentlemen that the famous heraldic bird called the Lever—that is, so called in heraldry, but nowhere else—may have had something to do with this much vexed question. In nature, which is quite a different thing from heraldry, the Lever would seem to be the Blue Duck, once common in Lancashire; still well known in Lancashire blazonry. In the latter case the Blue Duck becomes the Lever. A family of the name bore the bird on their shield. The Levers of Liverpool had for arms, argent, a lever azure, beak and legs gules. If this be not our old friend the Blue Duck, it is nothing, or anything. The Pool in which that respectable bird was once to be found in numbers to excite ecstasy in the most cautious of sportsmen used to be much talked of by that well-remembered individual, 'the oldest inhabitant.' But then persons who had no respect for 'oldest inhabitants' refused to accept the connection of Lever, or Blue Duck, with the Pool. They said that there were several pools, and that Lither-pool indicated the *lower* pool, on, near, or about which the city was built. But, again, a city so noted for what may be mildly called its *bumptiousness* was more likely to take the upper than the lower pool. After all, the best starting-point from which to descry some sort of meaning is to look at the first document in which the place is written down. Here we have it, in the charter granted by Henry II. One might also suppose that that monarch, who was not without humour (occasionally it was very ill-humour indeed), must have had some foresight of the establishing of such things as learned journals, in which etymological subjects, and the derivation of names especially, would be very much discussed. If Henry was really sagacious of that quarry from so far, he could not more effectually have puzzled posterity than he has done in the document to which one naturally resorts in order to discover if Liverpool was Liverpool, or by

what other name it may have been called in 1173.
'Know ye,' said the King, 'that the whole estuary of
the Mersey shall be for ever a port of the sea.' This
is clear, intelligible, and not without a dash of poetry
in the enouncement. When, however, etymologists
come to the name, they are flung on their backs; for
the place is described as one 'which the Lyrpul men
call Litherpul.' So St. Albans was a place which
the St. Albans men called Little London, but in the
latter case we can distinguish the true word from the
slang. We suppose that the Lyrpul men were referred to correctly, and that Litherpul was a corrupt
form of the proper name. However this may be,
the fact of what the Lyrpul men did call their town
is recorded in the charter; and Robert, Bishop of
London, and Thomas the Chancellor have put their
hand to the record as witnesses. Till the matter is
settled let us stick to the Blue Duck, the Lever of
heraldry. For want of a better origin, the Liver-
pudlians need not be ashamed of the source of the
name by which their town is now known.

Although Henry II. made the estuary of the
Mersey a port of the sea for ever, many years elapsed
before Liverpool grew into notice. Fuller has not a
word to give to it; he ignores the place altogether.
In the reign of William III. it was but a townlet,
slowly making itself. In 1699 the Lyrpool men
thought their place, which had so nobly resisted
Prince Rupert, was worthy of being something more
than a chapel-of-ease to Walton, which was two miles
off: they asserted that Liverpool was large enough
to be a parish of itself. Their assertion was allowed,

and William III. raised the town to the dignity of a parish. From that year, 1699, Liverpool has flourished and extended into several parishes. Its prosperity was of rapid growth. In thirteen years from its being parochialised it had a newspaper, as well as a parish church, of its own. In 1712 the *Liverpool Courant* was started, under the editorship of a Mr. Terry. It appeared twice a week, and was made up less of Lancashire news than of news for Lancashire people, consisting chiefly of abstracts from the London papers. The metropolitan half-sheets of that time were themselves made up of foreign news. There was a wonderfully dry letter from the Hague; a few paragraphs that seemed to be flung together from various corners of Europe, because they were worth nothing; and pleasant accounts of how the Londoners could not stir half a mile beyond the outskirts without being robbed and stripped naked, perhaps brutally murdered, by footpads or mounted highwaymen, whose ultimate inevitable ride in a cart to Tyburn gallows was told in a couple of sharp business-like lines, as a gratifying matter of fact. Such local news as was given in the *Courant* is of interest now, for it enables us to mark the progress of the place and of the port. In one number, containing three days' news, the *Courant* notifies the circumstance of 'one ship arrived,' and of another outward bound for Dublin. The great port of departure for the Irish capital at that time was Parkgate, on the Dee, near Chester. One of the two advertisements in the same number of the *Courant* shows that one lady at least in London had discovered the growing importance of Liverpool, and the new field which it offered to those whose old pastures had ceased to yield means whereby to live. The advertiser in question announces herself as a governess or female teacher from London. Reading and writing are not the only things she undertakes to impart. Young ladies who are now taught, or who at all events believe, that life is one of pleasures and not of duties, may laugh their bright little laugh of scorn at this London governess when she informs the Liverpool ladies, in a somewhat *robe-de-chambre* style of grammar, that ' she learneth young gentlewomen to mark, work, point, make plain work, flourishing, embroidery, and dressing of heads, after the newest mode and to the best advantage.' Excellent woman! and fit to add more witchery to the Lancashire Witches! But those times were singular. Butlers stated among their qualifications that they could play on the flute and violin; clerks had a better chance of attaining to office-stools if they could handle a fiddle with dexterity; and a young nobleman going abroad advertised for half a dozen young fellows who knew the ' hoboy,' and who could discourse music to him in unison as he traversed the seas, ascended the Rhine, or sailed on Como or Lucerne.

When the *Courant* was fairly established, and Liverpool was a parish, the next thing thought necessary and profitable was a dock. The inhabitants got parliamentary permission to construct one, and by 1720 we hear of a hundred and twenty vessels belonging to the port of Liverpool. A century and a half earlier all the shipping of the place consisted only of a few barks, which altogether amounted to little more than a couple of hundred tons. This, however, was in proportion to the population. In the latter half of the sixteenth century, Liverpool counted less than a hundred and forty householders and cottagers. Half that number were employed on the seas. Riches did not come till long after. As late as the middle of last century there was but a single carriage in the town, and that belonged to an old lady. But at that time the timber was ripe out of which scores of carriages were about to be constructed. London had given up the slave-trade; metropolitan merchants had a spice of morality in them. As soon as they discovered readier ways to wealth than by dealing in human flesh, they left the old paths as paths of iniquity, and took to pleasanter, more proper, and more profitable ways. What London left, Liverpool took up with. She had for competitor rich and righteous Bristol, which had been a slave-dealing city as early as the halcyon days when she could kidnap a shipful of Saxon boys and girls, send them over to Ireland for the service and pleasure of Irish chiefs, and receive in return heaps of ill-earned gold. Liverpool, envying modern Bristol, entered heartily into the trade in human flesh. When the first ship sailed from Liverpool to Africa, there was assured hope in the tender hearts of the owners that untold dollars would grow out of the traffic, but they never dreamed of the balances that would be embarrassing their bankers for lack of room wherein to store them. Pactolus flowed through their gardens, depositing gold-dust of a 'blood-red hue,' as the song has it. Wives and daughters were radiant with the wealth made out of the lives of men, women, girls, and boys who had the misfortune to be African and not Liverpool born. The songs and the dances and the luxurious living of Liverpool sprang from the groans and anguish and horrible sufferings of the slaves bought and sold by Liverpool merchants. The traffic had its warmest supporters in the local historians. There is something exquisitely sardonic in the complacent remark of one of these writers, who, even after the traffic was declared to be illegal, said of it, with a lingering love for the abominable thing, that, 'however repugnant it may have been to the feelings of humanity, it was productive of opulence.' Such was the *non olet* sort of morality applied to matters of very ill savour.

Riches constituted excuse and justification. What a pity it would be to check a trade which soon brought a quarter of a million annually into Liverpool, where the merchants subsequently boasted that they alone carried on more than half of that lucrative traffic! For the African and West Indian trade were built those splendid docks which are now used for nobler and not less lucrative purposes. As in Sussex there are still quaint old houses in picturesque but secluded positions, where local tradition says that large fortunes were made by smuggling and a chivalrous disregard of life, so in Liverpool report used to ring the changes upon names whose owners built up colossal wealth by unscrupulous perseverance in the slave-trade. The virtuous George Frederick Cooke, when too drunk to articulate intelligibly on the stage at Liverpool, was met with cries of 'Apology, apology!' The tipsy representative of Richard gravely walked down to the footlights, looked the Liverpool merchants and their ladies in the face, and said, with a haughty scorn and a halting logic, 'Apology! from *me* to *you?* Why, there isn't a brick in your town that is not cemented with the blood of a slave!'

Riches, in the case of Liverpool, did not bring with them any measure of refinement. Down to a comparatively recent period bears were baited at the election of mayors. The ceremony was, perhaps, symbolical of the sort of life his worship was likely to have of it during his year of office. Despite the brutality of these baitings, where the bear was less of a beast than any of his enemies, ladies attended in great numbers, and joined in the procession to church afterwards! It was a mercy that the bear was not made to go to church too. After one of the bull-baits that made lively the Liverpool season of 1782, and at which ladies attended like Spanish donnas at a tauromachia, the beast behaved so well that the biped brutes cast a halter of honour round his throat, and took him lovingly with them into the box circle of the royal theatre! This was the rude time when no lady in Liverpool dared walk abroad with a nosegay in her breast, as was then the fashion. However well attended she might be, she was sure to be assailed by ruffians, who made a point to tear away the flowers and carry off with them any article of value that could be easily secured. From men and manners of this quality has sprung a slang which would fill a dictionary of its own. We do not profess any intimate acquaintance with it; we cannot even guess why a Liverpool man is called a *Dickey-Sam*, or why all over Lancashire a horse is called a *cow*—a word which, everywhere else where slang prevails, is the cant term for a thousand pounds.

In the last century, moral philosophers thought that Liverpool rudeness might be cured by holding the mirror up to Nature on the stage. It was tried with indifferent success and much opposition. The Liverpool stage has gone through all the varieties of fortune, and indeed of misfortune, which belong to the history of provincial theatres generally. The local Thespis of the last century was a Mr. Kearns, who used yearly to bring his strollers for a brief sojourn—and for business—in the great commercial city. Gibson was the first reformer who gave respectability to the profession by opening a permanent little theatre in Drury-lane, as the place was appropriately named. It could *hold* 70l., as the stage slang says; but it seldom or never did; and then the Dissenters bought it, and filled it to the ceiling with people who delighted to hear of Liverpool delinquencies, and how difficult the rich man would find it to make good his entry into the kingdom of heaven. Exactly a hundred years ago, great efforts were being made to bring about what was afterwards accomplished—the erection of a suitable theatre in Williamson-square.

Other theatres have since raised their heads, and with floods of capricious fortune have found it more or less difficult to keep their heads above water.

Williamson-square Theatre is the old classical house, around which hang the more cherished memories of the local drama. Covent Garden Theatrical Fund and the yearly Sunday dinner of the managers are all the better for the bequest left by Gibson, who did not live to see the new house completed. In the latter Miss Farren made her first, and John Palmer, 'plausible Jack,' his last, appearance. On that stage the beautiful future Countess of Derby sprang into bright dramatic life and found herself famous. On the same stage Palmer was stricken down by sudden death; and out of the solemn circumstance has been woven a story which wants nothing but truth to make it instructive. It is amazing to find how falsehood has been deliberately adopted in order to tack a moral on to Palmer's death. At the present moment the falsehood lives, and an attempt is made to show the naughtiness of the drama by the assertion that Palmer fell dead on the stage after uttering the words (in the *Stranger*), 'There is another and a better world.' If this had been true, it would have proved nothing. Palmer died in the performance of his ordinary duty. The truth is that Palmer, in June 1798, left London, depressed by the death of his wife and of the most dearly loved of his sons. This double loss, and the anxiety he felt for the rest of his children, now dependent on him alone, seriously affected his health. On the night he played the Stranger for the last time, he was overwhelmed by the thoughts of those dear dead and of the equally dear living. He had long passed the scene in which the words occur, on uttering which he is said to have instantly fallen dead. He was in the middle of the opening scene in the fourth act, when to a query referring to his wife, put by Steinfort (played by Whitfield), he answered, 'I love her still.' He then replied to the question as to his children, 'I left them at a small town hard by.' The words fell falteringly from his lips, and as soon as Palmer had uttered them he fell dead at Whitfield's feet. This is the simple truth, and it is worth the telling, because it continues to be perverted for the sake of pointing a moral which is altogether inapplicable. Deaths like that of Palmer on the Liverpool stage are not uncommon, but they are not peculiar to members of the dramatic profession. In England, Spiller, Bond, Cassel, Baddeley, Margaret Woffington, and Harley died on the stage or after being attacked upon it by apoplexy or paralysis. Bricourt, Mondory, and Monfleury are among the French actors who have died of similar attacks; and the greatest of all English players, Betterton, died soon after the attack which he experienced on his benefit night, when playing Melantius in the *Maid's Tragedy*.

Neither the stage nor any other amusement ever diverted Liverpool men from that serious end and aim of life—money, and what it brings with it. One's breath is almost taken away when the cotton statistics are being read. Imagination sees the Pelion of it piled upon Ossa, and these upon Olympus, and the mountain still growing in height and breadth, and gold being coined out of it faster than the stamp could give it circulating value at the Mint. No wonder that the old prosperous farmers, who had (in those days it was so) risen from being industrious labourers, put their children in the 'manufacturing line.' The fields thus sent their sons to Liverpool; but Liverpool was not unbeneficial to the fields. Holt states in his *Survey* that a farmer who died in 1795 remembered that the first load of night-soil brought from Liverpool into the country part of the shire was by his father, 'who was paid for carting it the same price that theretofore had been paid for carting away this nuisance and throwing it into the Mersey.' There is a certain sort of propriety in the fact that Lancashire was the first English county in which the potato was grown; for John Hawkins, the dealer in slaves (the article which, with cotton, subsequently enriched Liverpool beyond all conception), got in 1565 the first potatoes for ship provisions from Santa Fé in New Spain. He introduced them into Ireland, whence they came into Lancashire, where curious chance promoted the cultivation of other useful and profitable vegetables. In 1756 we brought over from Canada the French neutrals in the war of the period. They resided some years in Liverpool, and, according to the fashion of their *cuisine* and the sanction of their appetites, they required so many vegetables that the prices went up in the markets for such things. This led to increase of production, and Liverpool was long famous for its good supply of fresh vegetables. In enriching the land for such purposes every sort of experiment was resorted to. Even mussels were applied to the forcing of the earth to bring forth fruits more abundantly. But it was found that mussels helped the land only to one crop, and then left it 'seedy' and weakened. Accordingly this method of farming was called by agricultural wits *dram*-husbandry! Liverpool imports, among a host of other things, that now precious, yet once almost useless drug—madder. The value of madder went up marvellously after the discovery of dyeing cotton a Turkey red. From a mere nominal price it rose to one varying from 50s. to 6l. a cwt. As England imports nearly 300,000 cwt. of madder and madder-root, it might be supposed that Turkey red was your only wear; but madder is applied to more uses than we have space to mention.

Liverpool has its intellectual glories as well as its material possessions. With the city the name of William Roscoe will be for ever connected. He was the son of a tavern-keeper; but the gentleman was innate in him, and his tastes could not but lead him to what he became. He laboured amid the turmoil of Liverpool, its pursuits, passions, triumphs, and calamities, as calmly as if he had been far away from the distracting din of men and their antagonisms; but there is something melancholy in the fact that, after all his intellectual labours, he made shipwreck of his fortunes by embarking and failing in business as a banker. It is painful to contemplate the author of *Lorenzo de' Medici* and *Leo the Tenth*, whose wealth as well as learning had been turned to the best purposes, meekly accepting 100l. a year from the Royal Literary Fund. We cannot say that George Stubbs, the animal painter of Liverpool in the last and beginning of the present century, was to Art what Roscoe was to Literature, but he was the foremost painter of his day in limning a horse; though his excellence was denied by critics who had tried to paint horses and could never succeed.

Liverpool had been for a long time great and flourishing before it was thought worth while to raise it, as it were, to the peerage. The county had furnished names which peers were proud to wear. The Queen is at this day Duchess of Lancaster. There were Earls of Lancaster from 1267, when Henry III. raised his second son, Edmund, to the dignity, till 1345, since which time, till the accession of Henry V., 1413, the ducal title was borne by four more Plantagenets. As Henry V., when Prince of Wales, had been also Duke of Aquitaine, Lancaster, and Cornwall, and Earl of Chester, those titles, at least the foreign ones, merged in the Crown, in which they have ever since remained. We must notice, however, that her Majesty's right to bear the title of Duchess of Lancaster has been hotly disputed by a semi-historical sort of lady, who dated her protest from 123 Kentish Town-road, N.W. Not wisely, but sillily, was the protest made on the occasion of the Queen's last visit to the Continent, when she travelled under the more easily borne dignity of Duchess of Lancaster. Whereupon the alleged true Duchess addressed this manifesto to the public: 'Her Majesty the Queen Victoria having on her visit to the Continent assumed—for it is really assumed' (the pleasing candour of the assurance is charming) '—the name and title of Duchess of Lancaster, I am called upon to contradict it, as I am the only person entitled by descent, by the late Princess of Cumberland and Duchess of Lancaster, who was my mother!

(Signed), Lavinia, Princess of Cumberland and Duchess of Lancaster, known as Mrs. Ryves.' We need hardly say that Mrs. Ryves's mother was the sharp, clever, Warwickshire woman, Olive, the discarded wife of Dominick Serres, the marine painter. Olive asserted that she was the legitimate issue of a marriage between the ultra-Dundreary of his day, Henry, Duke of Cumberland, and a Miss Wilmot. The claim broke down in the Court of Queen's Bench, and there are not two shreds of it that now hold together. Mrs. Ryves, however, is as pertinacious a woman as the Countess of Derwentwater; and if she should present her papers for the consideration of the British Association, the members will treat the communication with all the respect that is due to it.

Liverpool has not had the luck, because it has not had the long-standing, of Lancaster. Its name did not figure in the peerage till 1796. Charles Jenkinson, an individual who had owed his learning to the Charterhouse, his baronetcy to Lord Bute, and his barony of Hawkesbury to having in his youth made a copy of verses on the death of the Prince of Wales, who seized, in fact, every advantage they had brought him to raise himself higher—this Charles Jenkinson, in 1796, was created Earl of Liverpool, after having had what was called 'one leg in the House' for a considerable time. At last he got both in, and he became noted for his graceful wriggling in his exalted position. His two sons succeeded him in the title (the elder being the best known of the three earls as a statesman), and on the death of the younger, in 1851, the dignity became extinct, and Liverpool ceased, after half a century's enjoyment of such greatness, to grace the peerage-books with its highly respectable name.

At the time that Jenkinson was raised to the earldom of Liverpool he had held many offices, and he was accused of being one of 'the King's friends'— in other words, one of his secret and irresponsible advisers. England was then busily discussing the danger of the country, the power of aggressive France, and the worthlessness of our militia: Lord Sheffield expected that chaos was coming. He confided to Lord Auckland his views of what might ensue. 'The country,' he said, 'would be well pleased to part with Pitt as a substitute for Apollo Belvidere. The graceful wriggles of Lord Liverpool might entitle him to be a substitute for Laocoon, Ryder for the Hermaphrodite, Dundas for Mars. The French would not take the Duke of Portland for Jupiter Tonans. The Chancellor and Windham, having some expression of countenance, might be taken as pieces by Raphael; but I know not why I laugh, for I never was less disposed to it. I never was thoroughly alarmed before.' Such was the tone of the times—times having, in some measure, a resemblance to the critical period in which we are living; but Liverpool must needs have been a little nettled to see its brand-new earl so unceremoniously treated. The son and successor of this earl has a stronger hold on history, he having been Prime Minister from 1812, when Mr. Perceval was shot, to 1827, when paralysis disabled and death soon after relieved him. Such was the end. The beginning naturally led to it. Just a hundred years ago this Lord Liverpool was born—in 1770. At the Charterhouse he had his father's career before him. When a young fellow, on the *grand tour*, he was present at the taking of the Bastille, and he wrote accounts of the court, addressed to Pitt, which made the writer worthy of ranking with the most accomplished of modern special correspondents. From that time he was *safe*. His career is well known; his half-brother and successor had none worth mentioning. It is impossible to take up a periodical of the time without seeing in it a letter to Lord Liverpool, either printed or advertised. Letters fell upon him thick as leaves in Vallombrosa. They were upon every possible, and sometimes impossible, subject. Each writer could set the world straight and going, and was willing to show Lord Liverpool the way to do it. If it had been a matter of necessity for Lord Liverpool to read all the letters that were addressed to him, he *must* have died earlier. Had he survived till now, he would not have got through the task; and, everything considered, whatever is is best!

But neither Plantagenets who have been Earls or Dukes of Lancaster, or Jenkinsons who have been Earls of Liverpool, are to be prized by the old and the new town so highly as the Molyneux, who are now Earls of Sefton. When the quiet, proud, little, and aged and poor Breton lady heard some one extolling the Bourbon family for its antiquity, she remarked, with a hand significantly laid on her own bosom, 'There are older families than that of the

Bourbons!' So, what are the Plantagenets? The Molyneux were great men in Lancashire before the first Plantagenet was ever thought of. The 'cross moline, *or*,' on the azure shield, had threatened death before the *planta genista* had grown which the first of his house clapped into his bonnet for a sign. William de Molines was noble before the Conquest. His name is on the roll of Battle Abbey, and what he got thereby is still held in Lancashire by his descendants. One of the fighting sons of this fighting house was knighted by the Black Prince on the field of the battle of Navaret; and this knight's grandson was as meritorious a soldier at Agincourt. To make *him* Constable of Liverpool was only among the meaner consequences of his gallantry. Gallantry was in the very blood of the Molyneux. It was born in them. The two standards taken by a Molyneux at Flodden Field are still among the possessions of this noble Lancashire family. Since that period there has been no derogation. The barony and earldom of Sefton have been fairly and bravely won, and the Molyneux at the coming gathering at Liverpool will have no superior there, at least in what is called *position*. They are among the few families of the realm who can trace their ancestry beyond the Conquest; but Liverpool respects them for better things than mere length of lineage.

We cannot close these desultory reminiscences, called up by the approach of the meeting of the British Association at Liverpool, under the presidency of Professor Huxley, with the stereotyped phrase that there is nothing more to be said, for the subject admits of much more; but we have barely begun to illustrate it, when imperious calls on our space prohibit our going further. The subject is, in fact, inexhaustible, as visitors will find next week when they devote themselves to the discussion of science amid such temptations as will be offered them in one of the most interesting cities of the empire.

XII.
EDINBURGH.
1871.

EDINBURGH.

1871.

THE British Association may be congratulated on once again assembling in the Queen of Cities. Just a thousand years ago there was a hill-fort out of which the present Edinburgh has grown; and if this Queen of Capitals has lost some of her strength, she has increased in beauty. It was because of her strength that Edinburgh was made the capital of the nation. Kings gazed securely from their tower of safety over the thatched houses, till English law-breakers coveted their neighbour's house, his ox and his ass, his maid-servant and his man-servant, and all that was his. Bannockburn may be something for the Scots to be proud of; but, to our thinking, the trophy that they may lawfully prize above all others, and which, we believe, is still in the keeping of the Convener of Trades, is the 'Blue Blanket,' as they popularly call the banner which James III. conferred on the citizens for their effectual aid against Edward IV. Generous King! the privilege he bestowed on the citizens, for the blood they shed and the lives they sacrificed, was, that they might display this banner and shed more of their blood for him whenever he needed their succour! It is true that the Edinburgh people were a fighting people. They slew one another in private quarrel when there was no public excuse for fighting with foreign foes. In religious questions, they exacted life for the sake of conciliation and the love of God! Even a princely wooing brought Edinburgh woe. When the Regency declined to give the little Mary Stuart to little Edward Tudor, the father of the wooer, Henry VIII., sent a force to Edinburgh, and set it on fire in several places at once. This burning was to show, by its light, that the Regency was wrong,—just as Elizabeth subsequently proved, by stronger reasons than Knox ever produced, that Edinburgh and reformed tenets were logically correct, by using the argument of Protestant culverins successfully against Popish Leith and its artillery. We suppose that it is a fond boast of our Northern friends that when the first regular actors appeared in Edinburgh, in A.D. 1599, one Shakespeare was among them. It is somewhat truer that, four years later, James VI. annexed England to Scotland —for Scotland reaped the first profits—and it is undeniably true that James has all the merit of having inaugurated the first British Association that ever assembled in Auld Reekie.

Edinburgh was the cradle and home of a Philosophical Society centuries before the British Association paid it a visit. The President of the earlier Association was a King, of whom, however, it must be confessed that some men said there was in him less of Solomon than of Sir Fool. More than two centuries and a half have elapsed since James I. (of

England) presided over the body of Edinburgh professors who met in the Chapel Royal of Edinburgh Castle in 1617. King James was then on his second and last excursion to his native dominions. He sojourned at Stirling, Perth, St. Andrews, Stirling, again, and finally in Edinburgh. In the Scottish metropolis he called the philosophers about him. The meeting combined the pursuit of Social Science with the study of Nature. For example, one subject thoroughly discussed was, 'Ought Sheriffs and other inferior Magistrates to be Hereditary?' The question was one of great national interest at the time. The National Senate had taken it up, and James was opposed to magistracy being hereditary like monarchy. The professors who took the royal view of the case were supported by the outspoken opinions of the King. The question was decided in the negative. This did not legally abolish hereditary jurisdiction, but it was a step towards it, by proclaiming that such jurisdiction of the inferior magistracy ought to be abolished. There happened to be standing behind the King's chair in the Chapel Royal the hereditary sheriff of Clydesdale, the Marquis of Hamilton. The monarch turned to him, with an anticipatory feeling of triumph, and exclaimed, 'James, you see your cause is lost; and all that can be said for it is clearly answered and refuted.'

The next question, or thesis, at this early British Association was scientific,—' On the Nature of Local Motion.' In the discussion, the supporters of the thesis quoted so largely from Aristotle that James made the not very profound remark, ' These men know the mind of Aristotle as well as he did himself when alive.' The opponents of the thesis took this for sarcasm; the supporters took it for praise. Both sides were perfectly satisfied.

The third and last thesis broached in this philosophical assembly was, 'Concerning the Origin of Fountains or Springs.' Only three-quarters of an hour was allowed for the discussion; but as King James disputed the opinions of respondents and opponents alike, the limit was not observed. The royal President, however, was gratified at having had the opportunity of showing himself wiser than all the world beside. This gratification added heartiness to the manner in which James invited the philosophers to sup with him. After the banquet he displayed his wisdom the second time; he went through the disputations again and again. Finally, he made puns on the philosophers' names: they are so very commonplace as not to be worth repeating. The meanest capacity would have made as good out of such names as Adamson, Fairlie, Reid, King, Young, and Sands. We deferentially offer one sample of the royal wit. 'Mr. Reid,' said the King, 'need not be red with blushing for his acting this day!' Elated by his combined wit and philosophy, the royal chairman declared that he would be godfather to the College of Edinburgh, and that it should be called the College of King James. 'I will give it,' said the King, 'a royal god-bairn gift to enlarge its revenues.' Finally, the monarch fired a parting pun at wise and reticent Professor Charteris, to this effect: ' His name,' said James, 'agrees with his nature. Charters contain much matter, yet say nothing, and nevertheless put a great deal into men's minds.' The philosophers, delighted with the monarch's follies, hired a poet to immortalise the royal wit. The poet, accordingly, put all those bad puns into worse verse, and the Association broke up in a state of general jubilation.

Should the members of the present Association make an excursion to the old Culross coalworks, on the shore of the Firth of Forth, which, in ancient, profitable, active times, were worked by the proprietor, Sir George Bruce, they will only follow an example set by James, and will find no such grounds for fright as he is traditionally said to have done. The works extended beneath the sea to a little island, through which they were carried upwards; from this issue the coal was shipped for transportation. James was conducted through this curious passage; but when he came out upon the little island, and saw nothing but waves around him, he was so frightened that he began to shout *Treason!* lustily. Had there been any design upon him he might have been disposed of below. He was with difficulty pacified, as he saw a pinnace moored close by, and he was told that it was for the purpose of carrying him and the gentlemen with him to Sir George Bruce's mansion to dinner. 'Very good,' said the King; 'let us all go straight to the collier's house!' This rudely condescending wit put him in good-humour, and there was merriment with abounding cheer in the house which had been once the hospitable mansion of Bruce.

When all the royal and philosophic and, occasion-

T

ally, roistering excursions had come to an end, the Chancellor Dunfermline addressed a few farewell words to his Majesty,—and we trust that something like them in sentiment may be appropriately addressed to the members of the forthcoming Congress at their breaking up: 'In all the time of your Majesty's remaining in this kingdom, in sae many great companies, and sae many noblemen and great personages of twa nations convened, never ane action, word, or appearance of any discord, variance, or offence betwix any of the nations with other, for whatsomever cause. I doubt gif ever the like has been seen at sic occasion of so frequent a meeting of men, strangers, and unknown to each other.' May the like unanimity prevail next week! To help to that end, let no man argue that Mary Stuart was a murderess, that Wallace was a Welshman, that Robert Bruce was a genuine Yorkshire Tyke, that Ossian was Mr. Macpherson, or that the famous book of the Dean of Lismore refers to Irish and not Scottish subjects.

In the last year of the sixteenth century there was a Scientific Association assembled in St. Mary's College, St. Andrews, where one subject was discussed which spiritualists would not even now consider a folly, or count as lost time the period necessary for discussing it. The subject proposed by the bold presbyter, Andrew Melville, was, 'Whether bodies could be transported or transformed by divining, or by diabolical force of witches; whether souls could be temporarily released from bodies; and whether bodies transported or transformed, having the resemblance of a corpse, senseless and motionless, as if the soul were banished, was a simple lethargy, or a certain evidence of execrable demonomania.' Reduced to simple elements, this subject presented no difficulty at all. The question was, whether a person in a fit, trance, or lethargy was so by natural infirmity or by evil spiritual power. There were disputants who supported the demoniacal view, and others who saw only natural causes for a seeming unnatural suspension of sense. Every disputant derided his adversary, and held his own argument to be above dispute. But a philosophical meeting implies disputation. Disputation, to be effective, demands as good listeners as speakers. When Curion, the Piedmontese reformer, read his treatise, 'De Amplitudine beati Regni Dei,' to a company of Calvinist sages in Geneva, they heard him without anger, although (and the *although* seems a sarcasm) his object was to prove that the predestinate to eternal bliss numbered infinitely more than the reprobate. There was a time when Calvinistic philosophy in Scotland and in Holland would not have listened patiently to such a theory. But the stoutest Presbyterian in the North would now probably agree with Bishop Reynolds—yes, even with a bishop —that God would rather have His trees for fruit than for fuel. Indeed, we are all getting very much of the school of Socrates, in so far as one part of the confession of faith of all humble and earnest men is, *Scio quod nescio!* This confession of Socrates, if it be unacceptable because of the confessor, may recommend itself to the orthodox when they remember that it was the acknowledgment of St. Jerome to the religious philosophers to whom he addressed himself.

Lord Brougham's Autobiography has recently demonstrated that there was a time when philosophy in the North leant more towards Seneca than Socrates; that is to say, it was rather proud of its wisdom, while it adopted, to a certain extent, the teaching of Seneca, that to be occasionally tipsy was by no means an unsalubrious circumstance. In some philosophical disputations a phrase has been caught by an adversary in order to mar the fame of the utterer of it. We could never understand the anger of Bishop Sandford against an old Scottish physician of his day who, with what is called the mild appearance of an old lion with the toothache, expressed, says the prelate, 'this charitable wish:' 'I wish,' said he, 'that more people would die of diseases in the spleen, that men might know what purposes the spleen is intended to answer.' Nothing would have tempted the Bishop to trust himself in the hands of one whom he looked upon as an ogre. The wish was stigmatised as 'truly professional.' It was truly wise, though not wisely expressed. A knowledge of the uses of the spleen has saved more lives than were sacrificed when men died of splenetic disease, and doctors knew not wherefore. Observation and discussion have greatly furthered this result.

To conclude the subject of science, we may state that its light was long maintained in brilliancy and usefulness by the Royal Society of Edinburgh. That Society was, perhaps, in its own most brilliant and useful period towards the close of the last century, when the publication of its *Transactions* challenged and won the attention of the world of philosophy. At the same time, some of the professors in the University who figured honourably and to excellent purpose in those *Transactions* received their appointments as professors for very singular reasons. For instance, Lord Robert Manners, second son of that Marquis of Granby who in his day was on as many battle-fields as signboards, was killed in action, April 12, 1782, —that was the great naval action, when Rodney beat the Count de Grasse, saved Jamaica, and ruined for a time the naval power of France and Spain. It was the fight in which the Ville de Paris, of 112 guns, struck to Hood—the only first-rate man-of-war which, up to that date, had been taken and carried into port. Lord Robert Manners was among the valiant captains there who were mortally wounded. Till he died he was attended with infinite care by his ship's surgeon, a Dr. Blair. The grateful ducal family of Rutland would not allow Dr. Blair's services to go unrewarded. With generous alacrity, they importuned the Government to do something for him, and at their solicitation the Crown actually founded for Blair a Professorship of Practical Astronomy in the University of Edinburgh! The naval surgeon and physician had seen enough of the stars to know Orion's Belt from Charles's Wain; but had he been ignorant of both it would not have much mattered, as the Astronomical Professorship was a sort of nominal office, without any charge. But if Dr. Blair was not a practical astronomer, he was an experimental philosopher of great repute, and his experiments and observations on the refrangibility of light excited considerable interest in his own day, and may be read with profit even now, when philosophers and experiments have equally increased. Visitors and members of the Association may turn to Dr. Blair's papers in the *Transactions* in the Library, if claret-cup and the consumption of other creature comforts leave them the leisure—and the inclination. Hospitality has always had a cheerful home in the Scottish metropolis.

The splendour and the hospitality have occasionally been themes for mocking rhymers. They eagerly seized the opportunity when Edinburgh was running mad at the idea of gloriously receiving George IV., now half a century ago. From one of the pieces that then went about in manuscript we take a verse or two,—the suggestions in which are made in good-humoured ridicule of the king-worship then prevailing in the city. 'F.S.A.s of Scotland' are not the only bodies who will understand the allusions:

> 'Make your peers o' high degree,
> Crouching bow on bended knee,
> Greet him wi' a " *Wha wants me ?*"
>   Sawney, now the King's come!
>
> Show him a' your buildings braw,
> Your Castle, College, Briggs, and a',
> Your jail and royal *Forty-twa*,
>   Sawney, now the King's come!
>
> And when he rides Auld Reekie through,
> To bless you wi' a kingly view,
> Let him smell your *Gardy loo*,
>   Sawney, now the King's come!'

This was satirising, with happy humour, circumstances which no longer exist in Edinburgh. Other satirists wanting such themes have attacked what should have been above assault. It is a singular fact that universal as the respect of the wise has been for the philosophy and philosophers of Edinburgh, both have been violently satirised, and that, too, by a Scotsman! Mr. James Hannay, at least, had the courage of his opinions. He put his name to his winged darts, and here are two or three samples of the pungent matter with which they were tipped. Laughing at the phrase, 'Modern Athens,' he exclaims:

> 'You call this Athens! Well, the stranger sees
> Cleon, Hyperbolus, and such as these;
> But where are Plato, Phocion, Sophocles?'

And again :

> 'Why *Modern* Athens? That the world may know
> How 'tis you hate the ancient language so?
> * * * * * *
> "Athens, forsooth!" the wandering tourist growls;
> "I see no olive, and too many owls!"
> * * * * * *
> Pompous the boast, and yet a truth it speaks:
> A Modern Athens, fit for modern Greeks!'

In this way a clever son of the soil spits, as it were, on his native heather; but even he could not point an epigram against his country's hospitality. For this virtue it has always been famous; occasionally it has been eccentric or picturesque, especially in the mediæval days.

In connection with the Scottish hospitality of a bygone time a curious story is told, very characteristic of that Earl of Murray who gave such sumptuous dinners during his 'little day.' The Earl entertained, in 1554, the Patriarch of Apulia. The host displayed on his sideboard, not only all his famous silver plate, but a wonderful variety of Venetian glass, rare and costly beyond calculation. In the course of the banquet, the Earl's servants swept to the ground the whole of that gorgeous production from the Adriatic. At the accident, the whole company gave expression to their deep regret. The accident, however, was but seeming; it had taken place by the Earl's command. He ordered the fragments to be cleared away, and a new and richer supply of Venetian glass to be placed on the sideboard. The guests were lost in ecstasy. Such a trick in our days would brand the perpetrator of it as a very vulgar person—in popular phrase, a snob. In the succeeding century, magnificence and meanness were in close combination. In Ray's *Itinerary*, 1661, the author says: 'In the best Scottish houses, even in the king's palaces, the windows are not glazed throughout, but the upper part only. The lower have two wooden shuts or folds, to open at pleasure, and admit the fresh air.'

The capital, however, was famous in that century for the magnificence of its public shows. Our own sovereign now enters and leaves Edinburgh with as little ceremony as can save dignity. It was otherwise in the old days. When Charles I. visited the capital of Scotland, his retinue counted by hundreds of noble riders. His baggage was barbaric in splendour and in quantity. His welcome was an allegory, with a nymph in sea-green at the head of it, and the Municipal Council, with a bowl full of double golden angels, at the tail of it. The King laughed merrily at this conclusion, as he might have laughed at the wit in the tail of an epigram. He ceased, however, to be mirthful when the Marquis of Hamilton appropriated the whole of the golden angels to himself, by virtue of his office as Master of the Horse! Kings, in Great Britain at least, were often the victims of their greedy officers, whose posts were in profitable connection with privileges. When George I. came to this country, he was old enough and experienced enough not to be surprised at anything. When he first sat down to ombre, at Kensington Palace, the Groom Porter placed at the King's elbow a bowl full of guineas to play with. The courtly official then dipped his hand to the bottom of the bowl, and having brought it up to the surface, palm uppermost, he carried off the gold that lay upon the palm as his perquisite. The King stared, but he consoled himself by the winnings which he made with the guineas that were left. The bowl was piled up with them, and King George was looking on them with delight, when, to his utter astonishment, he saw the Groom Porter walk off with the whole, as his fee! The proverb of 'working for the King of Prussia' implied a bad thing enough—working *gratis* for somebody else; but for an English King to play that another somebody else might pocket all the King of England's winnings seemed to George of Hanover to divest gaming not only of its delights, but of all excuse for playing at all.

The Marquis of Hamilton, as Master of the Horse, appropriated all money-gifts made to Charles while the King was in the saddle and the Master was at his side. Perhaps the King felt it a greater calamity to have to listen to and answer speeches made at every turn by allegorical personages, including all Olympus and Arcadia, with Parnassus and nine pretty boys seated about it, dressed as nymphs, and trying to look like the Muses. The ceremonies lasted for days, and culminated by the King's coronation in the Abbey Kirk of Holyrood. Puritanism was much scandalised by the presence of a crucifix, and by the conduct of bishops as they passed it. 'They were seen,' says a contemporary writer, 'to bow their knee and back, which with their habit was noted, and bred gret fear of the in-bringing of popery.' It is observable that, at the 'Riding of the Parliament,' Charles rode in the robe-royal of James IV.; and he was much admired. On the following day he headed a procession on foot, walking so fast that he threw his footguard into a perspiration, and elicited from spectators the remark that there was 'nae better footman than the King in the whole city.' There was some admixture of unhappy incidents in this visit,—foreshadowings of sorrows to come, and present fatality to darken the passing hour. A little matter came of it which should interest the Zoological Section. One Graham was licensed to take a camel belonging to the King throughout Scotland, that it might be shown to the people ' by tack of drum or sound of trumpet.' This was done for edification. The keeper of this embryo menagerie was recommended to the protection of the authorities, while he himself was enjoined to be modest, and shut the camel up on Sundays! One may smile at people wondering at the sight of a camel; but they who can remember the entry of the giraffe into Paris, the capital of civilisation, will confess that Esquimaux could not have exhibited greater signs of wonder than the Parisians did on that remarkable occasion. The reference to the retired life of the camel on Sundays leads us to suggest that strangers 'in the land where Fingal fought and Ossian sung' had, perhaps, better refrain from being too hilarious on any day in any of the Sections. Joyous approval of what they may hear or see may seem to some spirits in Edinburgh as grave an offence as it seemed recently to a minister in Kincardineshire. The good man was addressing an audience of children — several hundreds — and they loudly laughed and applauded; whereupon he checked both by telling them that there was no laughing or clapping of hands in heaven, and that such manifestations were 'inconsistent with religion.'

The sanitary condition of the capital at this time was very unsatisfactory, but it was somewhat better than it had been in the previous reign. It may be safely asserted that at no period was the sarcasm of 'sweet Edinbro'' more applicable to the northern metropolis than in the last years of the reign of James I. of England. The offended sense of the nobility and persons of nice feeling at last revolted against it. They complained that they could not get to their homes or ascend the stairs except through a mass of filth of every odious description. The fact must have been, what they declared it to be, 'shameful and beastly,' for it is sickening only to read the details, and the pen refuses to write the loathsome record. The cleaner-minded persons expressed their wrath not only for purity's sake, but partly for that of the honour of the city. 'Strangers,' they said, 'beholding the same, are constrained, with reason, to give out many disgraceful speeches against this burgh, calling it a puddle of filth and uncleanness, the like whereof is not to be seen in no part of the world.' They threatened 'rather to make choice of lodgings in the Canongate and Leith, or some other parts about the town, than to abide the sight of this shameful uncleanliness and filthiness.'

Edinburgh flourished in spite of all impediments and obstructions. The '15 rebellion did not much affect its prosperity, but the young Chevalier, who thirty years later flashed such temporary brilliancy on Edina, left her all the more gloomy by the contrast of what followed. After the suppression of the outbreak of 1745 the old capital did not recover itself for some time. At the end of eighteen years Edina started again, with recovered energy, beauty, and strength. The progress made between 1763 and 1789 was astounding. It is carefully shown, in a work by the well-known Hugh Arnott, published in the latter year. We cull a few examples out of a mass affording hundreds. Between 1763 and 1786 the valued rents of houses in Edinburgh paying cess, or land-tax, had doubled! In twenty years the revenue of the Post Office had nearly quadrupled; and that arising from distilling of spirits had increased more than twentyfold—that is to say, in round numbers, from *plus* four thousand to *plus* ninety thousand pounds sterling! A half share in an Edinburgh newspaper, in 1740, was worth 35*l.*; in 1763 its value was 100*l.*;

in 1783 it was a bargain at 1300*l*. In a score of years, four-wheeled carriages paying duty had quadrupled; but in the same period the number of boys in the High School had not increased in proportion. It had risen from 200 to 500. 'In 1763,' says Mr. Arnott, referring to progress which seems to us to indicate something less satisfactory, 'people of quality and fashion lived in houses which in 1783 are inhabited by tradesmen and people in humble and ordinary life. The Lord President Craig's house is at present occupied by a saleswoman of old furniture. Lord Drunmore's house was lately left by a *chairman*, who lived in it since his lordship, for want of proper accommodation. The house of the Duke of Douglas, at the Union, is now possessed by a wheelwright.' In one sense the poor did not gain by the increase of wealth. The sole dancing assembly-room, in 1763, made over all its profits to the charity workhouse. In 1783 there were three such rooms: none of them contributed a shilling to the workhouse. Charity seems to have gone out with the graceful minuet, and thoughtlessness to have come in with romping country-dances. 'Dress,' says Mr. Arnott, in 1789, 'particularly by the men, is much neglected; and many of them reel from the tavern, drenched in wine, to an assembly of as elegant and beautiful women as any in Europe.' It is a grave Scottish witness who makes this deposition.

The New Town of Edinburgh was begun little more than a century ago. The first stone, in accordance with Mr. Craig's plan, was laid in 1767. That plan was carried out by 1815; but a fresh extension began in 1801, and this was accomplished in 1826, though Edinburgh does not cease to grow. Very difficult of access was the old city. In the year 1637, Taylor, the Water-Poet, published his *Carriers' Cosmographie*, for the information of all persons desiring to travel from or to London, by land or by water. In that curious tract we are told that 'Shipping from Scotland are to bee found at the *Armitage* or *Hermitage* below St. Katherines.' Further, 'At *Galley* Key, passage for Men and Carriage for Goods may bee had from *London* to *Barwicke.*' There does not appear to have been any regularly organised means of travelling by land to such remote parts. York was the farthest point that could be reached by any other means than by a man riding his own horse. 'The carriers of *Yorke*,' says Taylor, 'with some other parts neere *Yorke* (within that county), doe lodge at the signe of the Bell, or Bellsaloage without Ludgate; they come every fridaie, and goe away on saturday or munday. A Footeposte from *Yorke* doth come every second thursday to the Rose and Crowne in Saint Johns street.' Letters passed once a fortnight in this way, but more frequently once a week, by other means, to Edinburgh. 'Those that will send any letter to *Edenborough*,' says the same work, 'that so they may be conveyed to and fro to any parts of the Kingdome of Scotland, the poste doth lodge at the signe of the King's Armes (or the Cradle), at the upper end of Cheapside, from whence every monday any that have occasion may send.' There was one other resource, but it was hardly more promising than the above. 'All those that will send letters to the most parts of the habitable world, or to any parts of our King of Great Britaine's Dominions, let them repaire to the Generall Post-Master, *Thomas* Withering, at his house in *Sherburne* Lane, neere *Abchurch.*' How often the post went to Edinburgh is altogether uncertain.

And when a traveller reached that city, at the above period, he had nothing before him, picturesque as the view was, to be compared with the magnificence which greets the eye to-day. Hammond L'Estrange, who visited it at the period last indicated, describes the city as being 'but one entire street, very spacious, seated on the prone and descending part of a hill, protended in a right line from the Castle to Holyrood House.' The members of the Association and visitors will be able to see this cradle of the royal metropolis still, as distinctly as travellers see the old hunting-lodge on to which has grown the stately, yet over-praised, palace of Versailles.

In 1651 a certain Adam Woodcock obtained a license to run the first coach that was ever started between Edinburgh and Leith. In 1686 there was one coach only from Edinburgh to London, whence, after a season of rest and repair, it returned. It was a fashionable conveyance. Prelates and peers travelled by it, while younger sons and subalterns, with ladies of various quality, went by the wagon and played forfeits in the straw. In Fountainhale we read that in 1686 the Archbishop of St. Andrews and Bishop of Edinburgh departed for London 'in the *retour* coach, which had the week before brought down the Marquis of Athole and Sir William Bruce from thence.'

In 1763 there was still but one stage-coach between Edinburgh and London. It set out once a month, and took from a fortnight to eighteen days, according to the season, to complete the journey. A score of years later, sixty stage-coaches, requiring hundreds of horses for the service, were running to and from Edinburgh and London in the course of the month. The journey was then accomplished in sixty hours. When 'coaching' was about to cease, the road was traversed by the mails in about forty to eight-and-forty hours. Though they sometimes went fourteen miles an hour, stoppages and stiff bits of road very considerably reduced the average,—that is, to something like ten miles an hour. A single night or day, through which a man may sleep or read, now suffices to make the change from the Thames to the Firth of Forth.

Edinburgh, it is well known, gives its ducal title to the second son of the Queen, but it is not generally known that there is a Prince of Scotland. 'The Prince of Scotland?' it will be asked; 'who is he?' He is the Duke of Rothesay, Prince and Steward of Scotland,—in other words, the Prince of Wales. The principality has existed since the time that the eldest son of the King of Scotland was called by the above ducal title. It is true that historians differ as to whether the principality was founded in the fourteenth or fifteenth century. The Deed of Erection, as it was called, has perished, but the principality survives. The revenue and the land have nearly altogether disappeared, like the deed. The two together would now hardly pay for the kilt which the Prince wore when a boy, when he was announced by his Scotch title to his father, on the occasion of the birthday of the latter. Prince Albert was probably not so astonished as he is said to have been, however surprised he may have feigned to be. He knew his son's titles, and was doubtless aware that there was then, as there is now, an account in the Bank of England standing in the name of 'The Prince of Scotland,'— meaning thereby the Duke of Rothesay, that is, the Prince of Wales. The account is an extremely small one. The eminent stockbrokers in Threadneedle-street, who are in some way intrusted with the administration of this account, can accomplish all requisite duties in devoting five minutes to it annually. We may add here, that the especial title of Prince of Scotland (standing so in the Bank of England books) is included by the heralds in the general designation, 'Prince of the United Kingdoms of Great Britain and Ireland.' The Scottish titles of the Heir Apparent are Duke of Rothesay, Earl of Garrick, Baron of Renfrew, Lord of the Isles, and Steward of Scotland. The title of Duke of Edinburgh, under which designation Prince Alfred first took his seat as a peer of the realm in 1866, was created for Prince Frederick (son of George, Prince of Wales, afterwards George II.) in 1726, before his father came to the throne. Prince Frederick's son inherited it; but when that son, as George III., ascended the throne, the title became merged in the Crown. The Crown—that is, the King—conferred it on his brother Henry, but in rather a diminished state. Prince Henry was created Duke of Gloucester and Edinburgh,—a com-

U

pound title, to which his son succeeded, the good-natured duke who died childless in 1834, but memorable for leaving no more debts than he did children. Thirty-two years later, the Queen revived the title of Duke of Edinburgh in the person of her second son, the sailor-prince, whose presence was once hoped for at the meeting of the Association in the capital of Midlothian, which will be inaugurated by the Chairman, Sir William Thomson, on Wednesday next, the 2d of August.

And all will not end with the following week. The celebration of the Centenary of Walter Scott takes place in August, to the close of which month the Loan Exhibition, in commemoration of the poet and novelist, will remain open, in the galleries of the Royal Scottish Academy. Everything that could illustrate that glory of Scotland will be found there. Portraits, from boyhood to the brink of the grave; objects that he used to handle or to look upon; views of localities which the presence of such noble intellect sanctifies; with printed and manuscript copies of those works, the composition of which makes the world rejoice in the author's birthday, a hundred years ago, when he was born in that old College Wynd, for which pilgrims to the shrine will now look in vain.

XIII.
BRIGHTON.
1872.

BRIGHTON.

1872.

WHEN William de Warren entered into possession of the loot in land which was conferred on him by William the Conqueror, he might have rendered infinite service to the British Association, which is just about to meet at Brighton. Warren, however, neglected to do anything for posterity. He was too much occupied, that greedy Norman, with arranging his *Sussex* estate, and wearing proudly his new title of Earl of *Surrey*. There were eighteen of those earls, from the Conquest down to the year 1660, when the title of the Earl of Surrey was merged in the superior dignity of Duke of Norfolk.

What would the British Association have thanked the first Earl for? Why, for a fair account of his Brighton estate, and of the legends which had sprung out of it, from the time the early Sussex lover put on additional touches of woad, before he took his gift of some of the ripe fruit of the country, hips and haws, to the thick-tressed lady of his love, down to the era when Earl Godwin's boys took headers from their father's gilded barge. He might have included anything he could collect of the intervening time, when Romans had their villas here, and British youths, ashamed of their paint, adapted themselves to the language, costume, and the very worst manners of those irresistible foreigners.

What a discussion might have followed the production of such an early history! And what a disputing of facts! For there is nothing so apt for dispute as your fact. The very air and climate of Brighton have been rudely treated by the doubters and deniers of most things. Dr. Wigan, the kinsman of the actor so named, not only wrote on the Duality of the Mind, but on the Triality (if we may coin a word), the *threefold* excellence, of the Brighton atmosphere. But when Sir James Clark, on Climate, just suggested that the West Cliff was 'somewhat damp,' how deeply were the scientific men of Brighton grieved at his ignorance or audacity! The question being undecided, we hope it will come before one of the Sections. It is one easy to deal with, as statistics lend themselves to the general proving of anything.

Meanwhile leaving prehistoric times and much-vexed questions to the archæologists and other persons interested therein, we may remark that Brighton has not uninterruptedly progressed to its present condition. It has had its downs as well as its ups. When, in the reign of Charles I., it numbered five hundred families—over two thousand inhabitants— it held up its head with any town in the county of Sussex. The civil wars and the sea between them caused this pride to have a fall. Population decreased, and year after year the waves swallowed up a bit of land and two or three houses. It seemed to be nobody's business to check the inroad of the waters; and, indeed, when an occasional Good Samaritan presented himself with a plan for obviating the calamity, the easy-going people looked on him as a troublesome person. They soon found the ocean far the more troublesome of the two.

In the first quarter of the last century the sea, which had so often before swept the little town by sudden assaults, subsequently retiring, had permanently advanced to its very foot. Thence it made inroads into the streets, house after house falling upon their undermined foundations. It is no matter for surprise that lodgings in the little low-roofed houses were cheap; yet we may wonder at the tariff which let two sitting-rooms, a couple of bedrooms, and 'offices' for 5s. a week! A regular season for visitors began about the year 1736. It began as soon as the Sussex roads were passable; roads which were deservedly more ill-spoken of than any of the other highways of England. To Dr. Richard Russell the merit is generally awarded of having what is called 'founded' Brighton as a sanitary resort. In the middle of last century he certainly pointed out the advantages of the medical use of sea-water. To Brighton forthwith repaired not only the robust goddesses of the day, but the more fragile beauties who were 'fine by defect, and delicately weak.' A rather feeble epigrammatist advised swains to avoid the double dangers of those combined sirens, lest they should have to endure 'a pain from some bright sparkling eye, which Russell's skill can't cure.' A crabbed censor, at the same time, divided the visitors into 'Silken Folly and Bloated Disease.'

The town was not extensive even at a later period. It took something more than a doctor to invent fashionable Brighton. About a century ago Brighton consisted of half a dozen streets, several lanes, and a couple of 'spaces surrounded by houses, called by the inhabitants "squares,"'—that is to say, Castle-square and Little Castle-square. It had its defamers. In spite of the fun of looking at patients drinking sea-water, in spite of Brighton's primitive and harmless gaieties, some people could see nothing in it. William Gilpin had an eye to appreciate the picturesque fishing fleet abroad upon the waters, but in 1774 he calls Brighthelmstone a 'disagreeable place,' and adds, 'There is scarcely an object in it or near it of nature or of art that strikes the eye with any degree of beauty.' Just ninety years have expired since George, Prince of Wales, was first attracted to the spot which was odious to Gilpin. A piece of land which then cost four pounds would sell now for more than as many hundreds. The coming of the Prince did not immediately cause any extensive improvement in the town. In 1787 a lady of local celebrity complained that, as the doors of most of the houses opened directly into the sitting-rooms, it was impossible to be 'out' to any importunate visitor. The doorways, moreover, were low, and there was often a step down into the parlour. People then lived almost under ground. *Now*, in the lofty palaces fronting the sea, they look over the ocean from their seat in the clouds. We sympathise with all the Brighton historians who deplore the fact that tasteless architecture has, in the present century, made of the place a mere 'London-on-Sea,' instead of a beautiful and appropriate Queen of Watering-places. We agree with Mr. Erredge, a local historian deserving the highest praise, that a quaint old country-town High-street is more picturesque than the most uniform of streets and squares. There was a time when the local manners had a rough pleasantness about them, corresponding with the primitive simplicity of the place. When Miles (or Smoaker, as the Prince of Wales, and therefore everybody, called him) was chief bathing-man, he once saw his Royal Highness swimming too far, as Miles thought, out at sea. Miles hailed 'Mr. Prince' to come back. The Prince struck farther out. Thereupon Smoaker dashed in after him, and brought his Royal Highness back by the ear, exclaiming as he thus towed the princely freight, 'I arn't a-goen to let the King hang me for letten the Prince of Wales drown hisself; not I, to please nob-budy, I can tell 'e.' The Prince forgave the act in consideration of its motive. In remembrance of it he founded the Smoaker Stakes; and when they were first run for in 1806, the Prince of course won the race with his own horse Albion.

We have spoken above of the increase in the price of land in Brighton. The increase in the cost of medical attendance may be illustrated by a curious fact. In 1580 there was one solitary medical man in the then village, and we are rather surprised to find one there at such a period. His name was Matthews. There has come down to us his rate of charges in cases of midwifery. For attendance at

Portslade and Rottingdean, 5s.; at Blatchington, 3s. 6d.; in Brighthelmstone, 2s. 6d. The charges were sufficiently high, if we take into consideration the change in the value of money.

When Dr. Russell persuaded nervous persons to feel unwell, and then, having drunk Brighton water, to fancy themselves better, he was a little like Pope's inefficient artist friend in the *Guardian*, who, not being able to draw portraits after the life, used to paint faces at random, and look out afterwards for people whom he might persuade to be like them. Let not the British Association be deluded by the idea that Brighton was made by *any* medical man's discovery of the efficacy of its mineral wells and its salt waters. Let them not be led away by the assurance that it was invented by the Prince of Wales. Brighton was set upon the legs of prosperity by one of the silliest and most vicious of princes—that Duke of Cumberland who was brother to George III. The Duke was residing exactly ninety years ago at Grove House, where the young Prince of Wales, in a sort of youthful frolic, paid him a visit and 'stayed the night.' The consumption of candles and of clay to stick them in for the general illuminating process to do the Prince honour was enormous enough to raise the price in tallow and give a rise in the brick-market. If the Duke had not been residing there, the Prince would probably never have gone down to old Brighthelmstone. Let him have all the credit he can get by it. We cannot deny that soon after the princely meeting there was a significant increase in the publication of local guide-books, illustrated and otherwise, with elaborate instructions how to get to Brighton, how to pass your time there with the least amount of inevitable boredom (for one *does* weary of Thalatta after a while), and how to get safely home again. One at least of those guide-books was written in so magniloquent a style that a monthly reviewer thought it *must* have come from the pen of Mr. Christie the auctioneer—a remark which we hope will not do violence to the sensitive feelings of that gentleman's representatives.

To the Prince of Wales, no doubt, the town was and is greatly indebted. He bought in 1783 a small house of Mr. Kempe. It was the seed out of which grew that serio-comic Chinese pumpkin, or series of pumpkins, called the Marine Pavilion. That unparalleled edifice was like the Eternal City in one circumstance, namely, it was not built in a day. It was begun in 1784. Sanguine people, who jumped to conclusions too readily, looked at the work in 1787 and said, ' Behold, the Wonderful Thing is completed!' They were deceived. It took a portion of two centuries—adding turnip to turnip, bulb to bulb, and wings to centres—before Brighton could boast that the Thing was finished. It was then a very large Vauxhall Kiosk in a very small Vauxhall Garden. It was a Lodge in the Garden, and it left no space for cucumbers. Built in a hollow, and only one story high, it was sheltered from the pitiless winds, and it was convenient for royal highnesses not clever at getting up-stairs. Moreover, it had a sea-front, from which wicked calumny has said that the sea could not be seen. This is false. If a person in a first-floor room stood tiptoe on a chair he might catch sight of a wave, if he and the wave were only tall enough. But, in sober truth, a panoramic view of the wide expanse of ocean, to say nothing of the land, might be enjoyed by any of the Pavilion chimney-sweepers. They alone possessed the privilege which kings and kaisers felt obliged to forego. The master of the marine palace looked upon it as a *chef-d'œuvre* of architecture; but the first architectural masterpiece of which Brighton long boasted was not the palace, but the palace stables. It was only by degrees that the Prince found 'elbow-room' for himself and household by adding thereto such adjacent land as he could purchase. When something like a comfortable place was made of it, the royal proprietor grew weary of his splendid toy, and only assiduous housemaids prevented the spider from weaving his web in the princely apartments.

The worthiest action on the part of his Royal Highness during his residence was his receiving into it, with their goods, the family of a burnt-out baker. The basest—in which his next two brothers joined—was raising money on post-obit bonds, by which the cash received was to be repaid within six months after a certain event. As the certain event was the death of George III., the transaction had a treasonable tinge in it. The lenders of the money had a direct interest in the old King's death. The sooner he died the sooner they would be paid. With that consideration in their mind, they were incompetent to join in the national anthem of 'God save the King' —which to the hyper-loyal persons of that time was a crime or a misfortune too dreadful for contemplation. We can hardly realise at the present time the height and the bitterness of the ultra-loyalty of Brighton in the olden days, particularly when there was a shaking of the nations beyond sea, and England was sensible within herself of a certain uneasiness. The simplest of the men with the very purest of motives had to consider twice before he spoke, lest his words should be twisted into traitorous meanings. Even as a great lawyer said that, out of a common note of three lines, he could, if necessary, find matter which would lay the writer under a charge of high treason, so the listeners to speakers, in those dangerous days, seemed to detect the same high treason in common daily greetings, in the snatch of a song, or even in the text or the substance of a sermon.

There is an historical incident of this sort connected with Brighton which is more curious than any of its legendary stories or its chronicles of scandal. In the August of the revolutionary period of 1793 the once celebrated Rev. Dr. Vicesimus Knox happened to be sojourning in Brighton with his family. The Vicar asked the great Master of Tunbridge School 'to gratify the congregation' of the parish church, the only episcopalian edifice in the town, with a sermon on the following Sunday. The sermon was delivered on the text, 'The peace of God, which passeth all understanding.' That it was at once brief and solemn, we may infer from the fact that the Surrey Militia (quartered in Brighton), a numerous portion of the congregation, were highly satisfied and considerably impressed. More orthodox hearers had nothing but congratulations for themselves and the preacher; and Dr. Vicesimus Knox appeared on the following night at the Prince's birthday ball, 'at the Castle Tavern,' with that air of complacency which is born of the conviction that success has attended enterprise. The chief business of very many persons, at both ball and supper, seems to have consisted in worrying the Doctor into a consent, which was not very willingly given, to preach again on the succeeding Sunday.

At the period in question pretty well all the world was engaged in war. People rushed into warfare with alacrity, and other people read the accounts of the slaughter and suffering of their fellow-creatures with the satisfaction of men well out of both. Humanity seemed dying out, and a universal savagery was taking its place. Now good Dr. Knox was a man before his time; he thought arbitration a better means to a good end than cannon-shot. He would not, like a certain Bishop of Orleans, have told armies, about to destroy each other, that in cutting throats they must do murder without rancour. Vicesimus Knox would have had them refrain from mutual destruction altogether. Accordingly the good man thought he would put in a word for peace and charity, and he selected as the subject of his discourse, 'Glory to God in the highest, and on earth peace, good-will toward men.' He was listened to without any manifestation of dissent. Even the warlike militiamen emitted no murmur—but they may have been asleep! The Doctor felt as satisfied as the congregation seemed to be. A lady, however,

who walked by his side on leaving church, quietly
imparted to him that, pleased as she was herself, she
had observed hostile symptoms in certain of the
pews, occupied by people who hated peace, and who
were little addicted to forgiveness. The preacher
could hardly believe his ears, but they had to suffer
worse assault. From a whisper there grew loud
report, and at last public accusation, that this wicked
Master of Tunbridge School, having a church crowded
not only with militiamen, but with the regular army
—officers, rank and file from the camp near Brighton
(which was not true)—had dared to preach 'peace,'
when war was so much more preferable, and 'good-
will toward men,' when it was well known to be the
duty of every patriotic Englishman to hate his enemy
like the very devil! The Rev. Vicesimus Knox, D.D.,
meekly replied that he had only preached what the
Gospel imparted. He went to the camp, and walked
on the Steyne; and on the Tuesday night the Doctor,
his wife, son, and daughter went to the theatre, and
from a stage-box prepared to see the *Agreeable Surprise*. Alas, it was anything rather than agreeable.
The boxes were full of officers. There was a coming
and a going, loud murmurs, scornful pointings to the
Doctor and his party; and finally a note was delivered
to him, in which there was a denunciation of his
sermon, and an order to leave the theatre immediately. At the same time the Doctor's box was
filled with officers, a number of others surrounding
the door, and loading the inmates with most oppro-
brious names. Knox was a brave man. He at once
addressed the audience; he stated his case, denounced

the anonymous note as impertinent, and he declared his intention to remain with his family where he then was by right of payment. But the speech could not pacify those who came expressly to nourish their wrath. The Doctor had preached 'peace and goodwill;' therefore he was howled at, called a *democrat*, with several expletive adjectives before the epithet to embitter its quality. There was a proposal to turn him out, to whip him, to put him in irons, also to hang this messenger of peace. As he ultimately withdrew, the 'officers and gentlemen' grossly insulted not only Knox, but his wife and children. The son, a plucky little lad of fourteen years of age, boldly shook his fist at the assailants, cried 'Shame!' upon them, and complimented them satirically at their being twenty to one. But he was mistaken. One stalwart fellow was not afraid to oppose himself to the boy alone. He seized the lad, shook him violently, crying aloud at the same time, 'Who are you, you dog? You ought to be hanged as well as your father—if he *is* your father—and all such as hold his demoralised principles, you dog, you!' Finally, Dr. Knox withdrew from Brighton; and a report was at once circulated to the effect that a mutiny had broken out in the camp at Wick, in consequence of his democratic sermon. He received letters threatening his life; and the press thought that nothing was too bad for him. Dr. Knox published a solemn and serious asseveration of his loyalty and patriotism, and a sharply satirical, but now very rare, pamphlet, which we recommend to the notice of collectors, should it ever fall in their way. It is called *Prolegomena*. This publication ended an affair which shook not only Brighton, but Great Britain, though both soon forgot it, and slept their usual sleep:

'Et jam Nox humida cœlum
Præcipitat, suadentque cadentia sidera somnos.'

In, about, and around the Marine Pavilion there was a condition of things which the Rev. Dr. Vicesimus Knox would certainly have honestly denounced. We are not going to open the Brighton Chronicle of Scandal. Suffice it to say, that it shocked the cursing, swearing, blaspheming Lord Chancellor Thurlow. One day, on the Steyne, the Prince was walking between the rake, Lord Barrymore, and the vulgar fellow who taught the Prince to drive, Sir John Lade. *Vulgar?* Well, Lade was refinement itself in comparison with his lady. But vulgarity was 'Letty's' nature. She was born with it in St. Giles's. According to fame, Letty Lade had been the early free-love consort of Sixteen-String Jack; next, the Cynthia of the hour to the Duke of York; lastly, and fittingly, the wife of the Jewish-looking groom, Sir John Lade. Whenever the Prince wanted to give an idea of the particular blackguardism of one of his friends, his Royal Highness would politely say, 'He swears like Lætitia Lade!' With this siren's husband on one side of him, and ruffian Barrymore on the other, the graceless trio encountered Lord Thurlow. The Prince gaily rebuked the latter for not calling on him, and condescendingly invited him to name a day when he would come and dine at the Pavilion. 'I cannot do that, sir,' said

Thurlow, who was by no means extra-particular in the matter of companionship, 'I cannot do that until your Royal Highness keeps better company.' Company! The most fashionable London paper of the day seemed delighted to record that Brighton was full of 'little French milliners.' If a man had preached morality at St. Nicholas's, people would have shaken their heads at him, and have strongly suspected his loyalty. The 'French milliners' were at least more modestly dressed than some of the lady guests at the Marine Palace, who walked as *décolletées* on the Downs as when they sat down to dinner at the Pavilion. It was not of them that it was said, 'Illis ampla satis forma, pudicitia.'

Thurlow may well have been ashamed to go among some of the guests. Many of the latter had slang names, and slang generally prevailed among august and illustrious personages. Queen Charlotte visited the Pavilion but once, and that was only two or three years before the royal lady's death. If at her own table at Windsor or Buckingham House the Queen had often to strike in upon her princely son's audacious stories with a 'Fie, fie, George!' she was not likely to have less cause for the exercise of such censorship at the Pavilion. Perhaps during her brief sojourn the Prince invited only fitting company to wait on so virtuous a queen. At other times he could condescend to very questionable fellowship, to which, moreover, he gave the most eccentric of names. As an instance may be adduced the three brothers Barrymore and their sister. They were severally known, from respective characteristics, as

Hellgate, Newgate, and Cripplegate. The lady, who had not the soft voice which is so excellent a thing in woman, nor sentiment, which would be in 'a concatenation accordingly,' passed by the delicate appellation of Billingsgate. The dining-room in the old building was known to the Prince's friends, who in summer had the honour of being baked there in his company, as the Royal Oven. Colonel Hanger once pronounced it to be as hot as ——, the place touching which Sheridan observed, as they were all undoubtedly going thither, it were as well to have a thorough antepast of it before setting out. The observation was not ill-founded, notwithstanding that civility to heaven was combined with good service of the devil in a palace of which it was said, in the very coarsest terms, that there was a chapel at one end and a harem at the other.

In matters of conscience Brighton has never been very tolerant. That is to say, no religious party seems to have believed in the sincerity of contemporary parties differing only on small matters. There was much profession and small measure of practice; very many Christians, but no Christianity. The Quakers, instead of staying, moved or unmoved, in their meeting-houses, would rush into the churches and abuse the preacher or ridicule the prayers; and orthodox magistrates would condemn the offenders to stripes and imprisonment. On all sides there was 'too much zeal.' Erredge quotes from a publication, by a friend, a passage referring to the way in which the Sussex Episcopalians treated the Quakers, whose worship they were as ready to break in upon as they were indignant when their own was indecently interrupted by the Quakers. The latter scornfully called the steeple-house congregations 'the professors,' as if none observed Christian practice but themselves. That the professors could stoop to very unworthy practices, we gather from a passage in the volume above noticed, and bearing date 1658. From that we learn that Episcopalians, on their way from church, showed their religious zeal by attacking the meeting-house if worship happened to be going on. The assailants were guilty of many indecent acts to show their orthodoxy, and their contempt for those who held any other doxy. One perfect Christian, lively, and charitable old woman particularly distinguished herself on a certain Sunday. The sermon at Brighton Church had been to her as the gad-fly to the animal that it irritates and stimulates to mischief. That excellent old woman, on her way home from church, broke the Quakers' windows with her own Bible!

This lovely zealot should have been handed down to fame at least on her tombstone, but we fail to identify her by any record in the churchyard. In fact, there is not much to be learnt in the old churchyard of individuals, or of the poets by whom they have been celebrated. Some of the quaintest of the inscriptions have disappeared, often stones and all. The old easy-going bard, or indifferent sculptor, perhaps both, may be seen in an epitaph which says:

> 'They were two loving sisters
>   Who in this dust now ly, that
> Very day Anne was bury'd
>   Elizabeth did dy.'

Phœbe Hassel, who fought as a man at Fontenoy, and whose life touched, if chronicle be true, the reigns of Anne and of the fourth George, has a simple record which gives the length of her days as making up the sum of 108 years. Now and then there is an attempt at rather lugubrious fun. This is illustrated in an epitaph on Mr. Law, which jingles solemnly to this sort of tune:

> 'Stop, reader, and reflect with awe,
> For Sin and Death have conquered Law,
> Who in full hope resign'd his breath
> That Grace had conquered Sin and Death.'

Let us hope that the second line carries no reproof with it, and that Law was in a hopeful state in a better sense of the word when he tumbled over Brighton cliff and was killed.

The tomb of Captain Tattersell stands, and still bears the record that the captain successfully conveyed King Charles II. from near Brighton to France, 'after he had escaped the sword of his merciless rebels.' Other historical tombs have perished, or rather they were destroyed about twenty-eight years ago—the contents of the graves themselves not being respected—when the old church was enlarged. The antiquary has much to regret on this score. Meanwhile we may record, that besides medical men who discovered the salubrity of the waters and the advantages of attracting patients, besides princes for whom the honour is disputed of having at least shared with the doctors in inventing Brighton, there rests an individual in old Brighton churchyard whose epitaph claims for him the distinction of having produced the transformation scene in which Brighton passed from a fishing-village and rustic sea-bathing place to a city of marine palaces. The individual was Mr. Arnon Wilds, who died in 1833. 'Through his abilities and taste,' says the epitaph, 'the order of the ancient architecture of buildings in Brighton may be dated to have changed from its antiquated simplicity and rusticity.' This is rather finely put. What follows is a little obscure: ' He was a man of extensive genius and talent, and in his reputation for uprightness of conduct could only meet its parallel.' Indeed, matter that was perfectly intelligible does not seem to have been tolerated by authorities which were not particular about grammar or right spelling. When John Jordan, the hairdresser, was buried in old Brighton churchyard, about sixty years ago, these lines were added to the ordinary particulars:

'Say what you will, say what you can,
John Jordan was an honest man.'

This was plain, straightforward, but the clerical censor had the lines erased. Perhaps he thought them presumptuous; or John had, perhaps, been the object of some scandal, and it was thought unseemly that the hairdresser should send forth his note of aggravating assertion from his grave. Besides, it was making much ado about the honesty of one man, as if all the rest of Brighton were knaves. The talk about the chastity of Lucretia has always seemed to us an aspersion on the character of other Roman ladies, who were virtuous without fuss being made about it, and who, after all, would have compelled Tarquin himself to respect them. 'He comes too near who comes to be denied' is one of the many excellent adages to be found in Overbury.

But, speaking of honesty and knavery, as one or the other may be found in Brighton, the old church itself once had an emblem which was interpreted in an adverse sense. On the tower was a gilt arrow vane, but everybody said it looked like a shark; and a poet, adopting the conclusion, like another Polonius, wrote thus:

> 'Say, why on Brighton's church we see
>   A golden shark displayed,
> But that 'twas aptly meant to be
>   An emblem of its trade?
> Nor could the thing so well be told
>   In any other way;
> The town's a Shark that lives on gold,
>   The Company its prey.'

There is an illustration of the ruling passion strong in death—to be found in the old churchyard —which must not be passed over. Among the silent citizens of the Necropolis, is the once celebrated surgical-instrument maker, Mr. Weiss. The last instrument the great mechanician ever invented was borne with him to the grave, piercing the inventor's heart. It was placed there by an eminent surgeon of the time, Mr. Vallance; Mr. Weiss, who dreaded being buried alive, left a bequest to the surgeon, for the performance of a duty, which Mr. Vallance fulfilled. The most showy of monuments was erected here by Michael Kelly, 'composer of wine and importer of music,' to the most melodious of warblers, if not most exemplary of women—Mrs. Crouch (who used 'to do' one of the singing Witches in *Macbeth*, with hundreds of pounds' worth of lace in her dress). In contrast with this is a tomb with its inscription to the memory of John Pocock, who was nearly forty years clerk of the parish, and during about a dozen years the more dignified clerk of the Chapel Royal. John was above fourscore when he died. We are willing to believe that he was all that man and even parish clerk could be. But there seems to be some doubt on this point; and the epitaph adjourns the settlement of the question till the day of judgment. 'In the discharge of his duty,' says the inscription, 'how simple, upright, and affectionate he was, will alone be known at the last day.'

Among the departed whose memories are dear is that of Deryk Carver, the Flemish brewer, who brewed good ale in Brighton before the 'Tipper' was heard of, and who not only read the Scriptures in English, but interpreted them according to his doubly solid Anglo-Flemish and reasonable understanding; for which exercise of free inquiry Deryk has the honour of being the first martyr for religion's sake in the county of Sussex. He suffered in 1554. Deryk was rather rude, perhaps, when replying to the charges brought against him, particularly when dealing with transubstantiation. 'You say that you can make a God!' cried the bold brewer; 'you can make a pudding as well!'—which was more 'saucy' than logical. There is some part of Carver's story that has a very legendary aspect. The Bible which was taken from him at the stake is said to have suffered merely a slight discoloration on some of the pages from the smoke. At the same time we are told, in the same legend or tradition, that the blood of the martyr who was burnt is visible on several chapters of the Old Testament, but particularly on the 'Book of Ruth,' which, says Erredge, 'is very much splashed with the vital fluid.' We can understand marks of fire on this Bible, which is a '*Breeches Bible*;' but that splashes of blood are visible upon it we cannot believe—at least, as the accident and part circumstance of Deryk's burning.

But let us get back from Sussex martyrdoms and Brighton churchyard to the Dome, beneath which Dr. Carpenter will deliver his inaugural address on Wednesday evening. What a Nemesis has been ever seated there! Under that roof, where George IV. was, as *he* thought, 'every inch a king,' Thackeray held him up to the contempt of his hearers when he lectured at the Pavilion, and made the Georges look so disreputable in the reign of Victoria. Strange contrast!—but Brighton is full of them. Famed for its once reckless gaiety and noisy dissipation, it sent forth, in Robertson's sermons, a series of discourses the publication of which has been more popular and a greater financial success than any other collection of such homilies, except that of the sermons of Blair. The Pavilion itself is still the Palace of Contrasts. On one night Mrs. Scott-Siddons enchants her audience by her refinement and passion; on another, a person in a monk's dress preaches the Gospel 'for Jesus only,' at 4*s.*, 2*s.* 6*d.*, and 1*s.* admission, with opportunity to buy his photograph if you are so disposed.

Brighton may look forward to a successful meeting. The railway administration offer certain facilities which travellers will appreciate. The working men will have a lecture delivered to them, on 'Sunshine, Sea, and Sky,' which is a universal subject. Oppressed minds, brains that reel under excess of scientific delight at the evening lectures, may find rest and enjoyment at the two *soirées* and the concert at each. There are not less than nine excursions arranged for those who love to go inquiringly abroad, with good objects in view. For those who prefer to keep within the town, there is the great Aquarium, wherein many an innocent fish has, during the late dog-days, been literally done to death. There are numerous other objects of attraction, unnecessary for us to point out; and therewith an abiding hospitality, which has been, indeed, a Sussex virtue from the earliest times.

BRADFORD.
1873.

BRADFORD.

1873.

A CENTURY and a half ago, to speak in round numbers, Defoe published his *Tour through Great Britain, by a Gentleman*. It was the precursor of all the guide-books that have since shown to travellers the path in which they should go, and the objects worth looking at which they meet with in their journeys. This proto-guide, however, can hardly be called a manual. It is in four volumes.

In this book Defoe, of which he is thought to have written only the first volume, says, 'The first town we came to from Halifax was Bradford. It is a market-town, but is of no other note than having given birth to Dr. Sharp, the good Archbishop of York.' That was the sum of what Defoe had to say about Bradford in the West Riding of Yorkshire. In the same volume the same writer has to make mention of the condition of another Bradford—the town in a Wiltshire valley, on the slopes of the sweet-flowing Avon; and he does so in these words: 'Bradford and Trowbridge are two of the most eminent clothing towns in that part of the vale, for the making of the finest Spanish cloths and for the nicest mixtures. Bradford is well built of stone, and lies on the side of a hill.' 'The toune of Bradford (in Wilts),' said Leland, three centuries ago, 'stondith by clooth-making;' and the same may be said of it now. Both Bradfords also produced the smallest article in connection with their manufactures. In this, one is reminded of the Bradford in Massachusetts, which builds ships and makes shoes. We may notice also two Bradfords, North and South, in one English county, Shropshire. Between them they have furnished a territorial title to the Earls of Bradford—of the race of that Newport who drank with great Nassau, and of Orlando Bridgman, who was also a man not to be forgotten. The Wiltshire Bradford, in the first quarter of the last century, was the busy Bradford. The town of the same name in the Yorkshire Riding was comparatively silent or inactive. It had but one production to boast of—the brave and worthy son already named, that stout John Sharp, who was born in the Yorkshire Bradford in 1644, who *would* preach against Popery in spite of James II. and Ecclesiastical Commissions, and who got his reward, when the good time came, by being promoted to the archbishopric of York. He retained the primacy from 1691 to 1713, in which year he died. Sharp has the reputation of being the man whose influence with Queen Anne induced her to refuse making Swift a bishop after she had made him a dean, for abusing the Duchess of Marlborough in the *Examiner*. The story is as well worth remembering as the Bradford prelate's seven volumes of quaint sermons are still worth reading.

It is believed that the Roman was once busy in the neighbouring district, where iron abounded. There too the Briton wrung the sweat from his brow, gathered 'there by toil' for his lord and master. The place was a wild place through succeeding centuries. James, indeed, in his excellent *History of Bradford* (by the way, he complains that the Bradford people would not help him to publish it by their subscriptions), states that there may have been some weaving of coarse woollen cloths here before the Conquest; but the *Domesday Book* significantly speaks of the district as 'waste.' James is, however, quite sure that woollen goods were manufactured at Bradford before the time of Edward III. It is certain that at an early period the Yorkshire Bradford was a portion of the largest parish in England—the ancient parish of Dewsbury. According to Dr. Whitaker's *Loidis and Elmete*, that old parish had an area of four hundred miles, including the later parochial divisions of Thornhill, Mirfield, Kirkbarton, Almondbury, Kirkheaton, Huddersfield, Halifax, and Bradford. The great boast of this immense Yorkshire parish was that Paulinus had preached there in the year 627. In proof of which, it is said that the cross on the mother church of the now subdivided parish is after the model of one erected at an earlier date, in commemoration of the event. Such evidence is even weaker than that which is submitted to the traveller at Lorch on the Rhine. The rock there is perpendicular; but in proof that a knight once rode up the face of it, the wayfarer is gravely shown the rider's saddle and bridle.

There were few of the adventurers who 'came

over' with William who got more than the De Lacys. There were two of them. One, Ilbert de Lacy, was made happy and rich by the barony of Pontefract, and a hundred and a half of manors, of which Bradford was one. He was so grateful that his son founded Kirkstall Abbey to prove it. The other De Lacy, Walter (from whom the eminent actor of that name is not descended), manifested his gratitude in his lifetime by building the church of St. Peter's, Hereford. Walter ascended a ladder to view the building better, but he fell from the top and broke his neck. His grateful son Hugh founded the abbey of Llanthony in Wales. The De Lacys became Earls of Lincoln, by one of them wedding an heiress to that title; and the line went out in the person of a too lively lady, Alicia, last heiress of the house. She married and ran away, and returned and re-married; and is said to have practised a little poisoning before she died, childless, in 1348. Bradford and the one hundred and forty-nine other Yorkshire manors of the De Lacys would probably be heartily ashamed of this terrible Alicia, if they knew anything about her.

They probably know as little of 'old John of Gaunt, time-honoured Lancaster,' who once owned a very comfortable share of them, and in whose time a few men paid their rent by simply blowing a horn, which is what not every man *can* do. Bradford's first intimacy with the head of Royalty was when Richard II. did the town the honour of capturing it. The place was a quiet place till the death of Richard III.

Bradford, after the accession of Henry VII., attracted the attention of the astute King and his friends.

It was a time when half the property of England changed hands. Every man who had helped Richard III. in the slightest degree became the new king's 'rebel' or 'traitor,' and his lands, goods, or money was made forfeit to the Crown, because he had aided and abetted 'the late Duke of Gloucester, Richard, King of England in deed, but not in right.' Bradford belonged to the Duchy of Lancaster; and one Thomas Gellyem had been 'Grave of the Lordship of Bradford.' This servant of York shared the fate of hundreds of other officials. He was turned out, and was ordered to send to the royal treasury all moneys due from his office. The post of Grave or Steward of the Lordship was conferred on a Lancastrian soldier, 'knight for the King's body;' and in like manner many hundreds of such soldiers were rewarded for having shared with Henry in his 'glorious march and victorious field at Bosworth.' One Hugh Smyth had, for similar service, the minor posts of Bailiff of Bradford and of 'Parker of the Park of Cansewyk.' The Lordship of Bradford itself was granted to Nicholas Leventhorpe, with the manor, and all rents, farms of mills, shops, tolls, and 'perquisites of courts and towns.' Leventhorpe rendered annually to the King, for the same, 28*l*. 6*s*. 8*d*. Under Richard the fee was less by the shillings and pence; but thrifty Harry clapped on the additional 6*s*. 8*d*., and called it 'improved rent.'

Down to the reign of Charles I. Bradford had the right of holding a market on Thursdays by charter. The inhabitants, however, kept the right (as they still do), but they changed the day. They made

Sunday market-day; and they alternately did a little piety in church and a good deal of business at the market-standings. On one and the same day they made the best of both worlds. It was a bad world just then for poor folk, with more appetite than cash for its gratification.

In 1631 Yorkshire was not a little stirred by a proclamation of King Charles. The poor were bitterly complaining of the high price of corn, and of ill-supplied grain-markets, although harvests had been abundant. The proclamation promised remedy, and the remedy applied was very disagreeable to the wealthy persons who starved the markets by storing their corn. A Commission was established, the members of which were directed to examine into and make record of 'the surplusage of corn remaining and being in the custody and keeping of rich men.' Bradford was one of the places where rigorous inquiry was made. There was not a barn, garner, or storehouse in the district that was not overhauled, and note made of its contents, by an annoyance jury of constables and churchwardens. The subsequent report, however, proved the poverty of the place, and chronicled no villany on the part of forestallers and regraters. The report to the Commissioners was to this effect: 'Our country being mountainous and barren, and the inhabitants thereof living most by trading, have not more corn than is sufficient for sowing that little ground they have, and for maintenance of their families which now they have remaining in their houses.' The Temperance—or the Total Abstinence—Society will be glad to hear that the

Bradford magistrates of 1631, as a means of doing good to the poor, suppressed the greater part of the Bradford ale-houses, and set to work the idle men who loitered in or about them. As for idle lads,— idle involuntarily or in spite of themselves,—the parish authorities took them in hand, and bound them apprentices, as they say, 'with all men of ability within the several townships.' In a general crusade against the lazy, there was no idle delicacy about the liberty of the subject. Rogues and vagabonds, made to earn their bread, growled out sentiments referring to 'tyranny' and 'free-born Englishmen;' but the workmen who loved working instead of 'spouting,' and the impotent poor, who were more easily provided for from the general industry growing up around them, thought that the long-promised good time had come in their days, and that it was a blessed thing to live under such a gracious monarch as King Charles I.

From State Paper Office records it appears that while many ale-houses were suppressed in Yorkshire towns, licenses were given for the sale of a 'comodetye,' the use of which generally leads to, or is accompanied by, more or less drinking of ale or other beverages—namely, tobacco. It is curious to read that, as there were individuals who *would* retail tobacco publicly or privately, licenses were issued to permit them to do so with an aspect of legal propriety. These licenses were granted to grocers, innkeepers, mercers, oil-drawers, according to the population and their narcotic tastes. Huddersfield would have delighted the heart and nostrils of King James, who hated the weed and its 'stink.' 'John Hirst and the constable, Edward Cooper, report that one vendor is quite enough, as very little tobacco is used in the town. There had formerly been two other vendors, but they had quite given it up.' With Little Bradford the state of matters was quite different from what it was with Huddersfield. In the former place the weed was loved; and small as Bradford then was, no less than six dealers in tobacco are mentioned as there carrying on their trade.

'Little Bradford' was the pet name of the place in the seventeenth century. It was then growing into the bustling Bradford of to-day. It was springing into life and activity; and among the curious facts to be recorded of it is this, namely, that before King Charles's reign had run out, Turkey cushions and carpets were in fashion, and these foreign productions were manufactured at Bradford! It was a manufacture by which great profits were acquired; but trades and manufactures that had flourished in the early part of Charles's reign perished wholly, or in a great degree, in the struggle in which the King himself suffered shipwreck. The Bradford youths, who manufactured Turkey carpets, mostly took service under Fairfax. Sir Thomas's first fight was at Bradford, in 1643, whence he drove the royal troops towards Leeds, although he had but half their numbers, and was disadvantageously placed. What effect the civil war had on the prosperity of the county is told in a letter, from Bradford, 'to the Right Hon. my honoured father the Lord Fairfax.' 'These parts,' he says, 'grow very impatient of our delay to beat them out of Leeds and Wakefield, for by them all trade and provisions are stopped, so that the people in these clothing towns are not able to subsist; and, indeed, so pressing are their wants that some have told me if I would not stir with them, they must rise of necessity of themselves, in a thing of so great importance.' Fairfax had no doubt of finding aid in the Bradford district,—to something like the amount of four thousand men, with muskets or other weapons. Great, indeed, was the impatience of the Yorkshiremen at the breaking up of their trade and the closing of their markets. The Parliamentary general, Fairfax, himself a Yorkshireman, had been commissioned only to defend the district, not to assault the enemy; but he expressed his readiness to attack the foe, if the Right Hon. his very honoured father would authorise him to do so. Meanwhile, the Royalists assaulted Bradford; and that circumstance finished it, for trade and manufacturing, for many a long day. The Earl of Newcastle was the assailant. His lordship sent a trumpet with a command to surrender. Fairfax, finding himself hemmed in, and victory all but impossible, replied by sallying out, cutting his way through the Royalists, and keeping them at bay, as he turned and fought them mile by mile, till, wounded and nearly dying, covered with blood, without a shirt, and his clothes cut to rags, he stumbled safely into Hull, with his honour saved. In the sortie from Bradford, Fairfax lost what was as dear to him as honour — his wife; and he nearly lost his little daughter. In the *mêlée* Lady Fairfax was captured; and, from fright and fatigue, the little girl, who had this rough and fierce experience of war, fell into a fever, which threatened to be mortal. Both mother and child were restored to Fairfax. The ever polite Earl of Newcastle had the gallantry to send Lady Fairfax into Hull in his own coach, and he put a maid of honour into it to keep her company. The little daughter, who was then only five years old, lived to have a coach ordered for the carrying of her also to her father. This occurred when her husband, the Duke of Buckingham, brought the abandoned Countess of Shrewsbury to live under the same roof. 'I will not live in the same house with this woman!' said the outraged wife. 'I did not expect you would,' replied Buckingham, 'and so I have ordered my coach to take you to your father's house.' Remembering the misery of this poor lady's married life, one is almost sorry that she did not quietly die, in her childhood, of the consequences of the fright and fatigue in the bloody sortie from Bradford and the daily fierce battles which followed it.

In the days of Charles and of the Commonwealth, the communications of Bradford and Wakefield and adjacent parts with London were not daily maintained. On Wednesdays little groups of Yorkshire folk settled in London waited in front of the Bear, in Basinghall-street, for the arrival of the provincial carriers. Others went to the Axe, in Aldermanbury, where the carriers were to be treated with on Thursdays. The White Hart, in Coleman-street, was a third house of communication, but the carriers started and arrived only once a fortnight; and on every second Thursday a foot post arrived from the county of the Ridings, with his budget of letters and his news picked up by the way.

To Bradford those days brought a ruin from which the town has slowly recovered. It may now be said to be in a state of magnificent convalescence, and yearly increasing in exceedingly rude strength. In the first year of the present century it had a population of little over 13,000 persons; now the population is not far from 150,000. Bradford lay stunned and powerless for nearly a century, and exactly a hundred years have elapsed since, in 1773, it turned the corner and started on the career which it is still pursuing. The parish may not be so extensive as at the early period to which we have before referred, but it is more flourishing. The parish of Bradford —which has for its vicar an ex-Bishop (Ryan) of Mauritius—is in itself still of considerable extent. It is full sixteen miles long, and about half a dozen broad. The town, comprising four townships, is situated at the juncture of three valleys, which lie smiling before the traveller, who sees also one of the tributaries of the Aire in the stream flowing near. Take the situation altogether, and it would be difficult to say that the town is not rightly called the metropolis of the West Riding.

Its recovery commenced in 1773, but it may be said that its later importance dates only from 1831, when the Reform Bill helped to raise it to the dignity of a parliamentary borough, with the privilege of returning two members. The local newspapers of the time show most amusingly their sense, not only of increased dignity, but of increased responsibilities;

and there is an undisguised consciousness that the eyes of Europe (not to say of the world generally) are fixed upon the new borough, a municipal borough, with a worshipful Mayor and Corporation, who have since administered local government with the success that might be expected from Yorkshiremen.

It was only half a dozen years before Bradford acquired the dignity of a parliamentary borough that the artisans of the place ceased to observe one of their old festal anniversaries. Next to Norwich, nowhere was greater honour rendered to Blase, Bishop of Sebaste, than in Bradford. On the 3d of February the festival of the patron saint of wool-combers used to be observed with great display; but the observance ceased in 1825—but it has been renewed this year. Why the good Bishop, who was made a martyr in 316, became associated with wool-combing (save that he is said to have been partly combed to death by iron combs), or why he is supposed, in some mysterious way, to be good against sore-throats, the least scrupulous of hagiographers has not audacity enough to declare; but when Bradford omitted to honour Blase, the lovers of old customs in rival Leeds affected a sort of pious horror at such incivility—against they did not know whom.

It is worth recalling to mind what constituted a Radical in the days of the first Bradford election. Hardy and Lister were the Radical—Banks the Conservative—candidates. Lister was absent through illness; but Hardy made the Radical declaration at the nomination. He was for vote by ballot. That was all. He was against triennial parliaments, household suffrage, unlimited freedom of the press, and separation of Church and State. Banks was for limiting the hours of labour for women and children. *That* was *his* war-horse. The two Radicals (!) were elected. They sent their sons to be chaired, in place of themselves; and the roughs tossed the lads out of the cars, and smashed the chariots of triumph.

The Bradford 'man-folk' were always vigorous in arms as well as speech—sometimes cruel. In the old days of riot they burnt mills and broke up machines with a fury of delight. It was their way of arguing against matters which they thought injurious to their interests. The Marchioness of Hertford was not much more ignorantly blind when she prevented the construction of a railway between Bradford and Leeds because it would encroach on some land of hers which lay between. My lady did not tear up the rails, but she prevented them being laid down. Rails, mills, and machinery all now exist in spite of these ignorant individuals. Generally speaking, Bradford must have had the worst of it in strikes. That of the wool-combers and stuff-weavers in 1825 lasted three-and-twenty weeks, and was brought to an end by the disappearance of the treasurer with the funds.

With prosperity, something like the envy, or let us rather say the emulation, that exists, or used to exist, between Liverpool and Manchester moves, or is said to move, the susceptible and sensitive pulses of Leeds and Bradford respectively. The former triumphed when it not only built a lofty town-hall, but crowned it with a lofty tower. We know what anguish visited the heart of Lord Kenyon when a waggish but cruelly-disposed friend addressed a letter to the worthy Welsh judge—'Wales, near Cheshire.' In like painful manner was the heart of all Leeds stirred when it was known that a letter had reached the post-office there bearing the superscription, 'Leeds, near Bradford.' It was as if the Bradfordians had erected a loftier town-hall, and crowned it with a more majestic tower than the edifice of which Leeds was proud, as a symbol of its supremacy.

However, Bradford struggles to go ahead in both architecture and manufactures. Two-and-twenty years ago, at the time of the first Exhibition, Bradford asserted itself in a successful manner. As between Bradford and Leeds, the former was accepted as having the worsted manufacture for its staple employment; Leeds and its dependencies being the more immediate seat of the woollen manufacture. At that time it was said that Bradford was rapidly rising at the expense of Leeds; and among Bradfordians in their native walk, so to speak, at the proto-Crystal Palace, a passer-by caught the words, 'worsted yarns,' 'thousands employed,' 'largest mills in Yorkshire,' 'see our piece-hall on a Thursday,' 'Leeds can't dye stuffs as fast as Bradford can manufacture them,' 'Leeds people are leaving their town and setting up warehouses in ours.' Of course there were and are many trades carried on at Bradford dependent upon the woollen and worsted trades. All came out with credit in 1851. The importance of Bradford then may be measured by the space required by the Bradford exhibitors, 2000 square feet for their five classes, viz. worsted stuffs, cotton stuffs, iron, machinery, and miscellaneous. Serious people were pleased by the report that an indefatigable Bradford weaver had woven the four Gospels on cloth as a specimen of his skill!

Since the Exhibition of 1851, Bradford has continued to 'go ahead.' The progress is marked in one way by the large new mansions which seem to be squeezing the aboriginal, diminutive, but strong and sturdy, dwellings out of existence. The two are types of what the place was and what it has become. Mr. Walter White, in his record of a walk in Yorkshire, distinguishes between the glories of Leeds and Bradford, by describing Leeds as famous for broadcloth, and Bradford as really a grand mart for stuffs and worsted goods. It was probably a boy belonging to a Leeds school who replied to a query, put to him at an examination, as to what Bradford was famous for, by saying that Bradford was famous for shoddy! The Bradford merchants are accomplished business men. By a liberal dispensation of generous sherry they warm the business feelings of buyers; and where transactions without sherry would stop at 500*l.*, they run up with the wine to the more respectable figure of 1000*l.* As a sample, we suppose, of Bradford thrift, Mr. White introduces us to a wife of whom a physician, for attending on her sick husband, asked for a guinea fee. 'A guinea!' The thrifty dame turned to her moribund mate and exclaimed: 'If I were ye, I'd say no! like a Briton, and die first!'

In spite of many peculiar characteristics Bradford has failed to find a place among the local proverbs of

Yorkshire. Hull and Halifax have been bracketed with hell itself, in order to point an alliterative illustration; and the phrase, 'as true steel as Ripon rowels,' alludes to the manufacture of spurs, the rowels of which would strike through a shilling, and for which the town was famous when there was much riding between it and the Border. Though Scarborough Castle now never speaks in the flash and thunder of cannon from its mouldering ramparts, the proverbial 'Scarborough warning'—which was none at all—serves to remind us of the time when the Scarborough gunners fired cannon-shot into the sides of passing vessels, just to remind their captains that they had forgotten to haul down their colours by way of salute. Even 'Merry Wakefield' has an epithet which makes its old jollity live traditionally; but the town that, with equal justness, might have been called 'Busy Bradford' can only take its share in the general county proverb, 'A Yorkshire wee-bit,' which found its way into Scotland, where Jeannie Deans's 'five miles and a bittock,' as the Duke of Argyle explained it to Queen Caroline, meant five miles and as many more.

The 'better bringing up' of the youth of the district was an idea which took permanent shape about the close of the reign of Edward VI. The Free Grammar School is far advanced in the fourth century of its existence. When it was about a hundred years old it had done, however, so little of what it was intended it should do, that Charles II. has the credit of setting the school on its legs again, for the teaching, instructing, and still better bringing up than its first founders had devised ' of children and youth in grammar and other good learning and literature.' It was in this Free Grammar School that the Bradford boy, Sharp, laid the foundation of the knowledge which formed part of his qualifications for becoming an archbishop. Mr. Howard Staunton says that 'other eminent men were educated here;' and we hope Mr. Staunton may have the goodness to name them in his next edition of the *Great Schools of England*. Some good Bradfordians seem to have thought that there were parts of their parish where the classics might be profitably cultivated. Accordingly Christopher Scott endowed a school in the Haworth district for a schoolmaster able to teach Greek and Latin, so as to fit his scholars for Oxford or Cambridge. The Thornton district was also provided for. A hundred years ago a school was founded there *by subscription*, to teach Latin and English to likely lads of Thornton and Allerton; and it is satisfactory to add that these schools still exist, and with all their excellent instruction they have not, we rejoice to say, beaten out the native accent so dear to West Riding ears. That there is not only accent, but wit, humour, and pathos in the dialect, may be learnt by all who will look into native books; such, for instance, as *Poems and Songs*, by a Yorkshire 'Lik'nass Takker,' a capital little work, in the dialect of Bradford Dale. Here is one specimen. The minstrel is singing of the Apollo Belvidere, which he describes as being

> 'All reyt and strayt i' mak and shap,
> A mould for t' raace o' men;
> A dahnreyt, upreyht, bang oop chap,
> Not mitch unlike my sen !'

Among the many things creditable to Bradford may be reckoned, not merely its literary tastes, but its literary activity and influence. It is the headquarters of the Yorkshire Literary Union, and in the town is published the *Yorkshire Magazine*, a monthly journal, which deserves credit for its ability and usefulness. In the opening number, published in October 1871, there is an article on the dialect of Bradford Dale, by W. Cunningham, from which there is much to be learnt. It is there shown how greatly the local *patois* differs from that of Leeds and Halifax. Although the Bradford dialect has some words in common with other parts of the United Kingdom, and particularly with Lancashire and Scotland, there are words and expressions which Mr. Cunningham claims as 'indigenous to the town itself.' That there is great variety of sounds for a single letter on the lips of a Bradfordian cannot be doubted. *A* is short in 'shape,' which becomes *shap;* it takes a mincing sound of *e* in 'wash;' and in 'dance' it becomes a very round *o* indeed. While *a* becomes *e* in 'wash,' *e* becomes *a* in 'very,' and it doubles itself, becomes *ee* in 'wet;' and not only doubles itself, but claps an *a* on to the doubling in 'fret,' which is pronounced 'free-at.' In short, the vowels at Bradford are altogether of a very loose way of life. *I* is short and long, where in other places it is long and short; 'pink' is *peenk*, and 'blind' rhymes to 'pinn'd.' The remainder of the vowel family is equally perverse, and utterly never to be depended upon. The diphthongs imitate them in audacious lawlessness, and popular Bradford conversation startles the ear with such phrases as 'Shoo coom dahn stairs i' hur bare fit a wick ago, an's bin poorly ivver sin.' The dialect changes some words altogether, and every visitor may fairly say, in Bradford dialect if he can, 'I fecar it's noan so eeasy to leearn.'

Not only do vowels and diphthongs sound in the Bradford district as they sound nowhere else, but they continually 'dance the changes' there. Indeed, Mr. Cunningham tells us that the local dialect 'effects an absolute change in many words.' In common with most Yorkshire dialects, the Bradfordian reduces *the* to simply *t*, and 'He 's at t 'op o' t hahze rigg' stands, in every-day English, for 'He is at the top of the house roof.' In Bradford conjunctions are put to uses to which they are not elsewhere accustomed, and for which they were never intended. 'T' more I do for 'm, and t' worse I am for 't,' is an illustration how the Bradford conjunction is made to qualify as well as connect. Words, however, are described as having local uses which are turned to the same service throughout Cockneydom. Indeed, that ill-used dominion has been plundered of its richest treasures of speech, and they have been claimed as original property by the plunderers. 'I won't go without you go,' where 'without'='unless,' and 'It's better nor I expected,' where 'nor'='than,' are examples to the point. As a proof that Bradfordians themselves are anxious to fix the pronunciation of words that find various ways of utterance, a tale is told of two Bradford lads referring a dispute, as to whether 'either' should be pronounced as 'eether' or 'ither,' to an old Bradfordian, and the venerable sage at once replied that 'awther 'll do!' and so delightfully increased the local perplexity. Mr. Cunningham states that fine old English word 'anent' is still used for 'opposite.' We have heard of a public reader in London who advertised that he would recite the *Paradise Lost* through by heart. It was popularly said at the time that of the dozen people who formed the audience, three escaped at the end of the first hour, several were subsequently carried out, and a faithful couple who sat to the bitter end became hopelessly idiotic! If a Bradfordian were to announce that he was about to 'give a reading *through* Shakespeare,' no persons of the country born would suppose that the reader intended to treat them to the whole of the plays—a process which, like a Chinese state dinner, would last a month or six weeks: he would know that 'through' is Bradfordian for 'from,' and that the reading would consist of selections from Shakespeare's plays; and if it were said that 'the reader comes through Halifax,' every one would know that he came *from* that town, which produces so many pretty faces—and this must be accepted as said without any disparagement of the Bradford belles. If in the last examples you suggest that 'from' would be a better word to use than 'through,' the Bradfordian will think for a moment, as if he were courteously weighing your objection, and will gravely reply that he 'don't see a difference of meaning in one word through t' other.' When the Princess Victoria went her progress through the North with her mother, the Duchess of Kent, she stayed at Lord Fitzwilliam's, where the

Princess received a monition the morning after her arrival from the gardener, as she was walking out early, to be wary, 'it was varra *slape*.' The last word is the proper district word for 'slippery.' Many of the words are even more foreign to other English ears; for instance, 'pratty'=softly; 'lennock' =easily moved; 'enah'=by and by; 'drea'=slow; 'offald'=shabbily dressed; 'loppard'=sour (applied to milk), and so on. Lord Bacon has said that a man who goes on travel to a country, of the language of which he is ignorant, goes rather to school than to travel. So visitors to Bradford, however well skilled in English, may find themselves at school as far as Bradfordian English is concerned. In that dialect, 'a bonny fellow' is a bad fellow; for it is used satirically, as many other adjectives are. 'What,' asks Mr. Cunningham, 'can be more stinging than such an attack as the following from the mouth of an old town gossip?—"Thah 'rt a *bonny* tyke, thah art! Thah's made a *nice* job o' thy sen this time, thah hez that. It's *fair grand* to think on't, is'n't it nah?"' This sort of satire, however, is not foreign to other parts. What *is* peculiar to this Yorkshire dialect is to be found in another application of words; thus 'fairation' fairness. There is something poetical in the use of 'yonderly' for absent-minded, distraught. 'Tha' lewks varra yonderly to-day, lad,' would imply that the lad's thoughts were far away from present themes. If it be poetical, so is the word 'kallin' aptly satirical, for a woman who neglects her business to visit a neighbour for the sake of a gossip. A woman 'calling' is no strange event elsewhere, but the same ill meaning is not given to the fact as in Bradford. A Bradford man says he is 'hooined,' when another would say he is distressed. To be 'moidered' is equivalent to being perplexed; and probably many a visitor, before the week is out, will be what the Bradfordians call 'dulled'—otherwise fatigued; but such visitors must not grow querulous over it, or the local folk will say they are 'newky' as well as 'dulled.'

Then 'frame' is a great word. A Bradfordian frames to his business, frames to his amusements, frames to his everything; and he is a very poor creature of whom his fellows can say contemptuously that there is no 'framation' in him; and no 'gawm' or notice is taken of a being so afflicted with unfitness. 'Feshan' is as important a word as 'framation;' and a young damsel who swears her pretty oath that she 'can't feshan to lewk t' wey 'at he is,' insinuates her too great bashfulness to look Strephon in the face. Yet the same maiden can feshan to 'hug' anything, though not anybody, for 'hug' is Bradfordian for 'carry;' and if she goes abroad in the meadows with her sweetheart, Strephon will be too happy to 'go a gaiters wi' her,' or to set her on her road home.

There is much more to be said about Bradford, which we must leave unsaid. It is in this interesting town that the British Association will commence its next annual general meeting, under the presidency of Professor Williamson, in the place of Dr. Joule, whom ill health has compelled to withdraw from the honourable and responsible office of President. Visitors will find that steam has despoiled Bradford of its beauty, but has added to its power. If it was accounted 'quikke' as compared with Leeds, during the Wars of the Roses, it would be hard to find a word now to express its fastness. Its spirit grasps past and present, and extends a hand towards the future. After allowing Bishop Blase to sleep for nearly half a century, the wool-combers have exalted him again to the position of a patron saint. Their townsman, Archbishop Sharp, might have served them better. The old motto which figured on the buttons of the Bradford Volunteers in 1793—'Ready and Steady'—may still serve for the device of a town ready for every good purpose, and steady in carrying it to a successful issue. Visitors will find ample proof of this fact, and foreign guests will find as warm a welcome at the Bradford, Union, Junior, Liberal, Conservative, Chess, and Catholic Clubs as they will at the Anglo-French, the Schiller Verein, the German, and the Swiss Clubs. The last named is the only one which denies membership to any who are not of the nationality from which it takes its name. We have only to add that the Bradford district has (so to speak) annexed itself gloriously to literature. Few of the members and visitors who will be in the town during the meeting of the British Association are likely to neglect making a pilgrimage to the shrine of the Brontës at Haworth.

XV.
BELFAST.
1874.

BELFAST.

1874.

IN its way there are few, if any, more beautiful things in this beautiful world than the run, by sea, from Belfast to Greenock. There is, perhaps, only one excursion to equal it, and that is the run from Greenock to Belfast. That this should be one of the routes to or from the northern metropolis of Ireland is a matter to be impressed on all members of the British Association who are about to repair to Ireland, and between whose homes and whose trysting-place 'roll the dark waters of Eire's deep seas.'

The sand-bank which was once formed at the mouth of the Lagan, by the river stream meeting the ocean tide, no longer exists. It gave to the now flourishing city the name which it still bears. Belfast is a modern adaptation of Bel-feirsde, or ford of the *farset*, or sand-bank. Mr. Joyce, in his *Irish Names of Places*, says 'the term is pretty common, especially in the West, where these *farsets* are of considerable importance, as in many places they serve the inhabitants instead of bridges.' The name, in a form slightly modified from the original, Belfarsad, occurs in Mayo. 'There is now a bridge,' says Mr. Joyce, 'over the old sand-bank that gave name to the village of Farsid, near Aghada, or Cork harbour. The origin of this name is quite forgotten, and the people call it *Farside*, and interpret it as an English word; but the name of the adjacent town, Ballynafarsid (Town of the Sand-bank), proves, if proof were necessary, that it took its name from a *farset*.' Farsetmore, or the Great Sand-bank, is the name of a place on the Swilly, near Letterkenny, where such a bank once existed.

One of the most familiar examples of the readiness with which an English interpretation is given to an old Irish name offers itself in Rings-end, Dublin. Local guides will tell you it denotes the spot where the last of the row of piles stood with their mooring-rings for shipping to make fast to; whereas the name is Irish, 'Rin Ann,' or the Point of the Tide, exactly denoting a fact. Many other examples might be cited. Returning to the name Belfast, we perceive that in Murray's *Handbook* it is said that 'a fort is known to have existed at "Beula-Fearsad," the *Mouth of the Ford*, in 1178.' Between this interpretation and that given by Joyce our readers may safely be left to choose for themselves. At this Mouth of the Ford, or whatever else be the meaning of the old Irish name, there was, according to tradition, that sort of liveliness which results from much fighting between contending chiefs. In these fights nobody suffered so much as the people; and no class of Irish people suffered so much and so long as the people of Ulster, who were the last to be brought under English law, and who resisted to be so brought till resistance was utterly useless.

For this reason it is that Belfast, like so many other places in Ulster, belongs comparatively to modern history. In the olden time, when the occupiers of land (they were not the tenants; no such matters as tenants or tenures existed till English law made both) were the slaves of the chiefs, they held nothing but what the chiefs chose to leave them. Belfast Lough had then no fleets of merchant vessels on its waters. The huts at the mouth of the Lagan were inhabited by a few fishermen, and the hunter traversed the woods or plains on which has sprung up and grown into beauty and usefulness that city which is the just pride of the North, which is sometimes called second to Dublin, but which is far ahead of the chief capital in many respects. The Lagan is not like the Liffey. It is not the common sewer of the city. It does not spread disease and death as it slowly flows and greatly stinks. A stranger in Dublin is as certain to get the Liffey fever, if he tarry near the banks of the river, as a stranger tarrying in the Roman marshes is sure to be stricken, more or less severely, with the 'Roman fever.'

Any one interested in the subject may learn with ease, pleasure, and profit what Ulster was in the early part of the seventeenth century, what it became as that century progressed, and how it became so, by reading Mr. Brewer's historical Introduction to the edition (edited by himself and Mr. Bullen) of the *Calendar of the Carew Manuscripts, preserved in the Archiepiscopal Library at Lambeth.* Mr. Brewer traces the prosperity of Ulster to the fixed determination of the English Government to protect the people from the oppressions of their chiefs, after these had submitted to English law, accepted titles, and, with new distinctions, fancied they could exercise their old tyrannous absolutism. Ulster itself scarcely thanked the English Government for its intended beneficence. 'Never did any country,' says Mr. Brewer, 'more obstinately resist every measure from which it now dates its wealth, order, and industrial progress, or adhere more tenaciously to its original and primitive misrule.' He adds, in a note: 'The tenure of land in Ireland—of which, properly speaking, there is no trace to be found among the native Irish—was introduced from England, and subjected precisely to the same conditions as here.' And thence Ulster flourished.

And therefore, also, Belfast prospered. If the province really owes something to a Government, its superb capital owes a great deal to one man, and that man was Arthur Chichester, the Lord Deputy during a part of James's reign, who had his home for a time at Carrickfergus, and who (so to speak) helped Belfast to proudly rise and gloriously establish itself on the river and on the lough. Chichester is sometimes alluded to as a sort of Nobody; whereas he was a gentleman of ancient blood, a brave soldier who never despaired, and a fair scholar for his time and opportunities. He quartered the arms of some of the noblest and most ancient families in the West of England. When James sent him a knight to Ireland as Lord Deputy, he sent the second son of that wise old Sir John Chichester, who, more than half a century before, had been a high sheriff of Devonshire in the reign of Mary, and subsequently in that of Elizabeth. Sir Arthur was the first Lord Deputy who sent justices of assize into Connaught. He not only established this circuit, but he revived what was thought defiant of revivification, the old circuit of Munster. These circuits, once confined to the English *Pale,* soon extended over the whole kingdom. This was done with such effect, we are told, that in Chichester's days ' there were not found in all the Irish counties so many capital offenders as in the six shires of the western circuit in England.' Sir Arthur fairly earned, by his service as a soldier and as a statesman, all the rewards and honours heaped upon him. He received large grants of lands in Ulster; he was raised to the Irish peerage as Baron Chichester of Belfast; and it was during his deputyship that the Harp of Ireland was first marshalled with the arms of England. For many years Lord Chichester was a resident, and his mansion of Joymount at Carrickfergus was a home of splendour and hospitality, and a centre of prosperity as regarded the trade, labour, and industry of the district. Later in life Lord Chichester was in the Palatinate, where he bearded the ferocious Tilly, and sustained the honour of his country. This almost founder of Belfast died in London in 1624. The present Chichesters are not his lineal descendants, as the fine old ' Lord of Joymount' died childless.

The first Arthur Chichester was not the only one who made those names illustrious in bygone days. His brother, Sir Edward, succeeded to his vast wealth, and was thought worthy of being raised, therefore, to the dignity of Viscount Chichester of Carrickfergus. It was the viscount's son Arthur who was the renowned Colonel Chichester, and whose services, military and civil, in Ireland were rewarded by his elevation to the rank of Earl of Donegal. Dublin remembers him for other than martial services. When he was Governor of Carrickfergus he founded (1668) a mathematical lectureship in the metropolitan University. Of the four Earls Arthur who succeeded, the most distinguished was he who gloriously fell at Fort Montjuich in 1706; and the luckiest was the earl who was made a British Baron Fisherwick in 1790, and in the following year Marquis of Donegal in the Irish peerage. His descendant now inherits his titles, and this heir can hardly say that the family motto is applicable to his ancestor, 'Invitum sequitur honor.'

Be this as it may, the name of Chichester, though it be not so romantic or sentimental as that of Tyrconnel or Tyrone, of O'Neil or of O'Donnel, is an honourable name in the annals of this part of Ireland. That Belfast does not owe all its prosperous circumstance of the present day to the Arthur Chichesters of the olden time is quite true. Belfast, says an anonymous modern writer, 'is a city of essentially modern growth and appearance, and as such will surprise and please the traveller who visits it after any lengthened experience of Irish towns, on account of its spacious and well-arranged streets and squares, its general cleanliness and good order, and the beautiful examples of decorative architecture displayed so largely in its public buildings. Belfast appears to owe these advantages, in a great degree, to the fact that it is presided over and inhabited by a race which unites the Scottish thrift and decorum with the Irish impulsiveness and kindliness.' Let us not omit to add that Belfast is so sheltered by its lofty chain of hills as to make it a fitting place of sojourn for invalids. The temperature, it is said, is only one degree below that of Torquay.

The 'Englishman' who walked round Ireland in 1865, beginning at Belfast and ending there, in about a couple of months, completed his tour of the Emerald Isle with less personal danger than he would have encountered by daily crossing, for the same length of time, the perilous road between the Bank and the Mansion House. To what class of travellers he belonged may be learned from the fact that, among his first chronicling of small beer, he complains that the glass on his toilet-table *would* swing round with its reflecting surface away from him, that his first potato in Ireland was hard-boiled, and that his egg was not what eggs and Cæsar's wife should always be, namely, above suspicion. However, the city was worthy of praise, and the citizens what citizens naturally would be, namely, civil. But it rained when he arrived and when he left, and it was raining when he returned at the end of two months. His surprise was great; but not quite so great as that of the French traveller, who, returning to Pisa, remarked, 'What a dog of a country! It was raining when I left Pisa twenty years ago, and it is raining still. Dog of a country, go!' Few travellers, we believe, depart from Belfast with any feeling of dissatisfaction. They may say of most things there, as heralds say of the various divisions in the city shield of arms, 'all proper;' and, in a measure, 'all prosperous' too. A century ago there were but four hundred looms at work in Belfast; now in the linen and cotton factories the spindles are reckoned, like the Arabian 'Thousand and One,' applied to objects difficult to enumerate, by 'millions.' It is said that upwards of a hundred thousand a year is spent in the ornamental wrappers in which linen goods are despatched to their several destinations. Belfast deals with the whole world. Tribute to her industry is paid at the Antipodes. It is hard to say what this flourishing and beautiful city does *not* produce; not easy to discern at what loftiest objects her wise and energetic citizens do not aim. Linens, lawns, diapers, damasks, drills, cambrics, machinery, steam-engines,—the factories and foundries of Belfast are for ever busy in furnishing the above, and hundreds of other objects of ornament or use. From Belfast started the idea, and in Belfast has been realised the fact, that it would be more profitable to raise flax at home than purchase it from abroad at a cost of several millions sterling. As the Roman lady saw her brightest jewels in her children, so Belfast may glory in her flax-mills as the proudest ornaments of the district. A mill employing, directly and indirectly, 25,000 persons is a sight in itself; but it is only one of many to be witnessed in Belfast. Her influence extends practically and profitably over the whole province of Ulster. With commerce and manufactures, Belfast has cultivated art and learning, and with its factories, shipping, schools, and colleges it wears an air of the most satisfactory industry, progress, prosperity, and order.

Nowhere, however, in Ireland has religious party feeling raged with greater violence or to more mortal issue than in Belfast. A popular holiday once meant a day in which the brutes and bigots of one party would exasperate the brutes and bigots of the opposite party to madness. Thence came fierce fighting, destruction of houses and property, and loss of limb or life. These factions seemed to despise all restraint of law; but a little simple home-made legislation succeeded in binding both sides to good behaviour. Party processions were prohibited; and the law now stands—as it was described the other night, in one of the debates at the close of the session, when Mr. Macartney remarked, according to the newspaper reports—'that the only persons who had any reason to be afraid of the law were those who were anxious to break it. There was in existence a law in Belfast under which he, for walking into Belfast and saying he was a Protestant, might be fined forty shillings and costs, and an hon. gentleman opposite, for saying anything about the Pope or King William, might be mulcted in a similar fine. That was a local law passed for the purpose of preventing party riots, and he was not aware that any respectable inhabitant of Belfast had ever complained of the existence of that law, because experience had shown it to be a useful and salutary one. It was necessary sometimes to submit to harsh laws for the general good.'

Old-world customs were established in and about

Belfast with the old-world people, and they lingered as long there as they did anywhere. One of the last to die out was the Easter Monday revel at Cave Hill. Out of the revel generally grew riot, and out of riot bloodshed. The revel itself was in consequence of an earlier religious observance; just as the folly and fashion of Longchamp were the product of antiquated pilgrimages. At Cave Hill there would have been little to object to in the dancing, jumping, running, and climbing the rugged rocks, but for 'the drink, the drink, dear Hamlet.' This accursed thing had often mortal issue, but this was not more thought of than the murderous fights of Donnybrook. Both belong to the past; but when the Belfast Easter Monday was in full swing—*the* holiday of the whole year—the Belfast Theatre had a stock-piece in honour of the season, the *Humours of the Cave Hill*. The holiday without that drama would have been like an old Christmas Boxing-night in London without *George Barnwell* at both the patent theatres.

Literature and the drama in Belfast do not rest for renown solely on the pieces which illustrated the morals and customs of the Cave Hill revelries. Seventy-one years have elapsed this very week since a young actor made his first appearance on the stage of Belfast, and that actor is yet surviving amongst us! We allude to the 'Young Roscius,' Master Betty of Shrewsbury, who, happening to see (in 1801) Mrs. Siddons play Elvira in *Pizarro*, at the Belfast Theatre, made known to his family his intention of 'dying if he was not allowed to become an actor.' He was then ten years old; a boy with a will and decision of character, to whose desire his parents yielded consent; and after honouring their son in his wishes, his days have been long in the land. In his twelfth year he made his first appearance on any stage, at Belfast, on the 11th of August 1803, as Osmyn in *Zara*. The Irish manager, Atkins, watched the new player, and pronounced him to be 'an infant Garrick.' Master Betty's other characters in the northern Irish capital were Douglas, Rolla, and Romeo. After which, passing triumphantly over the boards of various cities in Ireland, Scotland, and England, he appeared in December 1804, at Covent Garden, as Selim in *Barbarossa*, upon which all London went suddenly mad, and kept up the frenzy long enough to help Master Betty to the fortune which Mr. Betty still enjoys.

It is only readers who are 'well up' in theatrical history who are aware of the fact that Mrs. Siddons and Edmund Kean once played together in the same piece. This, one of the old glories of the Irish stage, occurred at Belfast, two or three years after Master Betty had flashed his boyish promise there of becoming a Garrick. Edmund Kean was about nineteen years of age when, in the course of his wanderings, he played at Belfast Osmyn and young Norval to the Zara and Lady Randolph of the majestic Sarah. In the first part Edmund was slightly imperfect, and the Siddons shook her august head at the apparent cause—a cause which often marred the genius of the last great master of his art in later days. Sarah's judgment of the young fellow at Belfast has come down through the chroniclers to the present times.

'He plays well, very well,' said the Siddons, 'but there is too little of him ever to make a great actor.' And yet this lad at Belfast was destined to overthrow the Kemble school of tragedy to its very foundations.

There is one person connected with Belfast in whom literature and the drama are both illustrated, namely, Sheridan Knowles. Knowles was a native of Cork, had the Sheridan blood in him, and was both player and poet for years—player, part of the time, in the strolling company of which Kean was a member—before he achieved celebrity. He lived the hard life of wandering players, and, as a luxury and a rest, Knowles turned schoolmaster at Belfast, with his father for an assistant. But the Belfast stage was an obstacle to the success of the Belfast school. The smell of the lamps drew the schoolmaster from his classes, and the drama which Knowles wrote and produced there —*Brian Boromh*—made the Belfast citizens hope that a genius was amongst them; and let us add that the noble tragedy of *Caius Gracchus*, acted on the Belfast stage in 1815, converted the hope into a reality. This tragedy did not find its way to London till 1823. In November of that year, Macready brought it out at Drury Lane, playing the principal character. If it did not succeed so enthusiastically as at Belfast, eight years before, there is this to be said for it, that the licenser only gave his permission for the tragedy to be acted on condition that some too political passages should be omitted. It was like taking the sting out of the tail of an epigram.

The subject of Belfast literature cannot be passed over without noticing that in the first three-quarters of the last century the printing-presses of Blow, and next of Magee, ranked among the best in the three kingdoms. Blow was, perhaps, not the first who in Ireland printed the Bible in English (after English Bibles were sent for sale across the Irish Sea from Holland as well as England), but he printed an excellent edition of it, and his enemies accused him (falsely) of printing, for 'sin no more,' 'sin *on* more.' It was very carefully printed; not like the copy of the old careless Scotch monopolists, who, if report be true, frequently printed 'Judas' for 'Jesus.' The presses above named continued to issue books of theology, of history, romance, and song. Belfast produced its first newspaper, the *Belfast News-Letter*, in 1737. It has the honour of being foremost in recognising the genius of Burns. The first edition of his works ever published out of Scotland came from Magee's press, in 1787. The last serious effort at maintaining literary distinction was in 1825, in which year the *Belfast Magazine* was started, and in which it died. Its merits were very great. Its failure reflects discredit only on a careless local public.

Belfast, some sixty years ago, proved no exception to the rule that no man is considered a great prophet in his own country. Ireland always thought less of the Irish bard, Tom Moore, than England did, and Belfast thought still less of him than even Ireland did. That Dublin has erected an unpleasant statue to the poet—who is calling a cab from the neighbouring stand—is only a proof of the refined satire of those who raised it.

Belfast disparaged the author of the *Irish Melodies*,

or rather of songs set to melodies which Stevenson un-Irished from original native airs, because the northern capital boasted of a contemporary editor of old Irish melodies, who was a native of, or at all events a resident in, that metropolis of Ulster. The now unknown bard's name was Bunting. When Moore was at the high topgallant of his pride as a lyrist, a public dinner was given to Bunting in Belfast, at which he was fêted, honoured, cheered, and toasted, with Ulster enthusiasm and Kentish fire, as the author of the *Irish Melodies!* No more allusion was made to Moore himself than if he had never existed. Indeed, Bunting was bumpered at Belfast as *the* bard of Erin, and 'Faugh a ballagh!' was the uncomplimentary feeling, if not actual expression, applied to all other sweepers of the Irish lyre who put in claims for recognition, at a banquet given to celebrate Irish minstrelsy. Some of them were, indeed, named, but Moore was rigorously excluded, and nothing pricked Moore's fretful vanity more sharply than that he should have been enwrapped in contemptuous oblivion at a literary banquet in Belfast.

Twenty years later, Moore's *fidus Achates*, Lord John Russell, was entertained at a public dinner in Belfast, and Moore was *not* present. Perhaps he got the well-known Irish hint which keeps any man from going as a guest anywhere, and which consists in the said man not being invited. The hint was most likely received by Moore, for he affected to think that it was, after all, as well that he was not with Lord John, as ten to one he would have got into some scrape (he said) at this dinner, by saying too much or too little;

which is certainly what would have occurred at Bunting-glorifying Belfast.

Moore, however, had friends there whom he warmly regarded. He has, in a measure, immortalised one of them in a note to his 'Young May Moon.' This was a Belfast merchant named Brown, who, when a prisoner to the French in Mariegalante, at the time it was attacked by the English, was sent by his captors to the British to negotiate a surrender to the assailants. In the hurry and flutter of his joy, Brown approached the English outposts without a flag of truce, and, as he kept advancing in spite of challenge, the black outpost sentinel shot him dead, through the heart. This catastrophe, it must be noted, occurred long before the Bunting dinner; previous to which manifestation at Belfast, Moore was not above noticing the Belfast poet as well as the Belfast merchant. It is in allusion to 'Morna's Grove' that the note above referred to says: 'See, in Mr. Bunting's collection, a poem, translated from the Irish, by the late John Brown, one of my earliest college companions and friends, whose death was as singularly melancholy and unfortunate as his life had been amiable, honourable, and exemplary.' 'Both Mr. Bunting and Mr. Brown are now justly enrolled among the Belfast worthies. Properly speaking, Edward Bunting, although called 'bard' and 'minstrel' in Belfast, was rather the friend of bards than one himself. All who have music in their souls may thank him for his quarto, *General Collection of the Ancient Music of Ireland*, consisting of upwards of one hundred and sixty airs; and all will agree in the judgment often expressed, that it is a work of the utmost importance to a proper understanding of ancient Irish musical science. Belfast, after all, may be proud of this worthy.

To the old 'Mouth of the Ford' the wise and the learned and the curious are preparing to wend their way. Spenser states that Edward Bruce was there in the fourteenth century. When the castle was built no one knows. Kildare took, and lost, and took it again, in the sixteenth century. The castle and 'village of Belfast' were given to Sir Thomas Smith by Queen Elizabeth, but James awarded them to Sir Arthur Chichester. In the same century Belfast shot ahead of Carrickfergus by purchasing from the corporation of the latter place, for 2000*l.*, the exclusive privilege which Carrickfergus enjoyed of importing foreign goods at one-third of the duty payable at other ports. Carrickfergus rapidly fell into a sort of Sleepy Hollow. Monk was before the city of Belfast when he was a Parliamentary general, and the heavy guns of Schomberg broke through seven of the arches of the Long Bridge in 1692. The chief magistrate long bore the very high-sounding title of 'Sovereign of Belfast.' The saddest memory connected with the city was the destruction of its ancient and magnificent castle in the year 1708. This happened two years after the death of the third Earl of Donegal, who was killed at Fort Montjuich. Belfast Castle caught fire and was burnt to the ground. There perished in the flames three of the Earl's six daughters, and local bards have mourned the hapless fate of the beautiful ladies, Jane, Frances, and Henrietta Chichester.

XVI.
A TRIP TO LONDONDERRY.

A TRIP TO LONDONDERRY.

ON the breaking up of the Assembly, visitors who had sojourned at Belfast were naturally desirous to 'look in' on Londonderry. The famous siege, in its facts and traditions, still gives importance and dignity to the northern city. The visitors found an excellent guide to hallowed spots in the *Siege and History of Londonderry*, edited by one of the citizens, Mr. John Hempton.

From the earliest days, 'doomed cities,' before which the beleaguerers have sat down intent on their destruction, have excited the liveliest interest. They have all, more or less, been marked by particular circumstances. Even that of Azoth is remembered, because of the record of Herodotus, that the city offered a successful resistance during nine-and-twenty years, compared with which the fabulous ten years of Troy sink into insignificance. We still read with 'bated breath' of the beleaguering of Seville, about the middle of the thirteenth century, when one of the most obstinate resistances was made of the many that give life to Spanish history. In the following century the interest increases as we look upon that novel feature, the use of dread artillery, and see the flash and hear the boom of the cannon employed at Remorentin in 1356, and against the walls of Calais in 1388. In progress of time deadly inventions were rendered more deadly; and the horrors of the siege of Antwerp, in the last half of the sixteenth century, were increased by the employment of infernal machines, against which the bravest were as powerless as the most craven. It was, however, in the seventeenth century that science was most terribly active in devising means to destroy life and the fortune of man. In 1634 an English engineer invented bombshells, and taught the French how to throw them at the siege of Mothe. A little more than thirty years later, the Turks despatched huger and heavier cannon-shot against the defences of Candia than could be hurled by any European engineer from any of his own death-dealing machines. The latter, however, speedily improved upon the infidel, and at Stralsund, in 1675, red-hot shot were first thrown with anything like precision and certainty. About the same time the name of Vauban began to be known as that of a man skilled in the sciences alike of destruction and defence. Only eight years before the siege of Londonderry, bomb-vessels were first used by the French against Algiers; and only one year previous to the siege of the Irish city, the first essay was made at Philipsburg of firing artillery à ricochet. Early in the eighteenth century Tournay was famous for the best defence ever made by countermining. Later in the same century the first experiment at reducing a fortress by globes of compression was made at

Schweidnitz; and the invention of the covert way signalised the siege of Bommel. But the most remarkable sieges of that century were those of Ismael and Acre. Triumphing at the former, Suwarrow, who first taught the Russian soldier to have no mercy on a wounded foe, massacred the garrison, with 30,000 men and 6000 women, in that brave but hapless city. At Acre Napoleon Bonaparte encountered the first check in his victorious career, at the hands of Sir Sidney Smith, and found himself compelled to raise the siege, after two months of open trenches. In the present century the sieges most honourable to the assailed parties were those of Saragossa and Silistria. Yet of all those which we have enumerated there is not one that bears with it such a variety of romantic incident, human interest, and terrible reality as that of Londonderry in 1689, where James II. commenced that fatal contest which yielded to the men he had wantonly made his foes the triumphs of Derry and Newtown Butler, of Ballymore, Athlone, Aughrim, and of the final contest at Limerick. The three months' siege of Derry has been fruitful in a bright record of heroic deeds and names. The three years' siege of Ostend only added a fashionable tint to the varied hues of fashion: the *couleur Isabelle* was invented in honour of the Archduchess, whose linen, which she swore she would wear, and did wear, without changing till the town was relieved, was supposed to have become of that dirty buff which ladies and gallants wore in robes and mantles, scarfs, sword-knots, vests, and slashed hose.

Mr. Hempton has departed from the ordinary way of writing a guide-book or local history. He has reprinted the most important pamphlets, with extracts from larger works, from which Macaulay compiled his narrative of the siege. These comprise, among others, the accounts by Walker, Mackenzie, Ashe, and the author of the doggrel epic, the *Londeriados*—all of whom were sharers in the sufferings and the glory of the immortal defence. From a careful study of these documents, and as careful a perusal of the historian's narrative, the method of the latter's manipulation of his materials is easily discovered, and we see the historian's haste and errors. Macaulay states that in the corporation of Derry, appointed by James before the declaration against him, 'there was only one person of Anglo-Saxon extraction, and he had turned Papist.' The historian founds this assertion on the words in the *Londeriados*,

> ' In all the corporation not a man
> *Of British parents*, except Buchanan.'

Mr. Hempton remarks that Macaulay has misunderstood the author to whom he refers, and that because there was only one man of British parents in the corporation, we are not to infer that there was only one of Anglo-Saxon extraction. Indeed the names of some of the members, such as Manby, Burnside, Eady, Crookshanks, Ashe, and Broome, prove that there were several, though they formed but a small minority of the sixty-five. It is singular, too, that Macaulay knew nothing of the author of the *Lon-*

deriados. We find from the title-page that it was 'written in verse by Joseph Aickin,' and that it was printed in Dublin, 'at the back of Dick's Coffee-house, in Skinner-row, for the author, and sold by him at his school, near Essex Bridge, and by the booksellers of Dublin, 1699.' It is dedicated to Rochfort, Speaker of the House of Commons, a post which he ceased to fill in the year this epic was published.

Again, Mr. Hempton accuses Macaulay of giving currency to an unfavourable report circulated against a leading Covenanter called Hewson. Macaulay says he was 'a Scotch fanatic, who had exhorted the Presbyterians not to ally themselves with such as refused to subscribe the Covenant,' adding that he 'sank under the well-merited disgust and scorn of the whole Protestant community.' But Mr. Hempton points out that David Houston, as his name was properly written, 'is recorded by Walker as being among the defenders of Derry. If Houston and his adherents had not stayed till the relief came, his or their desertion would, no doubt, have been most faithfully chronicled.' As the Episcopalians and Dissenters of such denominations as were within the walls had the use of the cathedral alternately for their respective services, we may well believe that each minister preached in support of the principles in which he most implicitly trusted. There is every reason to believe that David preached stoutly, but fought stoutly too; and, indeed, Macaulay himself confesses that 'among themselves there was for the time entire harmony. All disputes about Church government, postures, and ceremonies were forgotten.'

The mutual sacrifice had its well-earned reward; and yet the besieging force looked with certainty to beginning the extirpation of the Protestant race in Ireland by the destruction of those of Derry. Everything seemed indeed against them; but their very calamities were turned into advantages. They were betrayed by their infamous Scottish governor, Lundy; but, getting rid of him, they got rid of many a traitor besides. When in want of fuel, they found it in the broken timber of houses crushed by the bombs. When their few thousands decreased, and the cruel commander of tens of thousands, besieging them, drove beneath their walls thousands of the Ulster Protestants, there to perish, the defenders contrived to let out the weakest men of the garrison, and to admit stronger men in their place. The crashing cannon-balls broke into cellars, and there occasionally turned up stores of food hitherto unknown to the defenders; and when the latter were at the last extremity with dysentery and famine, a mixture of starch and tallow, which went by the name of 'French butter,' was all they had for food; but it was found to have the effect not only of allaying hunger, but of curing the dysentery. The cruel cowardly Kirke did not allow the relief to approach them till he dared delay it no longer; and great as was the exultation throughout every Protestant country at the almost unexpected triumph of the Derry heroes, they were never recompensed in proportion with their merit and the nature of the struggle out of which they had issued victors. The Parliament voted ten thousand pounds as compensation for damage done to individuals; but the officers were for the most part neglected, and the pay claimed by those who had fought as soldiers of King William, amounting to above twenty thousand pounds, was, according to Mr. Hempton, never granted to the claimants or their survivors.

Macaulay states that the remains of the great captains who strove in this immortal contest were duly honoured by their descendants. This is so far from being altogether the case, that it was not till 1860 that this poor meed was paid. Any one who knew the churchyard of Derry as it existed in years past may remember that the dead of any time received little respect therein. Relics of mortality were sometimes literally 'kicked about' the locality. In the year we have mentioned some alterations were commenced, in making which remains of the dead were shovelled out of the ground and tossed into the high-road. At first disgust was excited; then shame was felt, as men remembered that the bones of the famine-stricken or slain defenders of the city lay in that portion of the cemetery; and finally, a cry of horror arose, when skulls or fragments of skulls were tossed up, with the hair attached thereto tied up in knots of orange-coloured ribbon. Then men hastened to avert the coming upon them of a more hideous disgrace, and the sacred relics of heroes and heroines were reverently collected and deposited within the church with suitable inscriptions; while of the earth wherein they were previously laid a pyramid was erected, fenced in, and given over to the public protection. The great monuments of the great dead, however, will be as long as they stand—and the citizens say they shall stand for ever—the ramparts, which were the great fighting-ground of the besieged and the field of their glory. We have frequently walked round them in a quarter of an hour, but never without recollecting that, if the space was limited, every inch of it had been consecrated by an exceeding glory. Of the twenty cannon recorded by Walker to have been on the walls, only nine remain there. Some others of the original twenty used at the siege 'serve as posts for fastening cables and protecting buildings.' The apprentice-boys of Derry, since the law prohibits any partisan celebration on the anniversary of the shutting of the gates, would be legally and laudably employed, under the sanction of the corporation, in quietly restoring the old culverins to their former position. The Russian gun from Sebastopol, now placed at the foot of Walker's Pillar, is an absurd incongruity; it should be wheeled away to the Diamond, or fixed on the hill leading to Ashbrook, overlooking Derry; and the ancient pieces should be restored to their old but silent companionship with 'Roaring Meg.'

One change in the habits of the city is indicated in the words, 'the old theatre at Widows' Row has been converted into a Presbyterian church.' Some thirty years since, this little house was very creditably managed and very fairly patronised. The managers, the O'Connors, with Fitzsimons, Cunningham, and O'Callaghan, Miss Villars and Miss M'Keevor, contrived to play, sing, and dance every variety of drama, opera, and ballet—though 'Drink to me only

with thine *eyes*' was not a duet to be selected by
Frank O'Connor and the last-named lady, as they
had but a couple between them. The great theatrical
feature of the Derry theatre in those bygone days
occurred as the curtain fell, when the united audience
used to call vociferously for 'Mac Taggart'—a gentleman who was always present, who invariably re-
sponded to the call, and in a comic-heroic, serio-
macaronic way entered into a full and unsparing
criticism of the play, players, and the intelligence
and judgment of the audience. There were merry
days in Derry then—

> 'Days that did borrow
> No part of their good morrow
> From a forespent night of sorrow;'

a sentiment which stout old Walker himself could
not have gainsaid, though he might have made a
sour grimace at the unorthodox source from whence
the words are quoted.

XVII.
BRISTOL.
1875.

BRISTOL.

1875.

The British Association for the Advancement of Science will assemble next week for the forty-fifth time. In 1831 the Association opened its proceedings, and much satire was showered on both by some of the newspapers of that period. Since the inaugural day Oxford, Cambridge, Birmingham, Liverpool, and Edinburgh have been thrice visited; Glasgow, Newcastle, Dublin, York, and Manchester have twice received the philosophers and the friends of philosophy within their borders; in 1836 Bristol gave them a hearty welcome, and that welcome the ancient city is about to repeat, after the lapse of forty years save one.

Thus more than a generation has passed since the Marquis of Northampton filled the chair at the Bristol meeting in place of the then Marquis of Lansdowne, who was unable to fulfil the duty through the illness and untimely death of his eldest son, the Earl of Kerry. The great feature of that meeting was to be found in the presence of, and the statements made by, Andrew Crosse the electrician. He had as long before as the year 1807 produced by electricity crystals of carbonate of lime; and he predicted that by application of the same electric force instantaneous communication with all parts of the world would one day be accomplished. The survivors of that time have got over the fright into which they fell when it was reported that mites were produced in the solution with which Mr. Crosse had been experimenting.

England then was under a king, William IV.; and the chronicling of that reign, or, to confine ourselves within convenient limits, of the year 1836, seems now to belong to ancient history. It is not so with foreign records, for one of the most important paragraphs of the King's speech on opening Parliament alluded with regret to the sanguinary civil contest which was then desolating the northern provinces of Spain, where the atrocities of one side stimulated those, as cruel and disgusting, of the other. It was the year in which the first blow was effectually dealt at the Newspaper Stamp Duty; and other salutary measures were achieved without causing, as some feared they would, the setting of the sun of England for ever. In that year, too, railways existed only as small experiments. There was none between Bristol and London. Reports of the proceedings of the Association were despatched in parcels by the mail; and the guard flung them into the arms of zealous journal proprietors or their representatives, who stood to receive them in Piccadilly. *Now*, a telegraph clerk or two can verify the prophecy which Mr. Crosse made at the meeting of 1836, and sitting down in Bristol instantaneously communicate the course of events to the world at large.

We may take for granted that every visitor, if he be ignorant of the history and manners of Bristol, will have his ignorance enlightened by carrying with him a local Guide, or Mr. Murray's *Handbook for Gloucestershire*. Suffice it to say here that Bristol, from very early times, drew profit from a slave-trade, and we doubt if William the Conqueror himself altogether stopped it. Kings and queens have passed that way: some have tarried there. It boasts of natives of the greatest distinction in commerce, literature, and other ennobling pursuits; and it is not only famous for its milk, but for its milkwoman poetess, Anne Yearsley, poetess, dramatist, novel-writer, whom Hannah More upheld for a time; but she ultimately set her heel upon 'Lactilla,' with as much stamp in it as her gentle Christianity would allow. The two women were not wider apart than the Bristolian bards, Cottle and Southey; but Bristol once admired Cottle as much as it did Anne Yearsley, further intelligence about whom, as well as on every other pertinent subject, may be found in the local Guides.

The father of these Guides was William of Worcester, A.D. 1480. Nearly four hundred years passed away before anything like a genuine Guide was published to help strangers through the city. Of all those of the last century, the best is the *New Bristol Guide*, published in 1799. It has no author's name on the title-page, but that author (the Rev. George Heath) was no common man. He was a highly accomplished Nonconformist minister; but he had a weakness. Among his objects of adoration was 'lovely woman.' The reverend gentleman loved not wisely, nor at all well. For some tempestuous gallantry towards a married lady his Nonconformist brother ministers expelled him from their society; but they allowed him an annuity of 15*l.* a year. It was enough to starve upon; but the ex-preacher turned his good voice to account, and figured as itinerant vocalist at public-houses, collecting largesse in an old hat after due exhibition of minstrelsy. Of course, this author of the *New Bristol Guide* died in a state of the utmost destitution. Mr. Edwardes, his publisher, used to tell this hapless fellow's story over the counter, and it certainly carries a moral with it—for ladies, ministers, and men generally.

And this reminds us that we must not overlook the fact that there was a time when the Bristol Venuses were not held in much estimation for their personal qualities. An artist would have described them as 'out of drawing.' Such, at least, is the tone of old tradition. This saucy legend goes so far as to assert that the Bristol bride-market was so slack of profitable business that a stimulus was given to it by offering the freedom of the city to any one who would venture to take to wife a Bristol maid or widow. Of course this was calumnious satire; and probably there was some protest made against it by the anonymous author of a comedy of James I.'s time, who gave to his play the significant name of the *Faire Mayd of Bristowe*. It was played before James and his Queen, Anne, at Hampton Court, to their great delight, in 1605; and a black-letter copy of the piece, that may have been in the hands of those illustrious personages

while the piece was being acted, is now before us.
The fair maid is one Annabel, of whom her lover
speaks as
> 'Fair Annabel, the idol of my thoughts,
> Fair Bristowe's mirror and my heart's delight.'

The maiden, however, lacks spirit, and is not a model
that the maidens of to-day may be recommended to
follow. Her filial obedience is a virtue which, by
being carried to excess, has the usual consequence—
it becomes almost a vice. Of two lovers, she prefers
one and accepts the other, under paternal pressure.
Annabel is (as regards her father) a mixture of Grizel
and Katharine subdued; and so little self-reliant is
she that, when the question of a husband seems almost
left for her own decision, she indolently exclaims,
'Faith! whosoever, sir, you shall think meet.' Whether
this comedy biassed Queen Anne's feelings in favour
of Bristol or not, is hardly worth inquiring; but it is
worth noting that James's consort paid the highest
compliment to Bristol ever paid by sovereign lady.
She not only visited the ancient city, but graciously
remarked to the worshipful Mayor, 'Nay, I could
not feel myself to be Queen till I came to Bristol.'
Queen Elizabeth was not half so civil when she went
to Bath. Her Majesty lifted her nose above the City
of the Springs, and very unpolitely conveyed her
opinion to the civic authorities that it was dirty as to
look, and nasty as to smell. Let us add, that this
practical woman put down a handful of angels
towards opening a subscription for the better drainage of the city, which would draw greater numbers
to the springs.

Bristol once disputed with Bath on this matter of springs. Bristol, or Clifton, Hot Wells had a short reign and a merry one. At the present day wells have sunk in the estimation of Fashion, and under such circumstances infirmity declines to stoop to be vulgarly cured. The waters at Bath, Bristol, Tunbridge, Cheltenham, &c., have as much virtue in them as ever, but few care to tempt or try that virtue. Some have gone out of knowledge altogether. The old efficacious Islington Well would now be harder to find than the head of the Nile; and probably not one Londoner in a thousand knows of the existence of the healing well at Acton, and how its springs were surrounded by the most aristocratic of invalids in the morning, and its assembly-rooms made brilliant at night by joyous young dancers of a *cotillon* or stately young couples walking majestically through a *minuet*.

In a similar way did things go 'once upon a time' at the Bristol Hot Wells, as those wells are still called, which are not strictly wells and never have been hot. In the season when 'Society' used to frequent the tepid springs in the Clifton suburb of Bristol, not only local but London publishers used to vend a visitors' list, which has no resemblance to it in any list of visitors sold at modern 'watering-places.' We have one of these lists for 1723. It is entitled *Characters at the Hot Wells, Bristol, in September 1723*, and it enables us to see what the quality of the company was that assembled on the banks of the Avon in the reign of George I. In this little quarto list there are a score of characters. All are glorified with that superabundant eulogy which it was the fashion to offer in dedications to the living and in epitaphs on the dead—especially on those who had belonged to the finer class of clay. We pass over all the triple-piled flattery, and merely pause to pick from it the peculiar traits that enable us to distinguish more clearly the fashionable individual who was of 'the Quality,' and who excited the envy of the folk at the Hot Wells.

First, there passes along the walk 'Sir R—— M——' (all the characters are designated by initial letters), and as he passes, our Guide tells us that we may see in him a fine distinction, a being in whom 'the humanity of the private Gentleman is tempered with the dignity of the Peer.' His sublimity is so above all mortal character of that kind that, happily for all beholders, no one need think the worse of himself for the superiority of this gentleman!—and so on. We find that the 'gentleman' is also a nobleman, for the writer says, 'It is Sir R—— M——, that is, Lord R——y.' With this clue, we readily detect this superlative visitor at the Wells, when England had a foreign King who was unable to speak English. He is Sir Robert Marsham, Bart., first Baron Romney, to which rank he was raised in 1716. His wife was one of the daughters of Sir Cloudesley Shovel; and after she became Lord Romney's widow she married with the Earl of Hyndford. The elegant and fragile lord never figured again at Bristol Wells. He died in 1724, and his son, who succeeded him, enjoyed the title for the long period of seventy years, dying in 1794.

Next passes, with peruke and clouded cane, 'Mr.

W――e,' who is so lucky as to be 'formed to please both men of sense and the ladies.' He discourses with ' Mr. W――m,' the very quintessence of courtesy and civility. We fear, if these two be orthodox men, they move uneasily away as ' the Rev. Mr. W――r' approaches, for the 'parson' is a man who might affright even a beau of George I.'s time, seeing that he has 'a lay behaviour in an ecclesiastical habit, and he thinks Reason, as well as Grace, the gift of Heaven;' which last was a very naughty thought in the year when Hugh Boulter, Bishop of Bristol, came down to the Wells for a leave-taking before he crossed to Ireland to take possession of the archbishopric of Armagh. Next, conspicuous in a group of listeners, is ' Dr. A――t:' as he talks, they admire the fashion in which he wears his hat, ' with a button on the right side of his head; it adds gravity to his air, and keeps his sagacity warm.' We suppose Dr. A――t may have been Arbuthnot, who in this year, 1723, was chosen second censor of the Royal College of Physicians. Pope said of him, that he was a good doctor for any one that was ill, and a better doctor for any one that was well. The writer of the 'Characters' seems to have had a bad opinion of the faculty generally. 'I am,' he says, 'of the Duchess of Marlborough's mind: whenever I am sick, I am resolved to die a natural death.' Among other fine gentlemen at the Wells we have only room to notice Sir D――y B――y, who was drinking the waters in order to recover from consumption, the sequel to living over-fast, the pace that kills. People cannot have their cake, Sir D――y B――y is rather roughly told, and eat it too; and, altogether, sympathy is not much moved in behalf of a knight who is described curiously as having 'very harsh features, with a very sweet countenance.' 'Mr. B——m' was not a favourite, or wherefore, in his case, have we the remark that 'a fine person without proper accomplishments is a rotten carcase in a brocade habit'? A compliment is paid to three youngsters, who properly mean, it is said, 'to be figures and not cyphers.'

Then, coming to the ladies, we find it remarked of Mistress J——gs, 'She will forgive me if I imagine she thinks herself made for man, and that her present condition is not her proper element.' To the credit of 'Mrs. Wh——r' it is written, 'I can't but add at present that she wears the best tasted and the comeliest hoop that I ever have yet seen worn by female.' We find 'Lady A——n G——y' (Lady Anne Grey, the Duchess of Kent's daughter) and 'Mrs. W——n' not ill-distinguished by their talent for silence; but eyes can speak as well as tongues. The mother of Lady Anne, 'L——y Dss. of K——t' (wife of the only gentleman beneath Royalty who ever bore the title of Duke of Kent, Henry Grey), is prettily alluded to. 'One wonders what has become of the *Duchess* while one is talking to her *Grace*. Every one ought to pray for a successful cure of the waters in her Grace, till it shall please Heav'n to bless the world with more Lord Crews to beget such daughters as her Grace of K——t and her sisters.' Those who are beneath the rank of the dazzling beauty, 'L——y D——a Sp——r,' are told that it is happy for them that while they can't pretend to her they can gaze at a respectful distance unhurt. 'She is formed for conquest,' adds the character-painter of the Duchess of Marlborough's granddaughter, Lady Di' Spencer, 'but I am afraid she will delight in cruelty.' That very celebrated Duchess was with her daughter at Bristol Wells, and in reference to 'L^y Dss. of M——h' the writer says: 'I have myself experienced her easy gracious condescension in conversation, and am a witness to her charity. If her Grace has not time to read sermons, who has?' Therewith ends the little book, which shows us what fine shadows figured for a brief while at the Bristol Hot Wells in the autumn of 1723.

And these shadows of quality lead us to consider in what way Bristol has been connected with the peerage. The connection only dates from 1622, when John Baron Digby was created Earl of Bristol. Did James's Queen Anne, who loved the city so well, make an earldom of it? John's son George was the more famous Earl. It was he who turned Roman Catholic when abroad, at the instigation (it is sometimes said) of Don John of Austria; but the correspondence between him and the more celebrated Sir Kenelm Digby tells the tale in quite another way. According to this version, Lord Bristol wrote letters to persuade Sir Kenelm to abandon the errors of Popery. Sir Kenelm's replies, however, so logically upset the Earl's persuasive pleadings, that Lord Bristol embraced Popery itself, and, as this course excluded him from office, he attributed the exclusion, not to the force of law, but to the opposition of the Chancellor, whose ruin is reported to have been the planning of the Earl. As Lord Bristol's father fought first for the King, then for the Parliament, and ended on the royal side at last, so the son was by turns of two Churches, and ended in the bosom of his original faith. In 1664, De Comminges, the French ambassador, wrote to Louis XIV. that on the last Sunday in January the 'Comte de Bristol,' at *Oulmilton*, as he calls Wimbledon, in presence of the congregation in the parish church, heartily renounced Popery, and afterwards took the minister and a few others to dine with him. He lived in the house that had belonged to Henrietta Maria. The French Count denounces the whole business in the words, 'L'action est insolente et téméraire.' An action of Digby's son John, the third and last Earl of the Digby line, seems to us to be far more rash and insolent—if it be true that he emptied the stone coffins of the monks at Sherborne, and used the materials for building the Digby mansion. That Digby line of Earls of Bristol failed for want of a male heir in 1698. In 1714 the title was conferred on the head of the family of Hervey; in 1803 the earl's coronet was changed for that of a marquis, and this is still borne by a descendant of the first Hervey. The Herveys were such a peculiar people, that a wit said mankind consisted of men, women, and Herveys. He was the luckiest of them who married Chesterfield's 'sweet Molly Lepel,' whose three sons succeeded to the earldom. The first of these was the well-known Lord-Lieutenant of Ireland; the second, Augustus, was the husband of Miss Chudleigh, who married the Duke of Kingston while her first husband was alive, and was much rejoiced to be so rid of her. The third was the eccentric Earl, who was also Bishop of Derry, and who astonished good people at home, and astounded those abroad, by his mountebank pranks. He half-starved his eldest son; kept a strange house in Italy; died on the Continent in the highest odour of eccentricity; and was brought home in a cask of rum, which was emptied by the sailors on the voyage of everything but the Bishop!

Neither the Digbys nor the Herveys have had any local or territorial connection with the Gloucestershire city from which they took their title; and though the Digbys may be said to have been of a higher intellectual stamp than the earlier Herveys, Bristol has no particular reason for being proud of the two families who have tacked the name of the city to the degree of their dignity. The citizens have some grounds to be prouder of their prelates than of their peers. The diocese was one of the six sees erected by Henry VIII. out of the spoils of the monasteries and other religious houses which that monarch dissolved. The first bishop was Paul Bushe, appointed in 1542; the forty-third and last was Joseph Allen, after whose translation to Ely, in 1836, an Order in Council united this see with that of Gloucester, the diocesan taking the title of Bishop of Gloucester and Bristol. This, however, was not the first time that the sees were held by one and the same bishop. Cheney (1562-1579) and Bullingham (1581-1589) held them united by dispensation. In the last-named year Bullingham resigned Bristol and retained Gloucester, like the wise man that he was. Occasionally Bristol has been without any bishop at all, and does not seem to have been much the worse for the deprivation. This deprivation lasted once for two years; once for three; a third time for ten years (1593-1603); and lastly, for fourteen years— from 1646, when Howell died, to 1660, when the elder Gilbert Ironside left his prebend at York and took charge of the see of Bristol. Among succeeding prelates in the western diocese there were some noteworthy men. One was Sir Jonathan Trelawney, Bart., who was very profane of speech, and who used to half justify it by saying that it was the baronet and not the bishop who scattered those very strong oaths; upon which it was pointed out to this idol of his fellow Cornishmen that the baronet alone would be damned, but that the bishop might feel an interest in that person's condition, nevertheless. Addison's friend, Smalridge, was bishop from 1714 to 1719. He had a love for the drama, and always maintained that *Cato* on the stage was as instructive as any sermon from the pulpit. Secker was here during the years 1735-37, whence he passed to Oxford, on his way to Canterbury. Secker was born and bred a Dissenter; he had, therefore, never been baptised according to the rites of the Church by law established, and to which he conformed, and in it took orders. Secker in 1738, when he was Bishop of Oxford, christened the young prince (born in Norfolk House, St. James's-square) who was afterwards George III.; and it is a fact that timid souls are yet to be found who have some uneasiness as to the validity of that baptism—conferred on a royal prince by an unbaptised bishop! In the very year in which the ceremony thus questioned took place, another ex-Dissenter was made Bishop of Bristol, namely, Joseph Butler, whom we forget as the schoolfellow of Secker, but whom we remember as the author of the famous *Analogy*, which has given many a headache to many a young curate, not to say men of more reverential dignity. In after time William Lort Mansell was seated on the bishop's throne at Bristol from 1808 to 1820; and perhaps, when seated there during unusually heavy discourses from the pulpit, made some of those neat and clever epigrams, the failing to collect which on the part of the prelate's friends so vexed the soul of the poet Rogers, who never troubled himself to contribute a single example. As worthy a man, as great a scholar, and as efficient a diocesan as any in the list of Bristol prelates was good, single-minded, simple-hearted John Kaye, who entered on his duties here in 1820, and who was translated to Lincoln in 1827. He was of humble birth, and one of his practices was to go occasionally to preach at Hammersmith, where he was born, and to encourage the aspiring, yet perhaps half-despairing, young people, by alluding to his own career, and showing what might be effected by unflagging perseverance in the pursuit of an object worth the attaining.

Let us now consider what testimony travellers have given as to the features of this ancient city. A foreigner, Don Gonzales (see his *Voyage*, in Osborne's *Collection*), in the seventeenth century, says, 'The shopkeepers of Bristol, who are in general wholesale men, have so great an inland trade that they maintain carriers, just as the London tradesmen do, not only to Bath and to Wells and Exeter, but to Rome, and all the principal counties and towns, from Southampton even to the banks of the Trent.' The Bristol tradesmen were in truth much more enterprising. 'It is remarkable there,' we are told in the *Life of Lord Keeper North*, 'that all men that are dealers, even in shop trades, launch into adventures by sea, chiefly to the West Indian plantations and Spain. A poor shopkeeper that sells candles will have a bale of stockings or a piece of stuff for Nevis or Virginia, &c.; and rather than fail, they trade in men, as when they sent small rogues taught to prey, and who accordingly received actual transportation, even before any indictment found against them, for which my Lord Jeffries scoured them. In a word, pride and ostentation are publicly professed. Christenings and burials pompous beyond imagination. A man who dies worth 300*l*. will order 200*l*. of it to be laid out in his funeral procession.' In more than one point the above witnesses are corroborated by Pepys, who was in Bristol in 1668, with wife and 'our girl Deb.' Deb. brought her uncle Butts to see Mr. and Mrs. Pepys, and he is thus spoken of: 'A sober merchant and very good company, and so like one of our wealthy, sober, London merchants, as pleased me mightily.' Butts, having escorted the visitors about the city, 'brought us,' says Pepys, 'a back way by surprise to his house, where a substantial good house and well furnished; and did give us good entertainment of strawberries, a whole venison pasty cold, and plenty of brave wine, and above all, Bristol milk. . . . Butts' wife a good woman, and so sober and substantial, as I was never more pleased anywhere. ... He with us through the city, where in walking I find the city pay him great respect, and he the like to the meanest, which pleased me mightily.' Pepys says of the city, 'It is in every respect another London, that one can hardly know it to stand in the country, any more than that. No carts, it standing generally on vaults; only dog-carts. ... Many good streets and very fair stone houses.' Pepys had a good word to say for everything in Bristol except the sermon he heard in the Great Church : 'A vain pragmatical fellow preached a ridiculous affected sermon and made me angry, and some gentlemen that sat near me.' And in the evening 'the same idle fellow preached, and I slept most of the sermon.'

A very celebrated individual, in the next century, was walking the same streets, or was seated at a desk, trying in vain to like learning to be a mercantile clerk—David Hume. That is all we know; except that Hume disliked the place as well as his apprenticeship, which he soon abandoned. In his History, under the date 1660, he gives an account of the mock triumphal entry into Bristol of the fanatic Quaker, Naylor, who bore a certain resemblance to the portrait given as that of Jesus. 'He entered Bristol mounted on a horse ; I suppose,' Hume adds sarcastically, 'from the difficulty in that place of finding an ass!' Probably David did not find the Bristolians hospitable. An English naval captain stationed there with his ship for the protection of the port had the same experience. It was when all roasting in kitchens was accomplished by the help of turnspit dogs. These dogs sported in the streets when not engaged in their vocation. The captain sent some of his men ashore, who captured the whole of them. The consequent dire distress was ultimately ended by treaty, and the surrender of the turnspits was followed by numerous invitations to the naval officers to dinners and balls!

The most unfavourable judgment on Bristol was made in the same century by a very fine gentleman, Horace Walpole. Writing in 1766, he says: 'I did go to Bristol, the dirtiest great shop I ever saw, with so foul a river that had I seen the least appearance of cleanliness I should have concluded they washed all their linen in it, as they do in Paris. Going into the town, I was struck by a large Gothic building, coal-black, and striped with white. I took it for the devil's cathedral. When I came nearer, I found it was an uniform castle, lately built, and serving for stables and offices to a smart false-Gothic house on the other side of the road!'

It has been said by a well-known *diseur* that there are only two events in history, the Siege of Troy and the French Revolution. Borrowing this form, we might fairly say that, prominent as Bristol has been, politically, socially, and commercially, *the* two events in *her* history are the Siege in the Civil Wars and the Riots of 1831. The pamphlets which were published about the year 1642, relating to the city's sufferings or triumphs, would form a library of themselves. The Bristol Riots of 1831 caused the fierce Jacobite riots of 1714 to be no longer spoken of, so much more ferocious were the animosities between reformers and anti-reformers of the later period than those of the Hanoverian Whigs and the Jacobite Tories of the days of George I. In comparing what the latter printed of their opponents with the record which Mr. Greville has made of the dragoons and the colliers, it would appear that at both times ferocity of spirit in commentators was as great as ferocity of action in incendiaries.

Better times have succeeded, when reforms may be obtained by legal means, not by torch and pike; and among the best reformers are the peaceful philosophers who upset old false theories on a basis of new facts. They are now assembled in the Queen of Western Cities—a city especially remarkable for the beauty of its ecclesiastical edifices, and indebted for the restoration of much of that beauty which had perished to the taste and judgment of Mr. George Godwin.

XVIII.
GLASGOW.
1876.

GLASGOW.

1876.

THE British Association for the Advancement of Science is about to meet for its forty-sixth session. The visit paid to Glasgow this year will form the eighth appearance of the Association in Scotland, and its third in Glasgow. It has held its meetings three times in Edinburgh (1834, 1850, 1871). The Association was in Glasgow in 1840 and in 1855. After a lapse of one-and-twenty years, the leading citizens are again about to welcome the great body of men of science; but they can hardly outdo in hospitality the welcome of Aberdeen in 1859, or of Dundee in 1867, or, indeed, of Edinburgh in the years above noted.

When the celebrated Dr. Adam Smith was in Dr. Johnson's company in London, he boasted of the beauty of Glasgow; but he was interrupted by the learned, but exceedingly rude, 'bear,' who asked the Scottish philosopher, 'Pray, sir, have you ever seen Brentford?' Boswell thought this query furnished a strong instance of Johnson's impatience and spirit of contradiction. It was, in truth, a disagreeable instance of his ill-breeding and his ignorance. Johnson had much of both, despite his occasional courtesy and his wide knowledge. However, Glasgow flourished, in spite of the harsh and impotent sarcasm. It was never in more flourishing condition than it is in at the present day; yet, side by side with its prosperous commerce and its seats of learning, it can show as much misery and can point to as much vice as any city of its size in the empire.

To this splendid city, where much of the squalid misery is imported matter, the British Association will next week betake itself; and we profit by the occasion to say a few words of both place and people. First, as to the name of the city, we need hardly say that there is the usual diversity of opinion among philologists as to the meaning of the word *Glasgow*. They mostly agree that it is a Keltic word, but they read it differently, and each thinks his various opponents to be little better than dunces. 'Glas Gow,' says one, 'is the White Smith;' and the smith is set down as 'probably' having had a forge here in early times, when his smithy was a trysting-place! This is contemptuously treated by others, who maintain that 'Glasgow' is the Gaelic *Clais-ghu*, equivalent to 'dark ravine,' near which St. Mungo, *alias* Kentigern, first pitched his tent. 'Glasgow,' we are told sententiously by others, 'is this, and cannot be anything else—*Eaglais dhu*=the Black Church (of the Blackfriars)'—and so they leave and have left it.

It must be confessed that St. Mungo, when he built his hut near the stream in the dark ravine, had very ugly neighbours. It was in the forest, on the site of the eastern quarter of the present city, that dwelt and flourished that irrepressible tribe or clan, the Attacotti. These Caledonians loved war, and had terrible appetites, especially for human flesh. They cared much less for a roasted sheep than for a roasted shepherd, if he were but young. Shepherd or shepherdess was all one to these proto-Glasgovians, who are said to have been very nice epicures, and to have had their favourite slices in the richest parts of their victims. But we leave further discussion on the derivation of the name of Mungo's dark, or gray, or green ravine, and of his friends and neighbours. The more the subject is studied, the further afield do philologists lead the perplexed student.

Over the arms of Glasgow interpreters differ as much as philologists do over the name. The shield bears an oak, with a bird on, and a bell hanging from, one of its branches, and a fish, with a ring in its mouth, across the trunk. Learned pundits affirm that the oak is the city; that the bird indicates the fine air, as the fish does the produce of the Clyde; while the bell stands for the cathedral, and the ring symbolises the happy union of all classes! More learned Thebans read in the hieroglyphic the story of a murdered maiden: the singing of the bird discovered the murderer; the fish with the ring the place of the murder; the bell does duty for the bell-rope, by which the assassin tried to escape; and the oak represents the tree, on a branch of which the rope got entangled, and the assassin was thereby hanged! Laconic scholars briefly remark, 'Ring and fish refer to St. Peter; and there is nothing more to be said about it!' Then comes the romantic interpreter, who tells you a legend of a lady who in crossing the Clyde lost her wedding-ring; but her ungallant husband accused her of having bestowed it on some lover. The virtuous lady told her story to St. Kentigern, or Mungo. The sympathising saint went down to the Clyde, and seeing a fisherman in mid-stream just about to commence fishing, Mungo called to him, 'I'll trouble you to hand me the first fish you happen to catch;' and when this was done, behold, the ring was in the fish's mouth! It was forwarded to the suspicious husband, and he 'supposed it must be all right;' but he asked, 'After all, what does it prove?' which, in those days, when saints did that sort of thing, was considered very bad manners. There is one circumstance connected with the arms of the city which must not be forgotten. The shield has a motto. It is familiar to us all as 'Let Glasgow flourish;' but this is only a mutilation of the old legend, which was, 'O Lord! let Glasgow flourish according to the preaching of Thy Word.' The Glasgow bodies have wiped out the Lord and the Word, and one would like to know who the daring innovator was who thought to get on without such aid and succour.

The founder of Glasgow was wanting in dignity of birth. His parents were august enough: his father was King Eugenius III., and his mother the Princess Thametis, daughter of the King of the Picts; but they so far anticipated Rousseau as to leave little Kentigern (or Mungo, as he was afterwards called, 'The Beloved'), their son, to be picked up by any chance person who might find him, and to be brought up by the State, if it cared to bring him up. At one time the bishopric of Glasgow extended over Cumberland, and fierce were the quarrels when England slipped from this overseership, and claimed supremacy over the Church in Scotland. Pope Alexander settled the controversy by exempting this Church from any jurisdiction but his own. But the disputes of prelate and clergy waxed all the hotter, and there seem to have been among them many Christians and little Christianity. Some of the bishops were intolerable tyrants, and one, at least, died mysteriously— Bishop Dandy, whose election was much disliked by the regulars. Going to Rome to be confirmed, he died by the way, not without suspicion of poison given him at a feast made by the friars predicant of Glasgow; but 'the credit of this,' as Spotswood says, on another occasion, 'we leave upon the reporters.' Perhaps the prelate the most hated by his clergy, and the people generally, was Bishop Cameron, who was as much detested for his cruelty and violence as he was despised for his covetousness; but Cameron was a weak creature, and was frightened to death, 'as fame goes,' by a dream or a trick. He was sleeping at his house at Lockwood, near Glasgow, on the Christmas-eve of 1446, when 'he seemed to hear a voice summoning him to appear before the tribunal of Christ, and give an account of his doings. Thereupon he awaked, and, being greatly terrified, did call his servants to bring lights, and sit by him. He himself took a book in his hand, and began to read; but the voice being again heard, struck all the servants with amazement. The same voice calling the third time far louder and more fearfully, the bishop, after a heavy groan, was found dead in his bed, his tongue hanging out of his mouth.'

In the time of Blacader the see was made archiepiscopal, which creation caused dire onslaught to be made on Blacader by Shevez, Archbishop of St. Andrews. Papal intervention cooled the combatants. Blacader died in 1550, on his way to Jerusalem, which was no easy way three centuries and a quarter ago. Under his third successor, and the thirtieth or, as some say, the thirty-second prelate, James Beaton, or Bethune, the Reformation burst forth, and a new order of things began. It was not invariably a better order of things; for in 1578 the magistracy resolved to demolish the cathedral, on the ground that it was the resort of superstitious people, that it was too large for a preacher to make himself heard, and that it was the only idolatrous monument left 'unruined' in Scotland. A promise, moreover, was given that with the materials various little churches should be built 'for the ease of the citizens.' On a certain morning the sound of a drum summoned the workmen hired for the purpose; but it awoke angry craftsmen generally; and these tumultuously rushed forth, with arms in their hands and savage words on their lips, and finally, gathering at the cathedral, they declared that the workman who moved the first stone should be slain and buried under it. And so the noble edifice was nobly saved.

There had been anxiety for its fate only a few years before, in July 1570, when, as we read in the *Domestic Occurrences*, published by the Maitland

Club, 'At 10 hours at night, there was ane earthquake in the city of Glasgow, and lastit but ane short space, but it causit the inhabitants of the said city to be in great terror and fear.' Neither the cathedral of St. Mungo nor the bridge built by one of the most active of his successors was injured; and it would be difficult to say which was held in the greater regard by the citizens.

That famous old bridge over the Clyde was the work of the famous Glasgow bishop, Rae. It was finished in 1345. For upwards of 300 years its eight stone arches breasted the strong flood without essential repairs; but suddenly, on one of the July Fair days, in 1671, the southernmost arch fell in at noon, but with sufficient warning to the crowd to prevent accident. This was, however, a calamity, for it cut off all communication between the north and south sides of the city and the surrounding villages and towns. The bridge was soon repaired; but that which was more than sufficient for the 2000 or 3000 inhabitants of the fourteenth century, for the 5000 of the sixteenth, or for the 14,000 of the end of the seventeenth, became too narrow, not to say too perilous, a pathway for the nearly half a million of inhabitants of the present century. Consequently an Act to erect the present granite bridge was passed in 1845, exactly five hundred years from the time when Bishop Rae spanned the Clyde with his noble octave of arches.

Some of the old families decayed like the old bridge. The Stewarts of Minto (for instance) were proud members of a brave knightly family; not 'carpet knights,' but successively knights created under the banner, as the saying was. Before the end of the first half of the last century, there was not one left of substance enough to buy a sword in defence either of old or young Pretender. The last of the family is said to have been a poor barefooted boy, who was glad to carry a letter for a 'consideration,' but whose quickness and deserts were noticed by the Duke of Hamilton. This so-called 'last of the Stewarts of Minto' was educated, and was ultimately sent out to Darien, where he was not the only Scottish adventurer who died. A rival family, the Elphinstones, who seldom met the Stewarts on the Glasgow causeway without broken crowns being the consequence, died out in as inglorious a fashion as the Stewarts of Minto. Even Sir George Elphinstone, who was a favourite of James I. (and at one time was Lord Justice-clerk), after having been Provost of the city, died so poor that his corpse was arrested by his creditors, and his friends buried him privately in his own chapel, adjoining his house. Of this line there is no representative now living.

Robert Chambers describes Glasgow, in the latter half of the sixteenth century, as a mere 'little town,' with the distinction of possessing a university, and of carrying on a small coasting trade. The townsmen, and indeed townswomen also, were a choleric race, given to cry loudly, to strike fiercely, and, moreover, to be as ready with sword or pistol as with fist and tongue. Shots were fired as 'promiscuously' in a crowded market-place as now among a Californian mob in the street, or a group liquoring up at an hotel bar. Glasgow tailors carried swords on their thighs like gentlemen, and angry Glasgow wives had words on their tongues not at all like those used by ladies. If a magistrate displeased a complainant, it was well for the former if he did not come to grief. Thus, one Herbertson assailed Bailie Elphinstone of Blythswood in the very Tolbooth (1574), 'giving him,' say the burgh records, 'many injurious words, sic as knave, skaybell, matteyne, and loon, and that he was gentiller nor he—having his hand on his whinger, rugging it halflings in and out, and that he cared him not, nor the hand that he had nowther.' The burgh record makes this ruffler as distinct and picturesque as a figure by Meissonier.

We have further illustration of old Glasgow men and manners in the record of a 'chirurgeon,' Mills, who probably found more patients than payers. He abused the magistracy, and called the place 'Hungry Glasgow,' which slander was quickly punished by dragging the scandal-monger to the market cross, where he openly confessed his fault. The turbulence of the people is also illustrated by the order, 'every booth-holder [shopkeeper] to have in readiness within the booth ane albert, jack, and steel bonnet, for eschewing of sic *inconveniences* as may happen.' One other record is worth noting. The citizens depended in a certain degree on influential nobles who were their neighbours. The favour of these nobles was bought by bribes. The Earl of Argyle was not above receiving seventeen gallons of wine, nor was Lord Boyd reluctant to take a couple of hogsheads; a Lord Provost was gratified by half a dozen quarts;

and for half that quantity 'the parson of Glasgow' rendered some honest service, worth paying for to that extent. On the other hand, Scottish nobles had no reluctance to become traders and manufacturers. In 1688 the Viscount Tarbat was chief partner in a little manufactory in the city, which paid very good dividends.

In former days it was the good old custom in Glasgow to inscribe some words of wisdom on the front of the houses (the usage has not gone out in some continental localities). About twenty years ago one was discovered, which had long been concealed under a coating of plaster. It ran thus:

'P. M. B.
God, by whose gift this worke I did begin,
Conserve the same, from skaith, from schame, and sin.
Lord, as this bvilding bvilt was by thy grace,
Mak it remaine stil with the bvilder's race.
God's Providence is myne inheritance. 1623.'

It is said that the property *is* still with the race of Patrick Maxwell Boyd, the original builder.

Such remains of the olden time are rare, but this is easily accounted for. In 1652 one of those calamities happened to Glasgow which are followed by good results. A fire broke out which destroyed nearly 11,000 houses. 'The like of this fire,' it was said, 'has not been formerly heard of in this nation.' Undoubtedly the ruin was universal, and some of the wealthiest burghers were reduced to beggary; but the fire purified the place,—its tongue of flame licked up the pestilence that was ever lurking or bursting forth. With aid from outside, and good-

will within, the city rose out of its ashes, and then
naturally, in 1657, the magistrates, following the
example of Edinburgh, bought an engine, 'for the
occasion of sudden fire, in spouting out of water
thereon.' Feeling that they could now sit down in a
certain security, the inhabitants began to be curious
about the world at large, and how it was going on.
Hitherto Glasgow had received from Edinburgh a
weekly sheet of intelligence; but this was not deemed
enough, and the magistrates ordered 'John Fleming
to write to his man who lies at London, to cause ane
diurnal to be sent for the town's use.' Next came a
printer, but there was little encouragement for the
same, and he wended his way whence he came; upon
which one Sandies was tempted to set up his press,
on the agreement that he was to receive 40*l*. (sterling) a year, for which he was to print gratis whatever the town (meaning, we suppose, the 'authorities')
required him to print! These were certainly behind-
hand in the matter of progress in another way, for
they did not allow a house-painter to exercise his
calling in the city till they were assured that there
was only one like him in the burgh, and not one
other in all the west of Scotland! But progress was
being steadily made, and in 1682 three Glasgow men
got permission to set up a manufactory for 'damatics,
fustines, and stripped vermilliones,' expecting great
advantage to the country therefrom, especially 'by
keeping much money therein which is sent out thereof for import of the same.' The checks to progress
were to be found in the frequent fires. The city
engine was always there, but it was always out of

gear. 'See,' says a Town Council Order in 1680, 'if it can be yet made use of in case of need.' Finally an engine was procured from London. One almost smiles at reading that a destructive fire broke out in Kelso, for the relief of whose destitute inhabitants Glasgow raised a considerable sum; but as this was about to be paid over, a fire broke out in Glasgow itself, and the subscription for Kelso was forthwith applied to the relief of the Glasgovians!

In the olden times religious toleration was not one of the Glasgow virtues. Papist, Presbyterian, and Episcopalian hated one another, and all three united in detesting the Quakers. In the seventeenth century especially, the members of the Society of Friends in Glasgow excited as much horror as mad dogs on the highway. Wherever detected they were hooted at, pelted, stoned, rolled in the mire, and dragged through it. This treatment they received at the hands of a Presbyterian ultra-orthodox rabble, people who had secured their own religious liberty, and would not tolerate such liberty in others. The magistracy winked at the offenders, and the persecuted Friends at last appealed to the Privy Council. They especially dwelt on one outrage. On a November night in 1691, while the Friends were holding a religious meeting in a hired house, a company of Presbyterian church-elders, with a mob at their heels, broke in upon the silent body, hurried most of them into prison, refusing bail unless the prisoners promised never to hold meetings there again, and allowing the hired house to be plundered and wrecked. All that the supreme Scottish Privy

Council did was to recommend that if the Quakers' wooden forms had survived wreck and plunder, it would be as well to restore them to the rightful owners! But we turn to better things.

In the last year of the seventeenth century a man appeared in Glasgow in whom the city found a benefactor, who has been rather ungratefully forgotten. His name was Wilson; he was born in Flakefield, and in as far as he is remembered at all, it is by the name of his birthplace. He had been a weaver before he served as a soldier in the continental wars; and while so serving in Germany his eye was one day attracted by a woven blue-and-white chequered handkerchief. It was a lucky moment for Glasgow when Flakefield bought this article. He stowed it away among his treasures, and he resolved 'some day' to weave one like it. In the year above named he and the prized handkerchief, with Flakefield's father and brother, settled in Glasgow, and there the ex-soldier, returning to his old calling, attempted to produce a woven blue-and-white chequered handkerchief. After some unsuccessful essays Flakefield succeeded, and the blue-and-white chequers were soon familiar all over the country. There was a rage for the novel handkerchief. Fresh set-up looms could hardly produce these articles fast enough, and on them the extensive linen manufacture of Glasgow was founded. Some years after the town-drummer of the city was a man who excited much sympathy. This humble official, in fact, was no other than Wilson of Flakefield, the old soldier and weaver, whose loom had started into life the above-named manufacture. But rival looms, whose owners had greater capital, beat out of the field the 'wabster body' who had done so much for Glasgow. He fell into poverty, and all that generous Glasgow could or would do for him was to make him useful (on small pay) in his old days—as town-drummer!

So runs the story, but it is to be suspected that there is a dash of romance in the details. About the time that Flakefield and his kinsmen settled in Glasgow the city was making rapid strides in manufacturing importance. From its 12,000 inhabitants, in 1695, a monthly cess was obtained for the expenses of the war, which amounted to 1800l. It seems incredible, but it can be proved. The amount of this tribute made Glasgow second only to Edinburgh, which contributed 3880l.; and thus, in the course of a century, Glasgow had advanced from the fifth to the second city in the kingdom of Scotland. Gibson, in his *History*, accounts for the comparative superiority of the wealth of Glasgow at this time, by stating that it had been for some years in possession of the sale of refined and raw sugars to the greater part of Scotland. The vendors were privileged to distil spirits from their own molasses, free from every sort of duty. Glasgow also exchanged with Bristol hides and linen for tobacco, which was manufactured into snuff. It was also said that 'they were the only people in Scotland who made soap.'

But with regard to manufactures, the late Robert Chambers points out that, in 1699, a copartnery (with Dunlop, Principal of the University, among them) was set up 'to make woollen stuffs of all sorts, . . . for men and women's apparel for summer or winter.'

To this end, the ablest workmen 'airtiests' were provided from 'the neighbouring nations.' The copartnery boasted that among resulting benefits would be a saving of above 10,000*l.* yearly in duties hitherto paid as import duty on such stuffs from Ireland, to say nothing of what was smuggled. In the same year an English company was established for the manufacture of every sort of hardware, from scythes to pins and needles. A rival and entirely native body of partners was allowed (for such matters went by Privy Council allowance) to establish a similar manufactory; and with these it is noticeable that the distilleries for every sort of spirituous liquor vastly increased, not purely for home, but for universal, consumption.

In the first quarter of the last century Glasgow opened a trade with Maryland, Virginia, and Barbadoes, not, however, in Scottish bottoms, but in vessels ·chartered from Whitehaven. The vessels carried mixed cargoes for sale, bringing back ship-loads of tobacco; or, if the goods were not all sold, as much of the plant as the vacant space would admit. The first Glasgow vessel that crossed the Atlantic was in the eleventh year of the union of England and Scotland—1718. In this tobacco trade Glasgow found a mine of wealth, and as the tobacco merchants could soon undersell those of Bristol, Liverpool, and Whitehaven, these latter traders persecuted their Scottish rivals in Parliament and courts of law, putting them to vast expense to refute accusations of fraud, and with such success as for a time to cripple their trade. Thousands of pounds were lost. 'Ah,' said pious

Woodrow, 'you don't understand the language of Providence. The Lord frowns upon your trade because you put it in the room of religion;' he also attributed the temporary decay to the establishment of the Union. It was only temporary, and enormous fortunes were founded or realised. Then came luxury, and lax morals, and laxer religion, and one meeting-house for prayer where of old there were forty, and a display of husseydom on the open street such as had been hitherto unknown, with ruin to some,—which Woodrow hoped would be sanctified to them. For the ruin that comes by mischance of honest trading there was sympathy enough, but in those good old times there was no mercy for the mercantile rogue. One of these, a certain George Cowan, of Glasgow, was pilloried, with this explanatory inscription: 'GEORGE COWAN, A NOTORIOUS FRAUDULENT BANKRUPT.' Meanwhile, commerce generally flourished, and as there was great prosperity, so great adversity, as is common, was there also. Woodrow rejoiced when misfortune could be sanctified; but the minister of Eastwood mourns over one great failure, simply for the reason that 'it was diffused over too many parties to be very sensibly felt.'

At this time Glasgow had not got any evil reputation for drinking. In the first quarter of the last century, the popular 'tap' was not whisky, but 'twopenny,' a light ale, so called because it was sold in pints, at 2d. each pint; but this was a *Scottish* pint, equal to half an English gallon. Let thirstiness in hot weather dream of two English quarts of wholesome ale (none of the stuff that is doctored by a barman who 'understands cellar-work') for 2d., and sigh for that good time. The Government of the day thought to profit from the extensive popular thirst by laying a tax of 6d. a bushel on malt. This was laying a penalty of 20,000l. a year on the twopenny drinkers. Glasgow broke into insurrection, the military opposed the insurgents, lives were lost, many persons were wounded in the fray, and savage were the feelings and the acts till at last Glasgow and twopenny triumphed. Triumph and prosperity make some men haughty. Glasgow men waxed fat and extravagant thereupon. Woodrow watched the city from his village adjacent to it, and groaned that no calamity befell it which it might take to heart. At length, however, a plague fell upon it which, he trusted, might prove wholesome. In October 1727 he writes: 'The vermin called bugs are at present extremely troublesome at Glasgow. They say they are come over with timber and other goods from Holland. They are in many houses there, and so extremely prolific there is no getting rid of them, though many ways have been tried. It is not twenty years since they were known, and such as had them kept them secret. These six or seven years they are more openly complained of, and now half of the town are plagued with them. This is chiefly attributed to the frequent alterations of servants, who bring them from house to house.' It must have been pretty well half a century later that Lady Murray came to the rescue, and advertised her bug poison as 'a secret and infallible mixture.'

When tranquillity reigned in Glasgow, after the

Jacobites had been vanquished and the Whigs (the city was mainly Whiggish) had grown weary of chorusing Hanoverian songs and quaffing toasts to 'Augustus' and 'Great Brunswick,' it fell into the head of the most absent of men and most abstruse of mathematicians, Dr. Simson, to found a club, the first known in Glasgow, which was called the Anderston Club. The members—sage men all—were wont to have a weekly outing every Saturday that it happened to be fine. They travelled a Sabbath-day's journey, gave themselves up to fun and frolic—surprising in philosophers—and from three to seven enjoyed hen-broth, rum-punch, and a reckless jollity, from which they all 'pulled up' till elders' hours warned the revellers to wend homeward in time for evening prayer. On other days there was grave talk to good listeners, now of Greek Odes, anon of Free-trade—a favourite subject in Glasgow, as might be expected, since Adam Smith was a member of the club, and was never tired of delivering himself on the subject of the wealth of nations. One of the most learned and most eccentric of the members was the founder himself; he invariably counted his footsteps from the college to Anderston's tavern-door, and liked not to be interrupted. On one of these passages, just as Dr. Simson had registered in his mind the number of steps he had made, a friend meeting him begged to be allowed to put to him *one* question. The doctor looked at him, and muttered, 'Five hundred and seventy-three!' The friend thought him too civil by half; and when, to other questions (concerning a law-pleading and how many nieces a certain uncle had), the doctor still answered, 'Five hundred and seventy-three,' the querist remembered the mathematician's humour, and left him to the further enjoyment of it. But we have a greater and a better man now to speak of.

One of the most thorough of Glasgow 'men,' of scholars, and of gentlemen of the last century was one who has been ungratefully forgotten, namely, the Rev. William Thom. He was the first man in Scotland who boldly championed those (then) slaves of the soil, the miserable down-trodden Scottish farmers. In his pulpit at St. Govan's, near Glasgow, he preached to congregations of farmers, and published his sermons. The old landlords must have thought Thom a pestilent agitator, who, through the tenant farmers, was going to turn the world upside down. In truth, however, the British Association may see in this bold and enlightened minister of the Gospel, and his audience the tenant farmers, the earliest sample of such an association in this part of Scotland. Thom and his congregation formed a section, and the former instructed the latter in the science with which they were the most concerned. He told them of the comparative value of land-rents in England and Scotland at that period. With praiseworthy audacity Thom exposed the system of rack-rent, the rouping of tacks and crops, and other ways of oppressing the cultivators of the land. Nothing that referred to humanity was above or below him. He helped to people America with emigrants of the best sort, and in the city mealmarket he kept a sharp eye on the dealings of the oatmeal-mongers and the levying of ladle dues. Here is a taste of his quality, taken from one of his sermons to farmers :

'I have spoke from principle, from abhorrence of rapacity, and from pity to the miserable. The subject is uncommon. I know of none who preached in this strain except the patron and ornament of Ireland, whom I should not dare to name, because I can never hope to imitate him, except in a tender concern for your wretched conditions.'

Here are two or three other words 'spoke' by this best of patriots to rouse his agricultural countrymen to exertion:

'The common people of Scotland, from time immemorial, have, by means and causes which I need not mention, been crushed down and held in miserable bondage. The free-spirited English farmer would disdain to drudge, and at the same time live so poorly, as our people would be content to do.'

The hearts of the farmers must have thumped under their waistcoats when Thom told them that the ordinary rent of the cornfields over all England was not more than two-ninths of their produce; and he added, 'Surely if 10s. is the rent of good land in England, 40s., 30s., or even 20s. an acre is too high a rent for ordinary land here.' So spoke in 1770, with no uncertain voice, this honest man, friend of his fellow-men, who found in him alone a whole association for the advancement of science and of themselves.

Three years after the last-named date, that is to say, in 1773, Johnson, at the age of sixty-four, arrived with Boswell at the Saracen Inn. He seated himself in the parlour, put a leg upon each side of the grate, and said, 'with a mock solemnity,' as Boswell calls it, 'by way of soliloquy, but loud enough for me to hear it, "Here am I, an *Englishman*, sitting by a coal fire!"' The wit of the remark is yet to seek, but to the utterer there speedily resorted some of the foremost men of brains in the city. Drs. Reid and Stevenson, with Mr. Anderson, breakfasted with the travellers. These, with Messrs. Foulis ('the Elzevirs of Glasgow'), dined and drank tea with them. The professors received Johnson most respectfully at the College, where he was congratulated on having successfully used his influence to have the New Testament translated into the Erse language, which the Scottish Society for Promoting Christian Knowledge had opposed, on the ground that it tended to keep up a distinction between Highlanders and Lowlanders. Generally the Glasgow professors were afraid of him, and were slow to enter into argument with him. The modest sage thought they were right, especially Robertson, who had 'a character to lose'! The brothers Foulis, however, seem to have irritated the amiable monster by illogical applications of expression. Johnson fled to Boswell for refuge, and Boswell was unwise enough to boast to Johnson of his resorting to him for shelter; but the former put him down with the assurance that he was merely the 'least' of two evils. Altogether the two or three October days spent in Glasgow were more pleasant to the guest than to the gentlemen whom he visited. Boswell, alluding to Johnson's comparison of Glasgow with Brentford, to the advantage of the latter, thought, now the doctor had seen the former, he must feel 'some remorse.' Johnson made no remark; and when, ten years later, Boswell ventured to suggest that so unfair a comparison was shocking, 'Why, then, sir,' he replied, 'you have never seen Brentford.'

When the celebrated statesman, William Windham, left Eton in 1766, before he was a statesman or celebrated, he was sent to Glasgow University, where he had for tutors the learned Anderson and 'Euclid' Simson. Windham, however, was not there more than a year, when he went to Oxford. Nearly twenty years later, that is, in 1785, he revisited the ancient city, without being much impressed. 'On the way,' he says in his diary, 'I had allowed myself to ramble too much from what should have been the subject of my thoughts, viz. the recollection of the period of my first being in this country. Indulged only in fancies. . . . . . . *Feel* at the sight of the College, and in general upon arriving here, not so strong as at return to Oxford; reason probably the interval too long, the stay not long enough, the character of the place too, perhaps, not so striking.' At the ceremony of Burke's admission, he notices that 'none but boys were present;' and on visiting the mathematical class, that it appeared to be much smaller than in his time. Of the society he had no reason to complain. He, with Burke and Lord Maitland, dined in the College Hall, with all the wise and hilarious men, Meek, Richardson, Hamilton, Young, Millar sen. and junr., and the Drs. Williamson, Stevenson, Wilson (and two sons), Irwin, Reid, and Taylor. How Windham pleased and *was* pleased he records in simple terms: 'I remained among the latest, finding in them so much wish that I should stay, and in myself so much satisfaction in my staying, that I was content to sacrifice to that motion time that would otherwise have been spent with Lady Harris.' Later in the day he had political business to transact at his inn; and, later still, he writes, 'From the inn we were conducted in grand and orderly procession, the windows on each side being lined, and a transparency with different inscriptions carried before us, to Dr. Stevenson's, where we were to sup.' There is no such honouring of scholars and politicians now, no such early banquets nor such late suppers, as was then the wont in Glasgow.

A year after Windham's visit to the commercial capital of Scotland a treaty of navigation and commerce was arranged between France and England. At the end of the first volume of Lord Auckland's *Correspondence* a copy of this treaty is inserted, and appended thereto are some acute observations written by a Glasgow merchant. Among them we find a couple of illustrations of Glasgow life and manners. 'There is a great distiller here,' says the writer, 'called Stein, who, by taking a few phials out of his pocket, will turn a bottle of our whiskey here in five minutes into rum, raki, or brandy, as you call for.' As an illustration of the easy adaptability of Glasgow workmen to any kind of work, the same writer tells us as follows: 'Mr. John Cross had a great rope-walk at Port Glasgow; he quarrelled with his men about wages, and about thirty of them left him. He did not mind it much at first, supposing they would come back again; but seeing nothing of them for some weeks, he inquired after them, and found they were all sitting on fine lawn-looms at Paisley.'

We have now to add a few words on one of the phases of the religious police of the city.

There was once a strict police supervision of the streets on Sundays, from midnight to midnight, for the better observance of the Sabbath. At twelve o'clock on Saturday night, when the Sabbath began, to twelve o'clock on Sunday night, when it finished, all the gates of the city were closed, and no one was allowed to pass in or out, save on very special necessity. In the daytime 'Compurgators,' 'Seizers,' or, as Andrew Fairservice calls them in *Rob Roy*, 'Searchers,' were appointed to take note of all persons idling on the highway or drinking in taverns, or even in their own houses, during kirk-hours. A man who shaved himself or a barber who dressed his wig on the Sabbath risked being had up before the Kirk Session, where, if he was not mulcted in twelve shillings Scots, he came in for a rebuke, which was often administered in the kirk itself, before a grinning majority of the congregation. It is said that the Compurgators were respectable and responsible men, who did their duty sternly, and were never tempted (in tavern or private house, when they came upon a company of ungodly tipplers) to put their lips to a pint stoup, wink their eye over the edge of it, and therewith make no unfavourable report to the Kirk authorities. It is clear, however, that a 'consideration,' or the lack of it, might influence the less honest searchers. The Sabbath regulation was carried to excess when even the sale of milk was forbidden on Sundays; but it hardly reached the Geneva rule, which forbade a man, under penalty, kissing his own wife on the Lord's-day.

At last rule and Compurgators came to an end, but both flourished till towards the end of the last century. Down to that time, and not in Glasgow alone, the *unco guid* cast a scornful eye on the unrighteous people who sought for fresh air in fields and meadows and country lanes. They would almost stone a man for whistling a call to his own dog on the Sabbath. At length the Glasgow Compurgators caught a Tartar. They found a Mr. Peter Blackburn (grandfather, it is said, of the judge) walking one Sabbath afternoon on 'the Green.' In a trice they had the Sabbath-breaking wretch in the guard-house. But Peter snapped his fingers at them. He did more; he 'raised an action' against them, recovered damages, and, as a consequence, brought the system, and, as some thought, the Sabbath itself, to an end for ever. The Dunfermline 'Seizers' had more vitality in them. They did not finally die out till about 1820. Yet can it be said that they have died out in Glasgow? Only about a month ago, a man was taken up and convicted for singing 'Willie brewed a peck o' maut,' in the street, on the Lord's-day; he pleaded that he sang the words to one of Moody and Sankey's hymn-tunes, but that did not save him from being mulcted in a fine for the offence in the words!

We must not omit to mention a social side of Glasgow life which is not yet extinct. We allude to the once famous Glasgow Clubs. One of the most renowned of those social clubs, and the longest lived of those founded in the last century, flourished long after the nineteenth century began. It was established by the very cream of the arrogant Tobacco Aristocracy, and they were so exclusive that the number of members was limited to nine. The name was democratic enough; it was 'The Hodge Podge,' and the title was better warranted when the roll was enlarged, and sages, wits, and men with various qualifications were admitted into membership. Among the first members who joined the Tobacco Lords was Dr. Moore, the author of *Zeluco* and the father of Sir John Moore. In later days the heroic son was made an honorary member among the old fellows, who still wore their scarlet cloaks, and were proud of the depth of their purses. Sir John, going on foreign expedition, gravely wrote to the fraternity: 'I am preparing to go to Sicily, where I hope to do nothing to render me unworthy of being a member of the Hodge Podge Club.'

Lord Ross's Club was the name of another society, which met in a tavern kept by one Ross. It was said that the man who began it did so out of sheer weariness of solemn evenings at home. Their jollity, however, seems to have been of an extremely moderate sort. According to Dr. Strang, the historian of the Glasgow Clubs, the members met 'over their tankard of twopenny and glass of Jamaica, running up a nightly score of from three to four pence each, or *at most to sixpence*.' There was more extravagance at the Morning and Evening Club, where the members foregathered twice a day and spent twice as much.

On London-newspaper day this club was at its liveliest. On that much-expected morning the firing of a gun announced the arrival of the post, and at the report every member turned out of bed, about 6 A.M., and rushed down to the then fashionable quarter, Currie's Close, and in the well-warmed parlour of the club drank the hot herb ale, read the papers, then joined his comrades in a debating assembly where the affairs of the nation were discussed, and finally they broke up at eight, when they hurried home to breakfast. They met again at night to talk of business, but not avoiding the affairs of neighbours, with which they had really nothing to do.

Indeed most matters seem to have been formerly entered upon over twopenny or Glenlivet. We hear of a reverend Glasgow divine, Dr. Hamilton, and one of his parishioners opening a conference in an alehouse over a gill of spirits and a piece of oat-cake. The pastor closed his eyes to ask a blessing, but he was so long in the doing of it that his fellow-townsman ate the cake and emptied the stoup. On addressing himself to the refreshment, the anger of the disappointed minister was aroused; but the lay citizen drily remarked that next time he would do well to watch as well as pray.

Of the other Glasgow Clubs we may notice the Gaelic, where the members were bound to speak the ancient tongue from seven to nine, that is, as long as they were sober. To the Accidental Club, of which any man might be a member by entering it, Dr. Ranken belonged. This was the modest historian who, wishing to know how his *France* was appreciated, once asked a librarian, to whom he was unknown, if Dr. Ranken's *France* were in. 'Sir,' was the reply, 'it never was *out!*' Club funerals were generally very merry meetings. Club dinners were sometimes monotonous. The Face Club never had any other dish but sheep's heads, and the standing dishes of the Sons of the Clergy in Glasgow were 'a haggis, a sheep's head, tripe, and black-puddings.' The Grey Club got drunk for the glory of Hanover. The Meridian boasted of the jolly good ale and old which they drank at their noon dinner. The Pig Club drank hard, played deeply, and encouraged piety to such an extent that, in a drunken fury against the drama, they set fire to the theatre, and, with the building, burnt the beautiful Mrs. Bellamy's wardrobe, worth nearly 1000*l.* Those old Glasgow tipplers had a sort of shame at their excess in drinking whisky; but Dr. Towers's remedy to conceal the odour of that spirit was generally adopted, and the whisky imbibers 'topped up' with a couple of glasses of rum, and then slowly moved home under the compound effect. However drunk they might seem, there was only sympathy for them, if they were moving homeward, at elders' hours, for prayer; whereas sober persons, wending to, or returning from, the playhouse and Shakespeare, had to run the gauntlet of coarse and orthodox ruffians. Playgoers were excluded from the What-you-please Club, where gluttony was looked upon as a virtue, especially if sucking-pig was in question. It is told of one Lingham, a member, that love for this viand was so strong in him, he once remained at a country inn, where there was a litter just ready for the spit, until he had finished the whole family of young porkers! The Medical Club, too, had its peculiar illustrations. One is to be found in a Dr. Woodward, who had a patient in another member, a gentleman who always had his fee in his hand to give to the doctor as he felt his pulse. One day Woodward arrived only to hear that a few minutes before his patient had died. 'Impossible!' cried the doctor, 'he cannot be dead yet. Let me see him; some trance or heavy sleep, perhaps.' The doctor accordingly went to the bedside in a darkened apartment. He felt the pulse, and also a couple of guineas in the dead man's hand, which he took quietly into his own as honestly earned. 'Ay! ay! Poor fellow,' said the doctor, 'he is dead. There is a *destiny* in all things! And with this tag of morality went on his way.

While on the subject of death, we may naturally add a word on that of funerals in Glasgow in the last century, and this can hardly be done more effectually than by copying an advertisement in the Glasgow local paper, 1747:

'James Hodge, who lives in the first closs above the Cross, on the west side of the High-street, continues to sell burying crapes ready made; and his wife's niece, who lives with him, dresses dead corpses at as cheap a rate as was formerly done by her aunt, having been educated by her and perfected at Edinburgh, whence she has lately arrived, and brought with her all the newest and best fashions.'

In 1789 we are informed that 'Miss Christy Dunlop, Leopard Closs, High-street, dresses the dead, as usual, in the most fashionable manner.'

Ten years later, 'Miss Christian Brown, at her shop at the west side of Hutcheson-street, carries on the business of making *dead flannels*, and getting up burial crapes, &c. She also carries on the mantua-making at her house in Duncan Closs, High-street, where a mangle is kept, as formerly.' Such are a few illustrations of the grimmer as well as the rollicking side of life in Glasgow in the last century, and, indeed, in the early years of the present one.

The old fashion of eccentric clubs has not died out in Glasgow. When Lord Palmerston visited the University there as Lord Rector, he met with an ovation. The captain of the Clyde boat, on the Prime Minister landing, gave him a salute of nineteen guns, and when asked to give a reason for it could find no better than that my lord was Lord Warden of the Cinque Ports! The Gaiter Club invited him to become a Gaiter; his gout was no obstacle, as the Gaiters did not undertake much walking, or, indeed, any. At his inauguration dinner, the rev. joker, Norman Macleod, professed to have come direct from Balmoral with the Queen's approval of the Premier being also a Gaiter, though her Majesty doubted whether the double honour was not too heavy a burden for proud but weak mortality. Lord Palmerston himself plunged into high jinks, and gloried in having become a single Gaiter. 'I don't know,' he said, 'whether the gaiters you wear be long or short, but my memory of this day will be as long as you can desire.' The aged statesman went into the fun of the thing with all the zest of youth.

The growth of the city is the most interesting

feature in its history. Half a million of people fight the battle of life round the spot where Mungo pitched his tent. For Bishop Rae's one bridge there are now five, and for the sixteen smelting furnaces of 1830 there are now nearly ten times the number. Iron, coal, cotton, and its dye of Turkey red enter largely into the causes of its prosperous industry; and if the Glasgow distilled whisky be of marvellous strength, there is there also the purest and sweetest of waters, brought from a distance of forty miles.

XIX.
PLYMOUTH.
1877.

PLYMOUTH.

1877.

THE Scientific Association, established in 1831 by Sir David Brewster and Sir Roderick Murchison, and set going in that year at York, will assemble next week at Plymouth, where the members previously met in 1841. In the latter year Plymouth succeeded to Glasgow. The same order of succession is now observed; but the Association has twice visited Glasgow since 1840, whereas the impending meeting will be held at Plymouth, where there has been no such Congress of Science for six-and-thirty years.

During that space of time a great change has come over the ancient town. The population of Plymouth, Stonehouse, and Devonport cannot now be much, if any, less than a hundred and fifty thousand. What were three towns are now, to all intents and purposes, one. The impulses communicated to them in the days of the great French war tended, so to speak, to weld them together, and to give them that force and cohesion which render them of such importance at the present time. From the dockyard to the citadel there is an endless and extremely significant succession of illustrations of the naval and military power of Great Britain. The nursing-mother of the present triple town has gone to decay; at least, it may be said that Plympton has become a sort of Sleepy Hollow, undisturbed as the remains of its once famous Augustinian Priory, and only existing in the memories of some of its distinguished sons, while Plym-mouthe has grown into the active restless town which we now behold. Here a solitary fisherman was wont to set his nets, and carry what the hauling of them brought in to the prior and brethren at St. Augustine's. How great is the contrast between the single priory fisherman in the earliest days of the brotherhood, and the admirals and captains, knights, princes, and men-at-arms, whom purpose of great moment has at various times here called together!

It is the general and self-evident assertion of all topographical writers on this especial subject, that Plymouth would never have been what it is but for the trifling circumstance of being *where* it is. Given the confluence of the Plym and the Tamar, with the surrounding heights, how could the town avoid growing into the harbour and naval station of to-day? Those who do not like to go far beyond the clouds for the origin of places, may be content with knowing, or rather with being told, that the fight on the Hoe between the giant Corinæus and Gogmagog represents the first struggle between the natives and foreign invaders. For a long series of years local history is furnished with details by those aids to antiquarian writers so familiar to us under the forms of 'probably,' 'doubtless,' 'it may be conjectured,' and so forth. One fact of an unquestionable kind turned up a dozen years ago, namely, the discovery of an extensive and ancient burial-ground near the town. The remains found were not at all discreditable to the anatomical development of the early Britons; and it may be a source of gratification to fine ladies and fine gentlemen in the neighbourhood to know that only fashionable personages were buried there. The remains of bracelets, fibulæ, bronze mirrors, &c., show that no vulgar individuals were interred. They all appear to have been distinguished members of society as it existed in their day.

After the Normans had got through their toughest bit of work in this part of England, the King and the Church helped themselves to what was best worth having; and the common folk settled down by the waters and took to fishing. The place and the vessels attracted the attention of 'superiors;' and progress was so remarkable that Plymouth (after being known by various names) at the end of the thirteenth century had a royal fleet of above three hundred ships anchored off the town, and a couple of highly intelligent gentlemen representing the borough in Parliament. One, at least, of the marine inspectors in the fifteenth century was a priest. His name was John Deverge —*Sir* John, by right of his clerical profession. In 1324, on occasion of confusion and backwardness in preparations on board the fleet, Sir John was despatched from London to survey the ships and to see that they were properly furnished with all necessary munitions and stores.

The first exceptionally notable fact with regard to the growth of Plymouth belongs to the year 1347.

Edward III. (for the siege of Calais) was furnished
with 700 ships, the tribute exacted from various
ports. Plymouth's contribution amounted to twenty
vessels. Liverpool then furnished one; but Dartmouth excelled Plymouth, her quota being thirty-one
ships. Hither came and hence went the most exalted
personages of the realm, bent on missions of good or
ill, as the case might be. The Black Prince brought
his royal and honest prisoner, King John of France,
some say, with likelihood, to Sandwich; others, to
Plymouth. Local history asserts that, after the landing of those personages, they were royally entertained
by the mayor—'ruinously' would, perhaps, be the
word in the mayor's private diary. To one of the
combatants who survived the bloody field of Poictiers
a rather extravagant reward was given, namely, the
right of levying toll at a ferry over the Tamar, and
20*l*. a year. The lucky soldier was one Lenche.
What the ferry was worth we do not know, but the
annuity in present value would be about 350*l*. a year;
and yet Lenche had only lost an eye. Chelsea,
Greenwich, and the War Office know nothing of such
largesse in these degenerate times.

It was not only the high mightinesses of the olden
times who made of Plymouth their port for outgoing
or incoming: the mixed companies of pilgrims, towards the close of the fourteenth century, became,
for the first time, legally entitled to pass this way to
or from continental shrines. Plymouth was soon
their favourite pilgrim port. Wherever many of
them came together there was no lack of jollity.
They must occasionally have made the town as full

of fun as an old man-of-war's crew just paid off, with plenty of prize-money in their pockets. No other reason is given for their long sojourning, save that it suited their humour. It is to be remembered that the prior and convent held the sole government of the town. The so-called mayor was their humble servant. So ill was the town governed and protected, that it was no unusual thing for a body of Frenchmen to land at night, set fire to a quarter, pillage it in the confusion, and fight their way back to their boats with their booty. But this was an outrage which was not accepted in a Christian-like temper. The Devon men had no idea, after the French had burnt one quarter of the town, of offering them the opportunity of burning another. Instead of turning the other cheek to be smitten, they sharpened their knives to slash that of the brigand invader. Stowe tells how the gallant William Wilford ('Esquire' —the title meant something then) headed the western navy, dashed over the seas to Brittany, and brought thence forty ships laden with iron, oil, soap, and a thousand tuns of wine of Rochelle. Thirty other ships of the foe Will Wilford destroyed by fire, as he did Penmarch and St. Matthieu, and towns and lordships along a coast-line of six leagues. The French, finding their favourite card trumped in this fashion, soon gave up the game, and were not successful when they renewed it.

The prior and convent followed the example— that is to say, they beat a retreat under compulsion. The townsmen left them no peace till they consented to be bought out of the government; and as a consequence, in 1439, Plymouth became an incorporated borough, with a mayor who was not a mere name and a shadow without substantial activity, like some called 'mayors' in the time of the priors. The name of the first borough mayor is reverentially remembered to this day, not for any particular wisdom or prudential rule, but for the wonderful pie with which he immortalised his inauguration-feast. It was composed of every sort of fish, flesh, and fowl that could be got for money. It was fourteen feet long, and an oven was built for the baking of it. We may suppose that it was not altogether so nasty as a knowledge of its component parts might warrant us in supposing; and the saying, 'as big as Ketherick's pie,' refers to the monster dish of the first real mayor of the borough.

The characteristics of some of the early mayors are noteworthy. One of them, Clovelly, wore a beard, under a vow that, having lost his wife, he would never shave chin or lip again; whereby the irreverent Plymouth youth only knew him as 'goat's face.' Another, Pollard, was facetiously called 'pullhard,' from his uncommon power in archery. Indeed the Plymouth folk seem to have been a mildly humorous folk. They sharpened their wit on their worshipful mayors' names. Shipley, for instance, being of saint-like qualities, they called *Sheepley;* this sort of anagrammatic wit being quite epidemic in this locality. But there were not wanting mayors who stood upon their dignity. Choleric Farcy struck the town-clerk for not addressing him as 'your worship.' He was fined for the blow; but he so far gained in dignity that he could never pass along the streets without the wicked boys calling after him, 'Worshipful Farcy!' Among the early magistrates there was one especially preëminent, the very Solomon of borough-magistrates, the Saul among the Plymouth prophets. His name was Nycoles. He was a shining light to the town at the close of the first half of the fifteenth century. When in office he gave this proof of his worshipful wisdom. He artfully detected a vile impostor who pretended to be dumb, and that by no other means than seeming to pity him, and asking 'how long he had been speechless;' to which the fellow unguardedly made answer 'that he was born so.' In the latter half of the same century, 'Yogge, mayor,' was blamed for lowering the magisterial dignity by carrying home the meat for which he chaffered in the market; but Yogge asserted that he was not proud, and he added, 'It's a poor horse that will not carry its own provender.' Altogether, it may be said, without fear of contradiction, that the record of the mayors of Plymouth is as profitable reading as the Chronicle of the Seven Sages, or the legends of the Champions of Christendom. They are full of illustrations of individual character and general manner. We might cite, as one instance out of many, the case of Paige, who was mayor in 1499. He is chronicled as a man very strict in his office, insomuch that the least violation of the laws, as far as came within his jurisdiction, was punished with much rigour. He was a great devotee, never missed matins or vespers, and took singular notice of those who absented from the mass on a Sunday. He had a rosary constantly in his pocket, and wore a silver crucifix continually beneath his band as a common appendix to his dress. In some country churches the custom is still kept up of looking after absentees from service; at least, so far as that the public-houses do not give them refuge. Country churchwardens show great alacrity in escaping from church, in order to search after others who have anticipated them by not repairing thither.

One other illustration of the doings of the old mayors deserves to be recorded. In 1455 Dirnford, the mayor, was at church on his 'opening day.' While there he had a fit of apoplexy, but at dinner he ate a fine Michaelmas goose, with the pleasant remark that his fit had given him quite an appetite. There are no mayors of this kind now. Paige was mayor several times; and he and the vicar were often at loggerheads about York and Lancaster, not knowing which side was to prove victorious in the end. For example, in 1462 Paige entertained the Duke of Clarence right royally, and drank to the health and prosperity of his brother, King Edward IV. Nine years later Margaret of Anjou and her son, whose career was to finish at Tewkesbury, landed at Plymouth with a body of auxiliaries, chiefly French. Mr. Mayor must have been sadly perplexed, for he was compelled to render a hospitality which King Edward and the Yorkists might construe afterwards as being nothing less than treason.

When the times seemed thick with perils for religious communities, there was not a prior in all England who had his wits more about him than John

Howe, who proved to be the last of the priors of
Plympton. He set about selling long leases of property, for which he obtained handsome fines, and on
which he laid charges of heavy pensions. In August
1534, Howe subscribed to the king's supremacy. On
St. David's-day in the following year he surrendered
the priory. For his prompt obedience, or, as some
might describe it, his subserviency, he was awarded
120*l.* a year—a very pretty annuity, having regard
to the value of money at the time. This, with the
ex-prior's fines and pensions, must have made John
Howe comfortable. For about ten years he seems to
have enjoyed himself in the world. In 1545 he
retired to Exeter College, Oxford, where he led so
very quiet a life that no chronicler seems to have
marked the hour at which he resigned it.

About the period in question there was but one
solitary house at Mount Wise. Where Devonport
now stands, deafening the senses with its noise and
confusion, there were green fields which extended
over the present dockyard, 'terminating,' says one of
the local historians, ' on a point at the mouth of the
present Camber, where the piled jetty still retains
the ancient name of "Froward Point."' In the progress of the town we observe a certain liberality on
the part of the bishops. For work done in building,
draining, fortifying, and so on, the wages were infinitesimally small; but then the prelates supplemented
low wages with high indulgences; and the labourers
went away with a poor penny in hand, but also
relieved from so many years of sojourn in purgatory.
For this relief much thanks may have been tendered

as heartily as when Francisco uttered the phrase on the platform at Elsinore. The townspeople were not ungrateful. Sooner than a heretic should not be burnt, they subscribed for the fagots, and generally burnt him at their own expense.

Plymouth has always been distinguished for its liking—we will not go so far as to say for its love—for the drama. This liking began early. In 1561—that is, three years before Shakespeare was born—'my L. Busshoppe's players' acted in Plymouth, and the mayor and commonalty of the borough patronised them to the extent of 13s. 4d. The same sum was expended on a 'Mr. Fortescue's players;' but the mayor and his counsellors made greater outlay when the Queen's players visited the town. No doubt this troupe, which had acted before Elizabeth, and which had her license to play where they would and earn what they might when she cared not to be amused by them, was a 'fashionable company;' and people of fashion thought it 'the thing' to witness their performances of an afternoon. The municipality actually spent one pound and an odd sixpence in going to see the Queen's actors. We should like to know how often they went, and how many entered each time, who the actors were, what they played, and what the audience thought of players and pieces. That three companies visited the borough in one and the same year shows the liveliness of the taste of the town. They probably succeeded each other, for we can hardly suppose that 'my L. Busshoppe's players' opposed her Majesty's. It is not unnoteworthy that if this Lord Bishop was Bishop of Exeter, he bore a very theatrical name — that of the actor Alleyn, who founded Dulwich College. The prelate, like many other persons of his time, had an *alias*—he is sometimes called Alley. He was of a long-lived family, one of whose members has already been noticed (p. 223), and who was as well worth recording as his (great?) grandfather, 'my L. Busshoppe,' whose players enlivened Plymouth, and who died in 1570.

In 1563 we find the Earl of Warwick's players and the Queen's company patronised by the mayor and corporation to the same extent as two years previously. In the following year came the Earl of Worcester's players. That was in 1564, when a boy was born up in the quiet home of Stratford-on-Avon whose mission it afterwards became to reform both plays and players, and his reward the homage of all mankind, save that of the maniacs who are inclined to ascribe Shakespeare's plays to anybody except Shakespeare. Subsequently came to this stage-loving town the players of various noblemen; among them the troupe of Lord Hunsdon, the nephew of Anne Boleyn, and first cousin to Elizabeth. It is observable that on St. John's-day the play seems generally to have been performed in the church; and that if the town cared for anybody rather than the players it was for the morrice-dancers, for whom there was not only liberal pay, but substantial pudding.

One of the most singular illustrations of the Plymouth drama and stage-managers in the middle of the last century is furnished by the footnote to a bill of the 16th of February 1759. On that night *Jane Shore* was played, with comic songs and dances between the lugubrious acts. This fashion of relieving the monotony of dramatic affliction was imported from London, where, for instance, Mr. Shuter played Henry VI. in Shakespeare's *Richard III.*, and between the acts sang a comic song, in which he gave imitations of all the cries of London! The footnote to which we have alluded is signed by 'Joseph and Maria Pittard;' the former is in the bill for Lord Hastings in the tragedy and for Puff in the farce of *Miss in her Teens.* The address to the public runs thus:

'Words cannot express our Acknowledgments for the Favours we have received from those Ladies and Gentlemen and Others of this Town, Stonehouse, and Dock, in favouring us with their Company on Tuesday last at the New Playhouse at Franckfort Gate; and it would have been a pleasure to us had our Performance been more to the Audience Satisfaction; but we are very sensible that the major Part of the Company came on purpose to help the Distress'd. And in order to make Amends for all past Favours, I have been over to *Launceston* to engage some of the best Performers belonging to the Company there; and I'm quite confident every Thing attempted next Thursday night will be entirely to the Audience Satisfaction, both in Playing, Dancing, and Singing; if not, I don't desire to have any more Favours from my Friends. I shall be at a great Expence (and am determin'd to spare none) in order to bring the Performers here, and I don't in the least fear but I shall meet with Encouragement from the Generous and Humane, which will be always gratefully acknowledg'd from their ever Oblig'd Humble Servants, Joseph and Maria Pittard.'

In all playbill literature we know nothing that in singularity, confusion, confidence, humility, bad logic, and equally loose grammar, can match this Plymouth address. Are there memories at either of the Garricks (senior or junior), at the Green Room, or the Beef-steaks, that can quote a parallel?

In other respects there is not much to say about the Plymouth drama. The present theatre is under the same roof with an hotel and assembly-rooms; in which arrangement there is this convenience, that if a fire should break out in any one of the three, the occupants of the other two would have the earliest notice of the fact. In the dramatic annals of the town the brightest name is that of a native actress, Miss Foote, who was highly distinguished in her day, inasmuch as that her career ended in her being a countess. In Plymouth another player terminated his career and uttered his last joke—Charles Mathews. He was complaining to his servant of internal pain. To console him, the man said he had once suffered similarly from inadvertently swallowing a quantity of ink. 'Did you?' said the dying actor; 'I hope you had plenty of blotting-paper at hand.'

And here we may as well localise one dramatic incident which has a hundred homes, but only one true one—Plymouth. The audiences there ever dearly loved a jest, and all the more if it interrupted stage business. One night Kemble was acting Hamlet. 'Will you play upon this pipe?' 'My lord, I cannot,' said Rosencrantz. 'I pray you!' 'Believe me,

I cannot.' Then Hamlet, turning to Guildenstern, said, 'I do beseech *you.*' 'Well,' replied the actor, in his own person, 'since you seem so much to wish it, I'll do my best to oblige you;' and thereupon he took the pipe, a flageolet (one-third of the orchestra instruments), and played the 'Black Joke.' This was the popular air of the day; it was set to some very vulgar words, and it was vivaciously country-danced to by active beaux and belles. The Plymouth audience heard it with delight, and John Kemble was of course, and reasonably, in a rage. Gilfillan says, in his *Dramatic Mirror,* that a gentleman who was present related this occurrence to him.

Let us now turn to another John, upon a wider stage. There is no name that occurs more frequently in the annals of the town, in the latter half of the sixteenth century, than that of Sir John Hawkins. No one will dispute his title to be called the great Devonshire admiral. But there is a blot upon this rather unscrupulous sailor's fame. It was not thought much of at the time, but it has grown darker and darker as years have succeeded to years. This glorious rear-admiral of the fleet which helped to destroy the Spanish Armada has left a reputation disgraced by the fact that he was the first European who carried off free Africans from their native homes to a cruel slavery in the West Indies. *There* Hawkins died, and brighter would have been his memory had he fallen fighting against the Armada. Sir John, however, was not the first European to carry on the inhuman traffic in human flesh.

If we were in search of a native of Plymouth who

presented the greatest contrast to Elizabeth's rear-admiral in most things, we should find what we looked for in the Plymouth workhouse. We allude to a boy born in Stillman-street, and in such humble circumstances as to make him a very willing inmate of the poor-house. That boy was stone deaf, a calamity which was the result of an accident which befell him while working with his father, a mason. Almost totally excluded from intercourse with men, he found a substitute in books. Thrown back upon himself, he was sufficient for himself. For conversation he had thoughts; instead of listening to suggestions from others, he lent himself to building up ideas of his own; and these ideas shaped themselves into realities more profitable, perhaps, to others than to himself, whereby he added so much to popular knowledge of the Bible, in that succession of works at the head of which stands his *Cyclopædia of Biblical Literature*, with his name and signs of distinction on the title-page, 'John Kitto, D.D., F.S.A.' Biblical personages of nearly the same sounding names are clearly distinguished one from another in this Plymouth youth's *Cyclopædia;* and there is nothing there of that Lemprière style of things which Macaulay ridiculed when he imagined a modern biographical dictionary done in the same fashion, and which would give results something like this: 'Jones, William, an eminent orientalist, and one of the judges of the Supreme Court of Judicature in Bengal; Jones, Davy, a fiend who destroys ships; Jones, Thomas, a foundling brought up by Mr. Allworthy.' Thirty years have elapsed since John Kitto read the revise of the last sheet of his *Cyclopædia* at Woking; and if it has been excelled since, it is only because fresh sources of information have been discovered and utilised. Plymouth may fairly be proud of John Kitto.

Plymouth furnishes one 'wise saw' to the roll of proverbs or popular sayings, namely, 'a Plymouth cloak,' that is, in the words of old Fuller, 'a staff; for gentlemen landing there, if unprovided, have leisure to repair to the next wood to cut a staff, when they are unable to recruit themselves with clothes.' This would indicate that Plymouth, with its princes and sovereigns passing to and fro, and its strange sojourners, whose first inn was a wood wherein to cut a staff, presented as wide contrasts as the county did in its gentry and its lowest inhabitants. Queen Elizabeth said of the former that 'they were all born courtiers with a becoming confidence.' This has been taken for praise; but there is in it a strong flavour of that satire in which Elizabeth loved to indulge. The contrast with the Devonshire gentry presented itself in the Devonshire 'Gubbings.' 'The Gubbings,' says Fuller, 'are a kind of Scythians within England, exempt from ecclesiastical jurisdiction and civil order, who have all things in common, and multiply without marriage, living by stealth, and securing themselves by their swiftness.' A few descendants of the wild Gubbings, free in their loves as in their lives, with extraordinary ideas as to their freehold property, of which they are deprived by the rightful owners, still survive—or were very recently alive and troublesome—in some part of the county.

The above-quoted proverb was the only one Plymouth furnished in Fuller's time. A second grew up in later days. In the last century, Dock (Devonport) had insufficiency of water for its increasing population. Plymouth steadily refused to help them with a single pailful. The Dock people consequently depended for the most part on rain, which was so joyous an advent that thence arose the saying, 'A Plymouth rain is a Dock fair.' Since then Devonport has brought water for itself from Dartmoor.

Plymouth may be said to be out of the peerage, where, however, it once gave, or seemed to give, territorial dignity to an earl. The first Earl of Plymouth was a slip of Royalty: he was that Charles Fitzcharles whose father was King Charles II., and whose mother was Catherine Peg. He was created earl in 1675, and was not a bad one, measured by the moral standard of the time. He enjoyed the dignity only five years. In 1680, in the affair at Tangiers, he was shot, and therewith ended his career. Not so that of his lively widow, the Countess of Plymouth, a daughter of the Duke of Leeds. Some years after, the Rev. Philip Bisse kissed her in the dark as she was slowly passing along the gallery at Whitehall. On being mildly rebuked by her, he protested, by way of excuse, that he had taken her for one of the Maids of Honour! The young fellow was forgiven; he married the countess, and, of course, he died a bishop—nay, twice a bishop, first of St. David's, and next of Hereford.

Two years after the death of Earl Charles Fitz-

Charles, the title of Earl of Plymouth was conferred on Lord Windsor, an old Cavalier who had spilt his blood for the first Charles, and had been mulcted of his land by Cromwell. He was of a mixed descent, coming on one side from William Fitz Otho, whom the Conqueror made Castellan of Windsor, and later, from Mr. Hickman of Kew. Nine of these Windsors (five of whom bore the Christian name of *Other*, which seems a barbarous mutilation of 'Otho') were in succession Earls of Plymouth—a place with which they were not otherwise connected. When the ninth earl died in 1843, the earldom became extinct; but the more ancient barony of Windsor still exists in the fourteenth and present lord, a descendant of Fitz Otho the Castellan, who is considered so dignified a personage to have for an ancestor and founder of a race, that he is claimed as a common father by the Cornish Carews and the Irish Fitzgeralds and Fitzmaurices.

Let us take our leave, looking at the arsenal, the breakwater, and Mount Edgecumbe. In 1812 'Mr. Pering, of his Majesty's Yard at Plymouth Dock,' startled the public, who had been used to the enjoyment of the signal successes of our fleets at sea, by a statement that the wooden walls of old England were in a very rotten state indeed. He published a work entitled *A Brief Enquiry into the Causes of Premature Decay in our Wooden Bulwarks; with an Examination of the Means best calculated to Prolong their Duration.* Mr. Pering showed that the shipbuilders were ignorant, and their materials next to worthless; the latter chiefly because North American oak was mixed with that of Britain, whereby the British heart of oak caught the dry-rot, which in eight or ten years brought a man-o'-war's career to an end. Mr. Pering mourned over the fact that British-grown oak was yearly becoming scarcer, and he asked, naturally enough from his point of view, where would Britannia be if her wooden bulwarks failed for want of oak with which to build them? Since Mr. Pering alarmed our grandfathers by his proclamation of danger ahead, the anxiety about oak has passed away—only for a time, perhaps—and shipbuilders hammer themselves deaf in riveting iron bulwarks. There is a popular idea that the wooden ships were not costly to build, and did not require a vast amount of oak for the purpose. The estimate, however, at Plymouth five-and-sixty years ago was by no means insignificant. For the building of a seventy-four-gun ship at least 2000 trees were required, of about two tons each; and the cost of a three-decker in the hull alone amounted to nearly 100,000*l*.

When the master of Plymouth Dockyard was much concerned about the building of ships, a project had been under consideration since 1806, founded on a suggestion of Admiral Earl St. Vincent, as to how they might ride in safety in adjacent perilous waters on a perilous coast. The project may now be seen substantially realised in that magnificent matter of fact, the Plymouth Breakwater. Looking at the great work now, it is hardly possible to conceive how vigorously the project was opposed. There are always opponents of great national projects; so far from blaming them, we think it is a lucky thing for the nation when such opposition exists. It insures a perfect weighing of objects before a decided course is taken, and it keeps at a distance unscrupulous projectors whose plans will not bear examination. The opposition to the construction of the Breakwater was based upon two grounds—that the Breakwater could not be constructed, and that it would be useless if it were.

While Mr. Pering was alarming the nation with the idea that, unless care were taken, there would be no navy at all, a Captain Manderson fired no less than 'Twelve Letters' at the head of the Right Hon. Spencer Percival. They were compressed into one volume, a sort of literary bombshell. It was composed of various missiles, one of which was a strong denunciation of the projected Plymouth Breakwater. To be of any use, the Captain maintained that it should be constructed at Falmouth! People remarked that a Falmouth Breakwater would be a poor protection for ships exposed off Plymouth. The Captain really meant that a new dockyard should be established at Falmouth, and that nothing should be done for the improvement of the anchorage at Plymouth. The Admiralty held that the vicinity of Plymouth Sound to a naval dockyard furnished a good reason for the construction of a breakwater to render the anchorage safe. Then arose the chorus of objectors: The water within the breakwater would progressively become shallower, and ships would at last have nothing to float upon! Obstructions raised against the natural course of the tides always had (so it was said) this effect. The answer was, there

will always be water (and safety) enough for thirty
sail of the line. 'Not safety,' said Sir Home Popham,
who asserted that not above half the number would
be safe there. And, murmured the grumblers, 'it
will cost a million and a half! Who is to pay for it?'
Captain Manderson affirmed that for half the above
sum Falmouth, with its natural advantages, might be
made one of the noblest harbours and the safest
anchorages in the world. Over the respective merits
of Plymouth and Falmouth angry opinions were uttered, and the two places showed to each other all the
significant hatred of a couple of rival Italian cities in
mediæval times.

The Admiralty settled the controversy, and celebrated the Prince Regent's birthday by lowering the
first block of granite into the water, on the 12th of
August 1812. There are nearly four millions of tons
of those granite blocks, and most of them are out of
sight. The least part of the gigantic work is that
which is visible. There is, indeed, a clear mile of it
stretching across the Sound, with a breadth of thirty
feet, but beneath the waves the base is more than ten
times as broad. Nearly a generation had passed
away before its completion in 1841. The work added
fresh lustre to the name of Rennie, father and son;
for those eminent engineering architects surmounted
what seemed insuperable difficulties. They had to
protect the breakwater which was to protect a navy
storm-driven behind it. They had to contend with
storms which lifted out of their places blocks of a
dozen or fourteen tons in weight. For this protection
of their work they constructed the 'foreshore,' in

completing which something like four million tons of rubble were deposited and secured. This platform of rubble is described as tripping up the heavy seas before they can reach the slope of the breakwater, and the thick coating of seaweed which covers the rubble shows the perfect repose of its angular stones. As wonderful as anything, the cost was according to estimate—a million and a half. But much has been spent on it since in the way of lighting and fortifying.

We have spoken of the fame of the architects; but what is fame? Does anybody remember Dummer? Yet it was once thought he had secured a never-to-be-forgotten reputation. In 1705 he was soliciting Government to pay him his due for great work done at Plymouth. 'There is not one of my brethren,' writes 'Charles Sergison,' chief at the Navy Office under Queen Anne, ' who does not think Mr. Dummer deserving of this and much more for his services in the navy. Not one in his post ever did anything like him. The new docks at Portsmouth and Plymouth will be lasting monuments of his great skill as well as services to the kingdom.'

Mount Edgecumbe is as beautiful as if it had never been despoiled by inexorable requirement. In 1779 'above one hundred ancient oaks, growing exactly where they ought, (were) felled to make way for a battery!' so writes Walpole.

'Oaks only!' exclaims Mrs. Delany; 'the finest beeches, the loveliest old oaks that Sir Francis Drake and Sir Walter Raleigh had seen perhaps; and these have their foes, and are now washed by the briny wave. O sad, O cruel war! How many French, how many Spanish noblemen have been hospitably and nobly entertained at that delightful place, and how much better a use that is to make of it than to form batteries to take off their heads!'

The battery is there, and the place is none the worse for it. Walpole, referring to it in 1780, speaks also of an Eastern question and a Russian difficulty in terms which are almost like present surrounding echoes. 'This is the third summer,' he writes to Lady Ossory, 'that our climate has been growing as Asiatic as our Government; and the Macphersons and Dalrymples, I suppose, will hail the epoch of the introduction of camels and dromedaries in lieu of flocks of sheep; yet a Russian fleet riding in the Downs is a little drawback on our Ottoman dignity.' With all the sacrifice of ancient oaks, Mount Edgecumbe remains as Lady Ossory described it,—'It has the beauties of all other places added to its own.'

THE END.

www.ingramcontent.com/pod-product-compliance
Lightning Source LLC
Chambersburg PA
CBHW032008300426
44117CB00008B/946